McGRAW·HILL
HEALTH

SENIOR AUTHORS
Susan C. Giarratano-Russell
Donna Lloyd-Kolkin

PROGRAM AUTHORS
Danny J. Ballard
Alisa Evans Debnam
Anthony Sancho

 **McGraw-Hill School Division**

New York   Farmington

PROGRAM AUTHORS

Susan C. Giarratano-Russell,
MSPH, Ed.D, CHES
Health Education Specialist
University Professor and Media Consultant
Glendale, California

Donna Lloyd-Kolkin, Ph.D.
Partner
Health & Education Communication
  Consultants
New Hope, Pennsylvania

Danny J. Ballard, Ed.D
Associate Professor, Health
Texas A & M University
College of Education
College Station, Texas

Alisa Evans Debnam, MPH
Health Education Supervisor
Cumberland County Schools
Fayetteville, North Carolina

Anthony Sancho, Ph.D.
Project Director
West Ed
Equity Center
Los Alamitos, California

PROGRAM REVIEWERS

Personal Health
Josey H. Templeton, Ed.D
Associate Professor
The Citadel, Military College of South Carolina
Charleston, South Carolina

Growth and Development
Jacqueline Ellis, M Ed, CHES
Health Education Consultant
Brunswick, Maine

Emotional and Intellectual Health
Donna Breitenstein, Ed.D
Professor of Health Education
Appalachian State University
Boone, North Carolina

Family and Social Health
Betty M. Hubbard, Ed.D, CHES
Professor, Department of Health Sciences
University of Central Arkansas
Conway, Arkansas

Nutrition
Celia J. Mir, Ed.D, RD, LD, CFCS
Associate Professor, Nutrition
University of Puerto Rico
Rio Piedras, Puerto Rico

Physical Fitness
James Robinson III, Ed.D
Visiting Professor of Health
Department of Health and Kinesiology
Texas A & M University
College Station, Texas

Disease Prevention and Control
Linda Stewart Campbell, MPH
Executive Director
Minority Task Force on AIDS
New York, New York

Alcohol, Tobacco, and Drugs
Kathleen Middleton, MS, CHES
Administrator for Health and Prevention
Monterey County Office of Education
Monterey County, California

Safety, Injury, and Violence Prevention
Philip R. Fine, Ph.D, MSPH
  Director
Wendy S. Horn, MPH
  Project Coordinator
Matthew D. Rousculp, MPH
  Assistant to the Director
University of Alabama at Birmingham
Birmingham, Alabama

Andrea D. Tomasek, MPH
Epidemiologist, Injury Prevention Division
Alabama Department of Public Health
Montgomery, Alabama

Community and Environmental Health
Martin Ayong Ayim, Ph.D, MPH,
  BSPH, CHES
Assistant Professor of Health Education
Grambling State University
Grambling, Louisiana

Teacher Reviewers
Judith Anne Charles
4th Grade Classroom Teacher
Blackstone School
Boston, Massachusetts

Deborah K. Wapner
4th Grade Classroom Teacher
Ashley River Creative Arts
  Elementary School
Charleston, South Carolina

Multicultural Reviewer
Joyce Buckner, Ed.D
Elementary Principal
Injury Control Research Center
Omaha Public Schools
Omaha, Nebraska

HEALTH ADVISORY BOARD MEMBERS

Lucinda Adams
State Advisor, Health Education
Former Director of Health
Dayton City Schools District
Dayton, Ohio

Clara Arch-Webster
Vice Principal
Duval County Schools
Jacksonville, Florida

Linda Carlton
Coordinator, Elementary Science & Health
Wichita, Kansas Public Schools USD 259
Wichita, Kansas

John Clayton
6th Grade Health Teacher
Orangewood Elementary School
Phoenix, Arizona

Pam Connolly
Subject Area Coordinator/HS Teacher
Diocese of Pittsburgh
Pittsburgh, Pennsylvania

Larry Herrold
Supervisor of Health Education, K–12
Baltimore County Public Schools
Baltimore, Maryland

Hollie Hinz
District Health Coordinator and
  Health Teacher
Menomonee Falls School District
Menomonee Falls, Wisconsin

Karen Mathews
5th Grade Teacher
Guilford County School
Greensboro, North Carolina

Patty O'Rourke
Health Coordinator
Cypress-Fairbanks I.S.D.
Houston, Texas

Sarah Roberts
6th Grade Health Teacher
McKinley Magnet School
Baton Rouge, Louisiana

Lindsay Shepheard
Health & Physical Education
  Program Coordinator
Virginia Beach City Public Schools
Virginia Beach, Virginia

Bob Wandberg
Health Education Curriculum & Instruction
Bloomington Public Schools
Bloomington, Minnesota

McGraw-Hill School Division ✖

A Division of The **McGraw-Hill** Companies

Copyright © 1999 McGraw-Hill School Division, a Division of the Educational and
Professional Publishing Group of The McGraw-Hill Companies, Inc.

McGraw-Hill School Division
1221 Avenue of the Americas
New York, New York 10020

Printed in the United States of America
ISBN 0-02-276418-6 / 4
    4 5 6 7 8 9 071 03 02 01 00 99

CONTENTS

LIFE SKILLS HANDBOOK

YOUR TEXTBOOK at a glance

McGraw-Hill Health has ten chapters, each one focusing on a special area of health. Every chapter has three or more lessons, plus special features for you to study and enjoy.

HEALTH ACTIVITY
Figure Out Food Labels

You will need: food labels from a variety of foods

1 Work with a group. List the nutrients from each label. Note which nutrient each food has the most of and the least of. Note the serving size and number of servings for each package.

2 Compare the facts for all the food labels. Decide which foods you think are the most healthful. Which would make the best snacks? Which might be good to include in a balanced diet?

3 Decide which foods are not good for you. What facts on the label led you to make this decision?

LESSON WRAP UP

Show What You Know

1. Why is it important to include fresh foods in your diet?

2. Why is it important to know the serving size shown on a food label?

3. Why is the list of ingredients on a food label important to consider when selecting a food?

4. **THINK CRITICALLY** Fresh foods are often considered better choices than similar packaged foods. In what ways might additives make packaged foods more healthful?

Show What You Can Do

5. **APPLY HEALTH ACTIVITY Make Decisions** Compare the food labels of two brands of your favorite cereal. Write a brief report explaining which brand is more healthful and why.

6. **PRACTICE LIFE SKILLS Practice Refusal Skills** Work with a partner. Write a skit to show how you would say "no" if someone offers you a snack that is not good for you. Take turns acting out your skit.

LESSON 3 · MAKING FOOD CHOICES **117**

HANDBOOK ● LIFE SKILLS pp. 276–287

Every lesson has a **Health Activity** to get you and your classmates actively involved in health issues. Every lesson also ends with a **Lesson Wrap-Up**.

Each lesson begins by highlighting **What You Will Learn** and the key lesson **Vocabulary**.

The **QUICK START** gives you a real-life problem to think about as you begin each lesson.

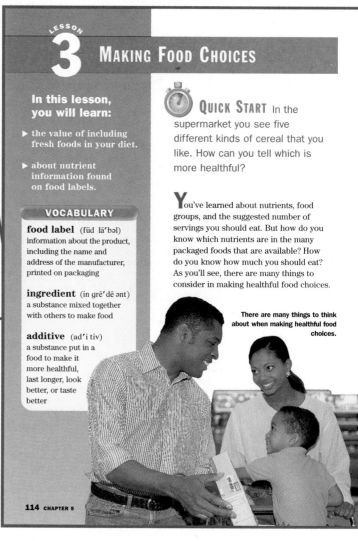

LESSON
3 MAKING FOOD CHOICES

In this lesson, you will learn:

▶ the value of including fresh foods in your diet.

▶ about nutrient information found on food labels.

VOCABULARY

food label (füd lā′bəl) information about the product, including the name and address of the manufacturer, printed on packaging

ingredient (in grē′dē ənt) a substance mixed together with others to make food

additive (ad′i tiv) a substance put in a food to make it more healthful, last longer, look better, or taste better

QUICK START In the supermarket you see five different kinds of cereal that you like. How can you tell which is more healthful?

You've learned about nutrients, food groups, and the suggested number of servings you should eat. But how do you know which nutrients are in the many packaged foods that are available? How do you know how much you should eat? As you'll see, there are many things to consider in making healthful food choices.

There are many things to think about when making healthful food choices.

114 CHAPTER 5

HEALTH FALLACY

Everyone needs 8 hours of sleep each night

This i̶   e needs
                  baby
                  d night.
                  u may

HEALTH FACT

Stress can give you extra strength.

This is true. Under s
releases a chemica
Adrenaline makes
work harder. That
more oxygen. Bl
brain and musc
become pale (
the help of a
have extra e
short time
ple have (
help oth

CULTURAL PERSPECTIVES

Rites of Passage

Many cultures celebrate becoming an adolescent with a special ceremony. These ceremo   *passage*. For might go throu mark her entry Thirteen-year-c might attend a synagogue. Do brations to ma into adolescen

HEALTHWISE CONSUMER

Pass the Sunscreen

Sunscreen products are rated according to the level of protection they provide from the sun's rays. The higher the SPF, the longer you can stay in the sun without burning.

Different sunscreen products suit dif-

A variety of features can be found within the lessons. **Health Fact** and **Health Fallacy** help you sort out the facts in health issues.

Do you wonder about health issues around the world? Check out **Cultural Perspectives** in each chapter.

Learn to be a **HealthWise Consumer** with tips on product safety and informed purchasing.

At the end of each chapter is a special page called **You Can Make a Difference**. Here you'll learn about health heroes who promote health and save lives, advances in health-related technology, or careers in health that might help you plan your future.

Infographics bring you information with pictures, diagrams, charts, and other visual clues.

INFOGRAPHIC

Dealing with Negative Influences

Saying "no" might not be easy—but sometimes it's a smart health choice. Following are some ways to handle negative influences. Think about which ones would work best for you.

Think about the possible results. Think about what might happen [if you] let yourself be influenced in a [negati]ve way. Some questions you might [ask y]ourself include "Might I, or someone [else, g]et sick or hurt if I do this? Might I [hurt s]omeone's feelings? The answers will [help y]ou decide what to do.

Think about your options. Saying "yes" or saying "no" may seem to be your only choices. But there may be other options. For example, suppose a friend wants you to climb up a dangerous hill. You might suggest a safer hill to climb. Or you might suggest playing a game or working on a hobby instead.

[... y]our values. [...]s important to you. [...] how you feel about [...] responsibility. [...]s according to what [...]ght—not what [...]say is right.

Remember that you are in charge of yourself. People may try to influence you by saying that you "have to" do something that you feel is unsafe or wrong. But you are in charge of yourself! Don't rush into things. If you have to, just walk away from the situation at that moment.

EMOTIONAL AND INTELLECTUAL HEALTH

HEALTHWISE CONSUMER

What's Not in an Ad?

Most food ads on TV or in magazines tell you very little about the actual nutrients in food. Instead, food ads often show people enjoying good times together, as if the food makes this happen. For the next week, pay special attention to food ads you see. Keep a record describing what the ads do and do not tell you.

Food Choices

As you grow older, you'll make more decisions about your life. You'll also make more choices as a consumer. Even today, you often decide for yourself what foods to eat. Perhaps you make your own breakfast. You may decide what lunch to buy or snacks to eat.

Eating fresh foods is one healthy food choice. Fresh foods do not have anything added to them. They have not been heated or frozen. Heating or freezing foods may destroy or break down some nutrients. Fresh fruits and vegetables are good food choices.

It's easier to make wise decisions if you have healthful choices in mind before you eat.

Healthful Food Choices	
Instead of . . .	**Choose . . .**
Potato Chips	Carrot Sticks
Ice Cream	Frozen Low-Fat Yogurt
Candy	Fresh Fruit
Soda	Unsweetened Juice or Water

Food Labels

Knowing how to read labels on food packages is important. It will help you make wise choices. The **food label** shows information that tells the buyer what is in the product and who made it. The law states that all packaged foods must have a label.

It takes time to read food labels, but your health is worth it. First you need to understand all the facts that are shown on food labels. Then you can judge whether or not a food is good for you. The food label shown on the next page is from a container of orange juice.

LIFE SKILL
PRACTICE REFUSAL SKILLS
What Would You Do?

Your sister is trying to talk you into buying some sweets on the way home from school. How would you tell her that you plan to make a more healthful choice? What would you choose?

HANDBOOK · LIFE SKILLS pp. 276–287   LESSON 3 · MAKING FOOD CHOICES **115**

▲ The **What Would You Do?** features help you apply life skills and what you've just learned.

The **Handbook** is a convenient reference tool with information on everything from setting health goals to performing first aid. It also lists health-related books, videos, and Web sites.

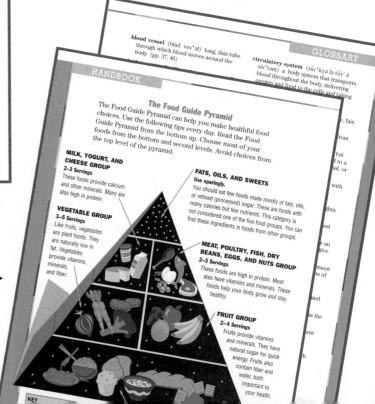

blood vessel (blud ves'əl) long, thin tube through which blood moves around the body (pp. 37, 46)

circulatory system (sûr'kyə lə tôr' ē sis'təm) a body system that transports blood throughout the body, delivering oxygen and food to the cells and taking

GLOSSARY

HANDBOOK

The Food Guide Pyramid

The Food Guide Pyramid can help you make healthful food choices. Use the following tips every day. Read the Food Guide Pyramid from the bottom up. Choose most of your foods from the bottom and second levels. Avoid choices from the top level of the pyramid.

MILK, YOGURT, AND CHEESE GROUP
2–3 Servings
These foods provide calcium and other minerals. Many are also high in protein.

FATS, OILS, AND SWEETS
Use sparingly.
You should eat few foods made mostly of fats, oils, or refined (processed) sugar. These are foods with many calories but few nutrients. This category is not considered one of the five food groups. You can find these ingredients in foods from other groups.

VEGETABLE GROUP
3–5 Servings
Like fruits, vegetables are plant foods. They are naturally low in fat. Vegetables provide vitamins, minerals, and fiber.

MEAT, POULTRY, FISH, DRY BEANS, EGGS, AND NUTS GROUP
2–3 Servings
These foods are high in protein. Most also have vitamins and minerals. These foods help your body grow and stay healthy.

FRUIT GROUP
2–4 Servings
Fruits provide vitamins and minerals. They have natural sugar for quick energy. Fruits also contain fiber and water, both important to your health.

KEY

McGraw-Hill Health and the Health Pyramid

McGraw-Hill Health was created to help you explore all aspects of your health. The lessons, features, questions, and activities are designed to help you be as healthy as you can be.

We've created the McGraw-Hill Health Pyramid to help you take charge of your health. It shows the skills and abilities that will help you attain the goal of health.

The "point" of this pyramid!

Five abilities you can build.

Six skills you will use throughout your life

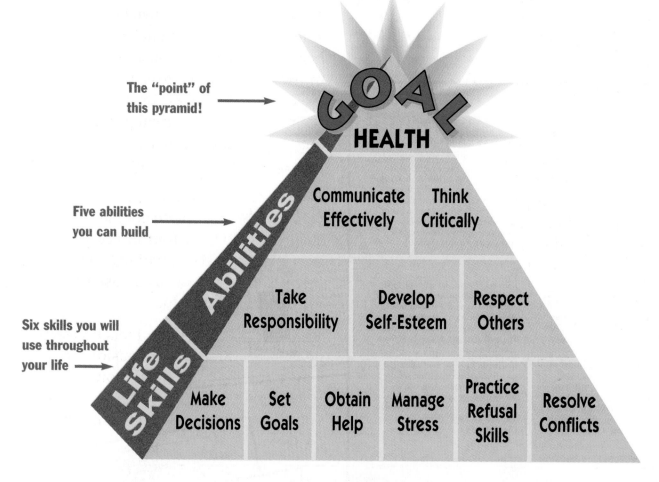

GOAL

HEALTH

Abilities

Communicate Effectively

Think Critically

Take Responsibility

Develop Self-Esteem

Respect Others

Life Skills

Make Decisions

Set Goals

Obtain Help

Manage Stress

Practice Refusal Skills

Resolve Conflicts

Five Abilities That Really Help

Communicate Effectively Talk and listen to people to share information, ideas, and feelings.

Think Critically Use your brain power to solve problems and make wise choices.

Take Responsibility Take charge of your life by protecting your rights and sticking to your responsibilities.

Develop Self-Esteem Build a positive and realistic picture of yourself.

Respect Others Consider how your decisions and actions affect other people.

What Are Life Skills?

The base of the pyramid shows six life skills that are the foundation of health. As you develop these skills, the abilities shown in the middle of the pyramid will also develop.

You will have many opportunities to practice the six life skills as you work with *McGraw-Hill Health*. The Handbook that begins on page 275 gives you more information about each skill.

Make Decisions Can't make up your mind? You need to practice decision making. You face decisions every day. What kind of after-school activities will you get involved in? How can you help your friend deal with a bully? What will you do Monday night?

Set Goals The best way to get something done is to set a goal and then figure out how to reach it. You might have individual goals, like learning how to swim, or group goals, like discovering a great place to explore with your family.

Obtain Help Getting help when you need it is a key part of health. Help might be first aid, advice, or factual information about an important topic. You can get help from many different people, including your family, teacher, and doctor.

Manage Stress Your teacher announces a surprise quiz. Does your hair stand on end because you're tense or nervous? That's stress, a feeling of tension you get when something bothers you. It's a normal part of life, but with practice, you can learn how to manage your stress wisely.

Practice Refusal Skills Being responsible for your health means saying "no" to unhealthy offers. If someone suggests something that you know isn't healthy, you can use your refusal skills to say "no."

Resolve Conflicts Conflicts between people create stress and tension. To stay healthy, you can learn how to resolve conflicts. These ideas can help you find solutions to even the hardest problems.

Am I Health Wise?

Health includes how you feel, how you act, and how you react. Your **physical health** relates to your body. Your **emotional and intellectual health** relates to your thoughts and feelings. Your **social health** has to do with your relationships with other people. On a separate piece of paper, try this quiz to see whether the three parts of your health are in balance.

PHYSICAL HEALTH

1. I eat well-balanced meals.	ALWAYS	SOMETIMES	NEVER
2. I eat healthful snacks.	ALWAYS	SOMETIMES	NEVER
3. I get enough sleep.	ALWAYS	SOMETIMES	NEVER
4. I am physically active.	ALWAYS	SOMETIMES	NEVER
5. I avoid alcohol, tobacco, and drugs.	ALWAYS	SOMETIMES	NEVER
6. I get regular checkups.	ALWAYS	SOMETIMES	NEVER

EMOTIONAL AND INTELLECTUAL HEALTH

1. I feel good about myself.	ALWAYS	SOMETIMES	NEVER
2. I do many things well.	ALWAYS	SOMETIMES	NEVER
3. I have people I can talk to.	ALWAYS	SOMETIMES	NEVER
4. I apologize when I'm wrong.	ALWAYS	SOMETIMES	NEVER
5. I can be angry without being violent.	ALWAYS	SOMETIMES	NEVER
6. I love learning new skills.	ALWAYS	SOMETIMES	NEVER

SOCIAL HEALTH

1. I make friends easily.	ALWAYS	SOMETIMES	NEVER
2. I can say "no" if necessary.	ALWAYS	SOMETIMES	NEVER
3. I get along with classmates.	ALWAYS	SOMETIMES	NEVER
4. I cooperate with others.	ALWAYS	SOMETIMES	NEVER
5. People seem to like me.	ALWAYS	SOMETIMES	NEVER
6. I can resolve conflicts without fighting.	ALWAYS	SOMETIMES	NEVER

Score 2 points for each ALWAYS, 1 point for each SOMETIMES, and 0 points for each NEVER. Add up your score for each category.

8–12 points:	4–7 points:	0–6 points:
HealthWise	Needs Improvement	Must Do Better

In which area do you score highest? Are your three scores balanced? Where could you use improvement?

PERSONAL HEALTH

CHAPTER 1

THE BIG IDEA

There are many things you can do to stay healthy. You can:

- make wise decisions that keep you healthy.

- keep a positive attitude.

- take care of your teeth, eyes, ears, skin, and hair so that you feel and look good.

CHAPTER CONTENTS

1 WHAT IS HEALTH?

In this lesson, you will learn:

▶ about the three different parts of health.

▶ the difference between healthful and risky behaviors.

VOCABULARY

physical health
(fiz′i kəl helth) health of the body

emotional and intellectual health
(i mō′shə nəl and in′tə lek′chü əl helth) health of the mind, having to do with feelings and thoughts

social health (sō′shəl helth) health having to do with relationships with other people

healthful (helth′fəl) good for your health

risk (risk) the chance of injury, damage, or loss

QUICK START What does being "healthy" mean to you?

You may think that being healthy means you have a healthy body—you are not sick and have no injuries. However, the health of your body is only one part of being healthy. Having a healthy mind and enjoying healthy relationships are important parts of good health, too.

Being healthy means having a healthy mind, healthy feelings, and healthy relationships.

The Three Parts of Health

Your body, your mind, and your relationships work together to make you a healthy person. The health of your body is your **physical health**. Your feelings and thoughts are part of your **emotional and intellectual health**. Your relationships with people are part of your **social health**.

Sometimes you may feel healthy in one way but not in others. Your body might feel fine, but you are unhappy. Perhaps you've had a fight with a good friend. These are health problems, too.

The way you feel in one part of your health can affect the other parts. Think about how you feel when you have the flu. Your body has many aches and pains. You can't play with your friends. All of this can put you in a bad mood. The next thing you know, you feel angry with your sister for no reason. Your physical health has affected other parts of your health.

CULTURAL PERSPECTIVES

Good Health Around the World

How you stay healthy is part of your *culture*, or way of life. Your clothes, your languages, your beliefs—all of these are parts of your culture, too.

People from different cultures take care of themselves in different ways. They may bathe in a stream or in a shower. They may sleep in a bed or on a mat on the floor. But people from all cultures share the goal of staying healthy.

MAKE DECISIONS
What Would You Do?

A friend says that biking is good physical activity. He wants you to ride with him on a busy road after dark. What would you decide to do?

Staying Healthy

No one is in perfect health all of the time. What matters is knowing how to stay healthy most of the time. You will learn a lot this year about how you can do the best for your own health.

The actions that you take can make a difference. Knowing how your body works and how to take care of it will affect your physical health. Using your mind to learn new things will affect your intellectual health. Understanding your feelings will affect your emotional and social health.

Acting in a way that harms you is not healthful. When you take a **risk**, you take a chance of injuring, damaging, or losing something or someone. Some risks—such as playing with matches—are clear. Others are not as clear. To stay healthy, you need to have *behaviors*, ways you act, that are healthful. You also need to avoid risky behaviors.

Healthful Behaviors

Risky Behaviors

PHYSICAL HEALTH

⭐ Regular physical activity

⭐ Eating healthful meals

⭐ Getting enough sleep

⭐ Taking medicine from the doctor

⭐ Using sport safety equipment

✖ Little or no physical activity

✖ Skipping meals

✖ Staying up late

✖ Taking illegal drugs

✖ Not using safety equipment

EMOTIONAL AND INTELLECTUAL HEALTH

⭐ Asking questions

⭐ Learning about new things

⭐ Talking about your problems

⭐ Dealing with your feelings

✖ Not asking a question when you have one

✖ Not being interested in new things

✖ Complaining all the time

✖ Ignoring your feelings

SOCIAL HEALTH

⭐ Being nice to neighbors

⭐ Cooperating with classmates

⭐ Sharing ideas with friends

✖ Being mean to neighbors

✖ Arguing with classmates

✖ Letting friends boss you around

Action Analysis

SET
GOALS

1 With the class, brainstorm examples of healthful and risky behaviors. Categorize the behaviors by the type of health it affects most.

2 Work with a partner. List six behaviors you have done or might do. Put these behaviors in order from most to least important. Decide which are healthful behaviors and which are risky.

3 Review your list. Make changes if you wish. Talk about goals you can set to practice the healthful behaviors and to avoid the risky behaviors. Share your ideas with the class.

LESSON WRAP UP

Show What You Know

1. What are the three parts of a person's health?

2. Name one healthful behavior and one risky behavior for each part of health.

3. **THINK CRITICALLY** Why would asking questions in class be considered a healthful habit?

Show What You Can Do

4. **APPLY HEALTH ACTIVITY**
   Set Goals Identify one risky behavior in your life. Write at least two goals that will help you change that behavior.

5. **PRACTICE LIFE SKILLS**
   Make Decisions Describe five behaviors that you saw on TV recently. Decide whether each is healthful or risky. How could these behaviors influence health?

2 PERSONAL HEALTH CARE

In this lesson, you will learn:

▶ how to develop responsibility for your own health.

▶ the importance of checkups, sleep and rest, and good posture.

VOCABULARY

responsible
(ri spon′sə bəl) being in charge, especially in taking care of your own health

behavior (bi hāv′yər) the way a person acts

attitude (at′i tüd′) thoughts and feelings about something

posture (pos′chər) the way a person holds or carries the body when sitting, standing, and walking

QUICK START You're playing in an important softball game tomorrow morning. You also want to stay up later to play a board game. "Losing a few hours' sleep doesn't matter," you think. Does it matter? Why or why not?

Being healthy means being at your best. In many ways you are **responsible** for, or in charge of, your own health. Your parents and other trusted adults may help set rules for you to follow. But it's up to you to know your strengths and weaknesses. It's up to you to learn good health habits.

How can staying up late to play a game affect your health?

What Affects Your Health

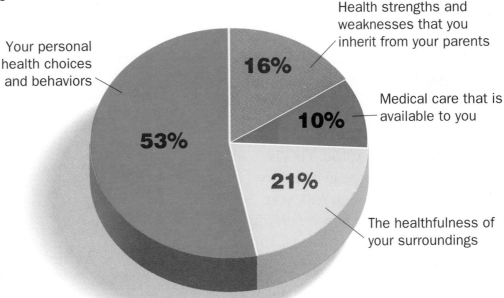

Your personal health choices and behaviors — **53%**

Health strengths and weaknesses that you inherit from your parents — **16%**

Medical care that is available to you — **10%**

The healthfulness of your surroundings — **21%**

The Importance of Your Actions

As the graph above shows, many things affect your health. You can't control everything about your own health. But you can control choices that you make. You can control your **behavior**, which is the way you act. Choosing the right food and getting enough sleep are behaviors that can help keep you healthy. Disobeying traffic rules is not a healthful behavior.

It's easy to see behavior. It's harder to see attitudes. **Attitudes** are ways of thinking and feeling about things. Your attitudes can affect your health. For example, you may think you will never fall while riding your bicycle. Maybe you think that wearing a bicycle helmet is silly. Those attitudes may lead you to take a serious risk.

You can change your attitudes and behaviors. Start by making a plan for good health. Set small goals that you can reach. Then move on to bigger goals. Every change will help you be healthier!

SET GOALS

What Would You Do?

It's your first day at a new school. You don't know anyone. You do know that having friends is part of being healthy. Think about healthful behaviors and attitudes about friendship. What is one healthful goal that you could set for yourself?

The Importance of Checkups

Getting good medical care is important too. It is another way people can be responsible for their own health. People of all ages need regular checkups with a doctor. Doctors and nurses can take care of you when you are sick or hurt. Doctors also can find health problems you may not even know you have. They can help you before these problems cause serious trouble. Regular checkups can help you stay healthy.

The Importance of Sleep and Rest

Getting enough sleep and rest is also important to being healthy. As you rest or sleep, your body slows down. Some of the energy you save is used to repair the body.

Your body stores energy, too. This is something like the charge in a battery. When you don't get enough rest, you aren't "charged up." You may be cranky or unable to pay attention in class. You may have headaches or very little energy.

Short rests or naps can help you have energy. But longer periods of sleep are even more important. A parent or other trusted adult can help you plan the right amount of sleep, rest, and activity. They can also help if noise, bad dreams, or other problems keep you from sleeping well.

HEALTH FALLACY

" Everyone needs 8 hours of sleep each night. "

This is not true. Not everyone needs the same amount of sleep. A baby sleeps for much of the day and night. Because you're still growing, you may need 9 to 10 hours of sleep. Many adults need about 7 to 8 hours of sleep each night. As adults grow older, they may need less sleep.

There's no "right" amount of sleep for everyone. The best way to tell if you're getting enough sleep is to "listen" to your body for signs of being tired.

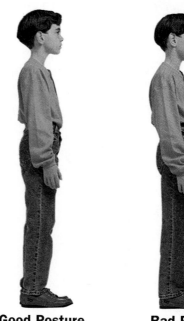

Good Posture   **Bad Posture**

Good posture is a healthful habit that shows the world that you feel good about yourself. What do you think bad posture shows?

The Importance of Good Posture

"Sit up straight!" Has anyone ever said that to you? You probably did not think that sitting up straight is important to your health. But it is. Your **posture** is the way that you hold or carry your body when you sit, stand, and walk. When you have good posture, you hold your back and shoulders straight. This helps you breathe deeply. If you have poor posture—if you slump or slouch— you become tired more easily.

Your posture also says something about you. When you stand up straight, with your shoulders back and your head high, you look like you feel good about yourself. Someone who slouches down in a chair does not look self-confident or happy. If you practice good posture, it will feel normal to you. Good posture helps you be healthy.

Health Behaviors

1 Take an inventory of your personal health behaviors. Make a chart like the one shown.

2 Which behaviors do you think you would like to improve? What goals can you set to do this?

3 Talk to a parent, teacher, or other trusted adult about the goals you set. Show them your chart. Ask them to help you make decisions about ways you can improve your health.

Health Behavior	Benefit	Do I Do It?	How Can I Improve?
wear bike helmet	protect my head and brain	most of the time	I really should wear my helmet whenever I ride.
brush and floss my teeth	no cavities, no bad breath	yes	I'm OK.

LESSON WRAP UP

Show What You Know

1. Name a healthful behavior.

2. Why is it important to get enough sleep and rest?

3. Suppose that a friend is slumping or slouching at her desk. How might this interfere with her school work?

4. **THINK CRITICALLY** What are some things you can do to show that you are responsible for your own health?

Show What You Can Do

5. **PORTFOLIO** **APPLY HEALTH ACTIVITY**
   Obtain Help With a partner, write a poem about how you can improve your health. Describe other people who can help you improve your health habits. Share your finished poem.

6. **PRACTICE LIFE SKILLS**
   Make Decisions Decide on two things you can do to improve your posture. Write your decisions and explain how they will help your posture.

3 ORAL HEALTH

In this lesson, you will learn:

▶ about the different kinds of teeth you have and what each kind does.

▶ the proper ways to care for your teeth and gums.

VOCABULARY

enamel (i nam′əl) the hard, white, protective outer layer of teeth

plaque (plak) a sticky film left on teeth by food and germs; if not removed, can harm tooth enamel

cavity (kav′i tē) a place that has worn away in a tooth; a hole in a tooth

tartar (tär′tər) a yellowish substance that forms on teeth when plaque hardens

fluoride (flùr′īd) a substance that strengthens tooth enamel and helps prevent cavities

QUICK START "Brush your teeth before bed," you're told. Brushing your teeth is important. Why is bedtime a good time to brush? What are some other times you should brush your teeth? Why?

Think about your favorite family pictures. In most of them, people are smiling. It's hard not to smile back! Your teeth play a big part in how you look. Even more important, your teeth chew the food you eat so that your body can use it. Good *oral health*—the health of your teeth and gums—is an important part of being healthy.

Parts of a Tooth

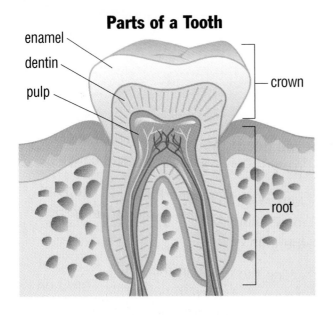

- enamel
- dentin
- pulp
- crown
- root

Your Teeth and Gums

People grow two sets of teeth. As a baby, you probably cried when your first set of teeth, your *primary teeth*, cut through your gums. You grew 20 primary teeth in all.

When you were about 6 years old, you began to lose some of your primary teeth. In their place grew *permanent teeth*. Right now, you probably have some primary teeth and some permanent teeth. Within the next

10 years or so, you should grow a total of 32 permanent teeth. You should take care of these teeth, because they are supposed to last for the rest of your life.

You can see the parts of a tooth in the drawing at the left. Each tooth is attached to your jawbone by its *root*. The root is hidden by your gums. The part of the tooth that you can see is the *crown*. The **enamel** covers the crown and protects the inside of the tooth. Much of the inside of a tooth is made of *dentin*, which covers the *pulp*. Inside the pulp are the blood vessels and nerves that keep the tooth alive.

Look at the four kinds of teeth shown below. Each kind does a different job. *Incisors* bite into food. *Cuspids* tear it apart. *Bicuspids* crush food, and *molars* grind it up. Then food is easily digested.

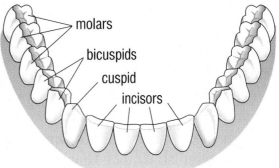

What are teeth good for other than smiling?

Types of Teeth

Upper teeth

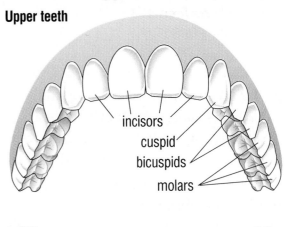

- incisors
- cuspid
- bicuspids
- molars

- molars
- bicuspids
- cuspid
- incisors

Lower teeth

HEALTH ACTIVITY
Cover Up

You will need: two pieces of chalk, clear nail polish, a glass of water, food coloring

1 Work with a partner. Put a few drops of food coloring in the glass of water. Set the glass aside.

2 Using the brush in the bottle, coat one piece of chalk with nail polish. Blow on that piece of chalk until the nail polish is dry.

3 Dip both pieces of chalk into the colored water for about 10 seconds. Take them out and look at them. How are they different? Talk about what the nail polish did. How is that like what enamel does for your teeth?

Caring for Your Teeth and Gums

If you want healthy teeth and gums, you should brush your teeth at least twice a day. Brush before you go to bed to clean away pieces of food left from your dinner. Try to brush or rinse your mouth with water after every meal.

Taking care of your teeth helps prevent tooth decay. Brushing removes **plaque**, a sticky film that forms on your teeth. Germs in plaque produce a chemical that can break through the enamel. This causes a **cavity**, or hole in your tooth. Plaque can harden into **tartar**, a hard, yellowish substance that can damage your gums.

Use toothpastes that contain fluoride. **Fluoride** strengthens tooth enamel and helps prevent cavities. Use dental floss to remove food and plaque from between your teeth. First wind the floss between your fingers. Then gently move it back and forth between all of your teeth.

LIFE SKILL

OBTAIN HELP

What Would You Do?

Suppose you have never used dental floss. Who could help you learn the right way to use it?

Visiting the Dentist

Have regular dental checkups at least once a year. During a checkup, your teeth will get a special cleaning. They may also be coated with fluoride. The dentist will examine your teeth and gums for problems. He or she may take x-rays of your teeth. X-rays can show problems that are hard to see. If there is a cavity, the dentist can clean and fill it. If there are other problems, the dentist will talk to you about them.

The dentist can show you the proper ways to brush and floss your teeth. He or she can tell you which kind of toothbrush or toothpaste is best for you to use.

Visit the dentist if you have sore gums or a toothache. Also see a dentist if you feel pain when you eat hot or cold foods. With a dentist's help, and with your own good health habits, you can expect your teeth to last a lifetime.

HEALTHWISE CONSUMER

Wired for Braces

When some people bite down, their upper and lower teeth do not line up properly. This can cause problems with biting and chewing. It can also wear down enamel.

Did you know that there are different kinds of dentists for different dental problems? If you need special dental services, your regular dentist can usually recommend the right person to see.

An *orthodontist* is a dentist who specializes in correcting bite problems. If teeth are crooked or don't line up properly, an orthodontist may fit them with braces. Braces push and pull teeth in order to line them up correctly. The length of time a person needs to wear braces will vary.

LESSON WRAP UP

Show What You Know

1. Tell how the four kinds of teeth help you eat.

2. Why is it important to brush and floss your teeth?

3. **THINK CRITICALLY** Over the past few days, you've noticed that your gums bleed a little when you brush your teeth. What might be the problem?

Show What You Can Do

4. **PORTFOLIO** **APPLY HEALTH ACTIVITY** **Science Connection** Write a funny story about germs on a person's teeth. Tell about the problems the germs would like to cause. Tell how the enamel and good oral health habits defeat the germs.

5. **LIFE SKILL** **PRACTICE LIFE SKILLS** **Set Goals** Think about how you could improve your oral health. Write two goals to help you make your teeth and gums healthier.

4 EYE CARE AND EAR CARE

In this lesson, you will learn:

▶ **how your eyes and ears help you see and hear.**

▶ **warning signs of vision and hearing problems.**

▶ **proper ways to care for your eyes and ears.**

VOCABULARY

vision (vizh′ən) the ability to see; eyesight

eardrum (îr′drum′) a thin membrane inside the ear that makes hearing possible by vibrating when sound waves hit it

nearsighted (nîr′sī′tid) being able to see objects that are near better than objects that are far away

farsighted (fär′sī′tid) being able to see objects that are far away better than objects that are near

QUICK START If you look at the faces of bicyclists in a race, you'll see that most riders are wearing goggles. Do you think all of the riders need glasses? Or is there another reason for the goggles?

Your eyes and ears collect information about the world around you. That's why it's important to take care of them. Without your eyes, you wouldn't be able to read a book, enjoy movies, or see a red traffic light. Healthy eyes provide you with **vision**, the ability to see.

Your ears let you hear what's going on in the world. You listen to your favorite music. You hear a friend whisper. You jump at the sound of a smoke alarm. Did you know that your ears even help you keep your balance?

How are these people using their eyes and ears?

How Eyes and Ears Work

You know that you see with your eyes and hear with your ears. Did you know that you couldn't see or hear without the help of your brain?

Suppose you see a friend in a red T-shirt. Muscles move your eyes to see the shirt as clearly as possible. Light bouncing off the shirt enters your eyes. The light carries information about color and shape. That information travels to your brain through the nerves that connect your eyes and brain. Your brain *interprets*, or makes sense of, that information.

Suppose your friend is listening to a song on the radio. How does your brain help you hear the music? The shape of your outer ear helps sound waves move inside. The sound waves move toward your eardrum. The **eardrum** is a thin membrane, or layer of skin, that vibrates. Those vibrations travel to nerves. The nerves carry the vibrations to the brain. Then your brain interprets what it hears.

Parts of the Ear

outer ear   middle ear   inner ear

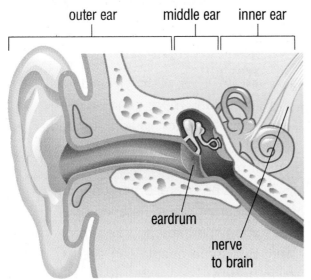

eardrum

nerve to brain

Common Eye and Ear Problems

Like the rest of your body, your eyes and ears need good care. Knowing about some common problems can help you keep your eyes and ears healthy.

To many people, some things look blurry. **Nearsighted** people can see objects that are near better than they can see objects that are far away. People who are **farsighted** can see objects that are far away better than objects that are near. Both problems can be corrected with glasses or with contact lenses.

Sometimes your eyes might feel itchy or become red or teary. Be sure to get help if this happens to you. You might have allergies, an infection, or some other problem. Also get help if a piece of dirt or anything else gets into your eye.

Tell an adult if you have trouble hearing—for example, if voices sound "fuzzy." You should also tell an adult if your ears hurt. Get help if you have a ringing sound in your ears. Infections or other illnesses often cause these problems.

LIFE SKILL

MAKE DECISIONS

What Would You Do?

Suppose you have just found out that you are farsighted. You start wearing glasses. A classmate says that glasses look dumb and that you shouldn't wear them. What would you decide to do?

Caring for Your Vision

These healthful habits will help you take good care of your vision.

- Read and work in well-lit areas.

- Don't rub your eyes.

- Wear sunglasses to protect your eyes from the harmful rays of the sun. Make sure you never look directly at the sun.

- Wear safety glasses or goggles when you play sports.

- Never put anything into your eyes unless a trusted adult says to.

- Sometimes a piece of dust or hair gets into your eye. Have an adult help you wash it out with water.

- If a hard object hits your eye, have a doctor check for injury.

- Have your vision checked every year. A doctor or school nurse can help make sure that your eyes are healthy. A doctor can send you to someone who can fit you with glasses if you need them.

Caring for Your Hearing

Following are some tips for taking good care of your hearing.

- Avoid loud noises. Don't listen to music that is played very loudly, especially not through headphones.

- Wear a helmet when you play sports such as football or baseball.

- Never put objects in your ear. They may damage your eardrum. If they get stuck, a doctor or nurse would have to remove them. Germs on the objects might also cause ear infections or other illnesses.

- Never use a cotton swab to clean inside your ears.

- If you think you have a lot of wax inside your ears, or if you have an earache, get help from an adult.

- To help avoid ear infections, dry your ears well after swimming.

- See your doctor or school nurse for a regular hearing checkup every year.

HEALTH FACT

" **No one has perfect eyesight.** "

This is true. There is no such thing as "perfect" vision. Instead, we say that people with 20/20 vision have normal vision. Normal vision is what an average person can see clearly from a distance of 20 feet. Many people can't see that well. But some people can see even better!

HEALTH ACTIVITY
Ask an Expert

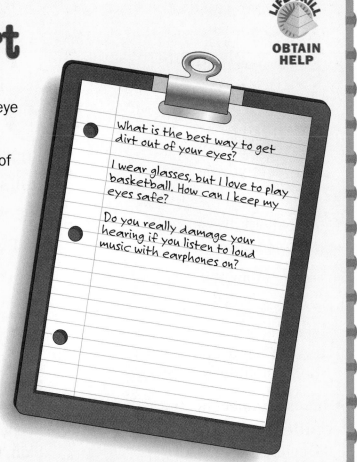

LIFE SKILL

OBTAIN HELP

1 What questions do you have about eye and ear safety?

2 Work with your class to make a list of questions.

3 Invite a teacher, doctor, nurse, or other expert to speak to your class and answer your questions. Or include your questions in a letter from your class to one of these people.

4 If a speaker visits your class, listen politely. Talk about what you are learning. Afterward, send the speaker a thank-you note from the class.

What is the best way to get dirt out of your eyes?

I wear glasses, but I love to play basketball. How can I keep my eyes safe?

Do you really damage your hearing if you listen to loud music with earphones on?

LESSON WRAP UP

Show What You Know

1. Explain how you get information from your eyes and ears.

2. Describe one vision or hearing problem that needs a doctor's care.

3. List three rules each for eye and ear care.

4. **THINK CRITICALLY** Why should you read in an area that has good lighting?

Show What You Can Do

5. **PORTFOLIO** **APPLY HEALTH ACTIVITY** **Obtain Help** With a partner, make a question-and-answer booklet about eye and ear safety. Ask a health expert to review and comment on your booklet.

6. **LIFE SKILL** **PRACTICE LIFE SKILLS** **Manage Stress** With a partner, list some sounds that most people can hear. Order the list from softest to loudest. Which sounds are stressful to you? Tell what you can do to deal with the stress.

5 SKIN, HAIR, AND NAIL CARE

In this lesson, you will learn:

▶ about the layers of the skin.

▶ the purpose of skin, hair, and nails.

▶ proper ways to care for your skin, hair, and nails.

VOCABULARY

epidermis (ep'i dûr'mis) the outer layer of skin

pore (pôr) a tiny opening in the skin, through which liquids such as oil or sweat move

dermis (dûr'mis) the layer of skin just beneath the epidermis

gland (gland) a part of the body that produces substances needed by the body, including liquids such as sweat or oil

QUICK START You probably know some people who bite their nails. You might even be one of them! Why is it a healthy decision to stop biting your nails?

Keeping your nails, skin, and hair neat and clean helps you look good. When you look good, you usually feel good about yourself. But did you know that there are also important health reasons for keeping your nails, hair, and skin clean? Skin, hair, and nails that are not cared for can cause problems. The good news is that taking good care of these parts of your body is easy!

Taking a bath is a healthful habit that feels good, too!

Parts of Your Skin

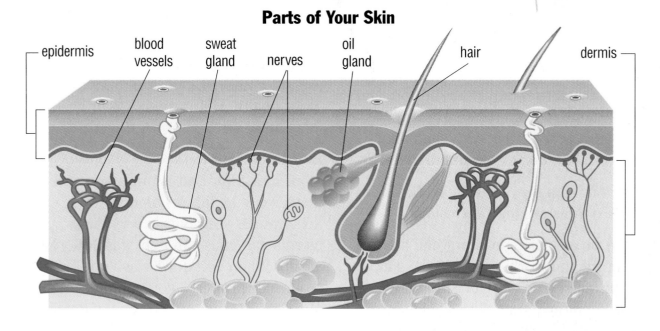

epidermis   blood vessels   sweat gland   nerves   oil gland   hair   dermis

Your Skin

Like most people, you probably take your skin for granted. In fact, it's as important to your health as your heart or lungs. Your skin is your body's first line of defense against illness. It also helps protect the organs inside your body.

The outer layer of skin is the **epidermis**. Nerves in the epidermis send messages to your brain. Your brain recognizes the things that touch your skin as being hot or cold, rough or smooth, and so on.

The epidermis is where melanin is made. *Melanin* gives your skin color. Darker skin has more melanin than lighter skin. In fact, freckles are areas of skin made darker by melanin.

Although the epidermis is nearly waterproof, it contains tiny holes. These are called pores. **Pores** link the epidermis to the layer of skin below it. This layer, the largest part of the skin, is the **dermis**. The dermis contains nerves and blood vessels. The hair on your body is rooted to the dermis.

Pores lead to glands in the dermis. **Glands** produce substances needed by the body, such as oil and sweat. Oil from the dermis keeps your skin from drying out. Sweat helps your body cool off. When air dries the sweat on your skin, you feel cooler. Your skin's sweat glands also help your body get rid of wastes.

Of course, you couldn't live without your skin! Your skin has some defenses that help protect it. You have read about melanin. One of the jobs of melanin is to protect your skin from the sun's radiation. When you stay in the sun, your skin makes more melanin. That can make your skin look darker.

Some people like to get a suntan. However, they are taking a serious risk with their health. Too much sun can cause skin cancers. It also can make your skin more wrinkled. It is up to you to protect yourself from getting too much sun. Look at the list on the next page to see some ways you can take care of your skin.

Taking Care of Your Skin

Following are some tips for taking good care of your skin.

- Wash well to remove the dirt, oil, and germs that collect on your skin. Wash at least twice a day with soap and water. Pat, don't rub your skin dry.

- If your skin becomes dry and cracked, use a moisturizing skin cream.

- Put on a sunscreen about half an hour before you work or play in the sun. Use sunscreen with an SPF (sun protection factor) of 15 or higher. Reapply it every 2 hours and after washing, swimming, or heavy sweating. Wear protective clothing.

- Watch what you eat. Healthful foods help all parts of your body, including your skin.

- Get enough rest and sleep. This helps your skin look good, too.

HEALTHWISE CONSUMER

Pass the Sunscreen

Sunscreen products are rated according to the level of protection they provide from the sun's rays. The higher the SPF, the longer you can stay in the sun without burning.

Different sunscreen products suit different needs. For example, you can use a waterproof sunscreen if you plan to swim. Also, sunscreens are sometimes combined with other health products. For example, you might want to use a sunscreen with insect repellent while hiking or camping.

Your Hair

Healthy hair helps you look and feel better. But hair is more than something to cut, comb, or curl. It plays a role in your health. Hair protects your scalp. It also helps keep your head warm.

It is important to take good care of your hair. Hair that is not taken care of can create health problems. For example, if your hair is very dirty, germs can cause an itchy rash on your scalp. When you don't wash and brush your hair properly, you could get dandruff. *Dandruff*—pieces of dead scalp—can be seen in your hair and on your clothes. Very oily hair can collect dirt. It makes a good place for germs to grow. Very dry hair can break.

If you use the comb or brush of someone who has *head lice*, you could get head lice too. You can also get head lice if you wear the hat or cap of someone who has head lice. These tiny, flat insects without wings can live on a person's scalp. You can get rid of head lice with special shampoos and combs. But it's better not to get them at all!

Taking Care of Your Hair

Following are some tips for taking good care of your hair.

- Choose a shampoo that is made for your kind of hair. How often you should wash your hair depends on the kind of hair you have. Most hair should be washed at least a few times a week.

- Wash your hair properly. Lather well at the roots. Then let the suds run through the rest of your hair. Rinse your hair completely. Gently towel-dry your hair.

- Be careful about using a blow-dryer. If the air is too hot, it can cause your hair to become too dry and break.

- At least once a day, brush your hair to get rid of dirt and dandruff. Brushing spreads oil from your scalp through your hair. This can help keep your hair from drying out and breaking. But be careful not to brush too hard. Also, do not share your brush with others.

Your Nails

You feel much of the world through your fingers and toes. So it's important to protect them. Your fingernails and toenails give you some natural protection. Made of hard *keratin*, your nails cover and protect the soft *nail bed* under the nail. Good nail care makes that protection even better.

Taking Care of Your Nails

Following are some tips for taking good care of your nails.

- Don't bite your nails. Biting nails damages them. It can also break the skin and cause infections. If stopping this habit seems too hard, ask an adult for help.

- Keep your nails clean. Scrub well with a nail brush. Remember to scrub under your nails, too.

- Trim your nails carefully. Use a nail clipper or nail scissors to cut them to a safe length—just a little beyond your fingertips.

- Smooth the edges of your nails with a nail file or emery board. File in one direction. Leave the sides of the nail straight. Round the top of each nail a little.

 LIFE SKILL

MAKE DECISIONS

What Would You Do?

One of your fingernails breaks below the nail bed. It bleeds a little. Ouch! It hurts, too! What would you do?

Taking Care of Me!

SET
GOALS

Grooming Tips	Reasons	Results
Don't over dry your hair with a blow dryer.	Don't want to damage my hair.	Used the dryer for 5 minutes, then I let my hair dry by itself. It looked great!

1 Think about the kind of skin, hair, and nails that you have. Look at the tips on pages 20–21 for ideas about taking care of these parts of your body. Which tips do you use already?

2 Think about the tips that you don't already use. Then divide your paper into three columns. In the first column, write two tips that you think you could try. In the second column, write why you want to try each one.

3 For the next week, try using those tips. Then review your goals. In the third column, write how well you did.

LESSON WRAP UP

Show What You Know

1. Name the layers of the skin.

2. How do skin, hair, and nails protect the body?

3. Name two ways to care for each of the following—skin, hair, and nails.

4. **THINK CRITICALLY** "Oil can be both good and bad for your hair." How is this statement true?

Show What You Can Do

5. **PORTFOLIO** **APPLY HEALTH ACTIVITY**
Set Goals Create a brochure for younger students about personal grooming habits. Help them determine whether they are taking good care of their skin, hair, and nails. Give them grooming tips.

6. **PRACTICE LIFE SKILLS**
Obtain Help For three days, the skin on your arm has been dry and red, with small bumps that itch. Why is it important to obtain help from an adult?

Technology Testers

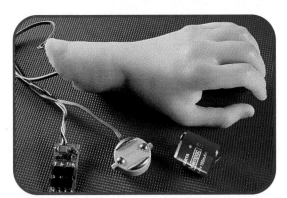

Equipment like this helps people with disabilities.

A program in Wilmington, Delaware, hires children with disabilities to test equipment. The equipment is designed to promote the health of people with disabilities. The children attend meetings with engineers and give them feedback about the new inventions.

Bern Gavlick has cerebral palsy. He gets around with a wheelchair, but his hand and arm movements are limited. He was asked to test a special robot arm that attaches to his wheelchair.

C. J. Marconi, who is deaf, tested a system that changes sign language into spoken or written words and vice versa. When this system is perfected, it will allow a person who does not sign to communicate with a person who does.

All of the technology testers take their jobs very seriously. They know that with their help, inventions such as these can make life easier for people with disabilities.

SCIENCE CONNECTION

INVENT A HIGH-TECH TOOL

Work with a partner to dream up a tool that could help people with a disability. Identify a disability and the kind of help a person might need. Draw a picture of the tool and label its parts. Report to the class on how it might be used.

1 REVIEW

VOCABULARY

**Write the word from the box that best completes each sentence.
Use each word only once.**

dermis

epidermis

farsighted

fluoride

nearsighted

physical

plaque

responsible

1. The three parts of health are ___?___ health, emotional and intellectual health, and social health. (Lesson 1)

2. Making sure that you get enough sleep shows that you are ___?___ for your own health. (Lesson 2)

3. You can get cavities if ___?___ is not removed from your teeth. (Lesson 3)

4. People who see close objects better than distant objects are ___?___. (Lesson 4)

5. The outer layer of skin is called the ___?___. (Lesson 5)

REVIEW HEALTH IDEAS

Use your knowledge of proper health care from Chapter 1 to answer these questions.

1. How can the three parts of health affect each other? (Lesson 1)

2. Why is it important to engage in healthful behaviors and also avoid risky behaviors? (Lesson 1)

3. Why should you have regular medical checkups? (Lesson 2)

4. What kinds of problems are caused by not getting enough rest and sleep? (Lesson 2)

5. Why is it important to brush your teeth at least twice a day? (Lesson 3)

6. Name four types of teeth and the purpose of each. (Lesson 3)

7. What are three things that you can do to take care of your eyes? (Lesson 4)

8. What is the proper way to use a cotton swab to clean your ears? (Lesson 4)

9. Why is it smart to avoid getting a suntan? (Lesson 5)

10. What can you do to take care of your hair and nails? (Lesson 5)

APPLY HEALTH IDEAS

1. A friend likes to listen to music with the sound turned up high. What would you tell your friend? (Lesson 4)

2. You have a toothache. Your friend says it will go away on its own, so you don't have to do anything. Explain why you agree or disagree. (Lesson 3)

3. Should you use a friend's comb to get ready for a class picture? Why or why not? (Lesson 5)

4. **PORTFOLIO** **SET GOALS** Draw a picture with yourself at the center. Add circles to show your physical, emotional and intellectual, and social health. In each circle, write one goal you can set to improve that part of your health. (Lesson 1)

5. **LIFE SKILLS** **RESOLVE CONFLICTS** A friend says he won't ride his bicycle with you if you wear a safety helmet. What can you tell him to resolve the conflict? (Lesson 2)

YOUR HEALTH AT HOME

Which personal health care activities should you do every day? Which should you do every week?

Use a sheet of paper to make a schedule. Your schedule might look like the one at the right.

Put the schedule in a place where you can see it. Check off each activity as you complete it.

Personal Health Activities	Each Day	Each Week
1. Brush teeth	3 times	
2. Floss	once	
3. Wash hair		3 times

Write True or False for each statement. If false, change the underlined word or phrase to make it true.

1. Listening to loud music through <u>headphones</u> can harm your hearing.

2. If you are a good bike rider, not wearing a bicycle helmet <u>is not risky behavior</u>.

3. If you are <u>responsible</u> for your own health, you know yourself and choose good health habits.

4. A biting tooth is a <u>molar</u>.

5. To help protect your skin from the harmful rays of the sun, use a sunscreen with an SPF of <u>6</u> or higher.

6. As you sleep, your body <u>stores energy and repairs itself</u>.

7. The three parts of health are <u>physical, family, and intellectual and emotional</u>.

8. Brushing teeth <u>at least twice a day</u> can help avoid some dental problems.

9. Nerves carry vibrations <u>from your eardrum to your brain</u>.

10. A <u>pore</u> is one of the layers of skin.

Write a sentence to answer each question.

11. Why is good posture important?

12–13. Name some warning signs of vision problems and of hearing problems.

14. What are some of the functions of skin?

15. What is tooth enamel and what does it do?

16. What are the functions of your hair?

17–18. How can you take good care of your vision and hearing?

19. What can you do to take good care of your hair?

20. What is the purpose of fingernails?

Performance Assessment

PORTFOLIO You have been voted Healthy Fourth-Grader of the Month! Now you have a special job. You will visit each kindergarten class to tell the students about good personal health care. Write a plan of what you will say.

GROWTH AND DEVELOPMENT

CHAPTER 2

THE BIG IDEA

People grow and change during life. Understanding how growth and development take place helps you to:

- learn about how the parts of your body work together.

- take care of your body so that it can work well.

GROWTH AND HEREDITY

In this lesson, you will learn:

▶ about the life cycle and how people change at different stages of it.

▶ how heredity, environment, and hormones affect your growth and development.

VOCABULARY

puberty (pū′bər tē) time during which a person first becomes able to reproduce

heredity (hə red′i tē) passing of traits from parents to children

environment (en vī′rən mənt) everything in your surroundings that influences you

hormones (hôr′mōnz) chemicals made by your body that control growth and some body processes

QUICK START Suppose you found a photo of yourself taken one year ago. Would you look the same? How have you changed in the past year? What changes would not show up in a photograph?

Growing up means more than getting bigger and stronger. You have probably grown taller and heavier in the past year. But you have also developed new skills that help you move, play games, make decisions, solve problems, and get along better with others. You will grow and develop new skills for the rest of your life. This lesson is about the different things that affect your growth and development.

Infancy is the first year after birth.

Growth continues throughout childhood.

The Cycle of Life

You've gone through some amazing changes in your life. Your body grew from a single cell. At birth, you probably weighed 7 or 8 pounds and were less than 2 feet tall. You kept growing and developing after you were born. You're not done yet! You'll keep growing until you're an adult. Even as an adult, your body will continue to change.

Everyone grows at different rates. But we all go through the same life cycle. A *life cycle* is the stages, or steps, of growth and development throughout a person's life. The main life cycle stages after birth are infancy, childhood, adolescence, and adulthood. A person's life cycle ends when the person dies.

Adolescence is the stage of life from puberty to adulthood.

Adulthood begins when physical development is complete.

Physical Changes

Infancy is a time of rapid physical growth and change. You probably tripled your weight and grew about a foot by your first birthday. You developed many skills. You learned to crawl, laugh, and maybe say a few words.

After a year, infancy ends and childhood begins. Children don't grow as fast as infants. But they do improve and develop new physical skills quickly. Just think about all you've learned since the age of 1.

Childhood ends when physical growth speeds up again at puberty, usually between the ages of 11 and 14. **Puberty** is the time during which boys and girls become able to *reproduce*, or have babies. They begin to develop the adult characteristics of their *gender*, or sex.

The stage of life called adolescence begins at puberty and lasts several years. After puberty, growth slows down and usually stops at adulthood. Adulthood begins somewhere between ages 17 and 19 for girls and 18 and 20 for boys.

Your body continues to change even in adulthood. Adults often gain weight as they grow older. Their hair may turn gray or white. Their bones may lose calcium and become easier to break. Their heart and lungs may not work as well. Many of these changes can be slowed by regular physical activity and proper nutrition.

Intellectual, Emotional, and Social Changes

Infants need to be fed, cleaned, and loved. As infants grow into children, they quickly pick up more and more *intellectual skills*. These skills include talking, solving problems, reading, and writing. As children grow, they also develop *emotional* and *social skills* that help them control feelings and get along with others.

The Adolescent Years

There's more to adolescence than just physical changes. Adolescents undergo emotional, intellectual, and social changes, too. Adolescents often experience mood changes—happy one hour, sad or angry the next. Usually these changes are caused by chemical changes in the body.

Adolescents also change intellectually. They begin thinking more about long-term goals—who they are and what they want to be. They also learn better ways to solve problems with family and friends in their daily lives.

Socially, adolescents begin to see themselves more as individuals. Often they feel a desire for independence from their families.

Friendships are a very important part of adolescence. At first, many adolescents are influenced by what their friends like, how they dress, and the way they behave. But by the end of adolescence, most teens have learned to balance their own needs, responsibilities, and viewpoints with those of their family and friends.

Taking Responsibility

Adulthood begins when physical growth has ended, usually between the ages of 17 and 20. In the early years of adulthood, most people learn how to make smarter choices. They learn how to develop stronger friendships. They may finish their education and begin to work. They may marry and set up families, taking on the responsibility of raising a new person to adulthood.

CULTURAL PERSPECTIVES

Rites of Passage

Many cultures celebrate becoming an adolescent with a special ceremony. These ceremonies are called *rites of passage*. For example, an Apache girl might go through a four-day rite to mark her entry into womanhood.

Thirteen-year-old Jewish boys and girls might attend a rite of passage at a synagogue. Do you know of any celebrations to mark a child's passage into adolescence?

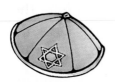

HEALTH ACTIVITY
What Did You Get?

You will need: chart paper, markers

1 Work with a group. Conduct a class poll of inherited traits. List traits to study, such as hair color, eye color, and attached or unattached earlobes.

2 Take one trait at a time, such as hair color. How many classmates have brown, black, blond, or red hair? Use a chart to record data.

3 Make a bar graph using the data you collected. Which color is most common?

4 Repeat with other traits.

Heredity and Growth

Have you ever noticed that family members sometimes look like each other? Children often have many of the same *traits*, or characteristics, as their parents.

Children look like their parents because of heredity. **Heredity** is the passing of traits from parents to children. Traits that are passed from parent to child are called *inherited traits*. The color of your hair, skin, and eyes are all inherited traits. Heredity also affects how you grow and develop. For example, it can determine how tall you might be.

Of course, no one looks *exactly* like a parent. That's because you get some of your traits from your mother and some from your father. Your eye color might be like your mother's. The shape of your nose might be like your father's. Some traits may skip generations— perhaps your chin is just like your grandmother's.

Some characteristics might be a combination of both parents' traits. If the mother has dark brown hair and the father has blond hair, the children might have dark hair, blond hair, or light brown hair.

Environment and Growth

You can't do much to change your inherited traits. But heredity is not the only thing that influences your growth. Your **environment**, or everything that's around you, also affects your growth and development. Your environment includes other people, the air you breathe, the water you drink, and the food you eat.

Family, friends, and other people around you help your social growth. They also influence your intellectual and emotional growth. You might learn how to share from a friend, how to multiply and divide from a teacher, and how to trust others from a parent.

You also need a healthy physical environment. For example, air pollution can cause lung diseases and other health problems.

Even the food you eat can affect your growth and development. For example, you must eat a variety of healthy foods to get everything your body needs to grow and function.

Steps to a Healthier Environment

You can't control everything in your environment. But you can decide to do things that make it healthier. Following are some ways you can make a difference. Can you think of any more?

- Reduce conflicts with friends and family. If you respect others, they will usually respect you.

- Avoid pollution when possible. Try to reduce solid wastes and water pollution by recycling. Try to use the least harmful materials for a job.

- Eat a variety of healthful foods from the different food groups. These are covered in detail in Chapter 6.

LIFE SKILL

MAKE DECISIONS

What Would You Do?

Clearville City has a dangerous amount of air pollution from cars and trucks. How could the people of Clearville City reduce air pollution and create a healthier environment?

Recycling helps keep the environment cleaner and healthier for everyone. What items do you recycle?

Hormones and Growth

How does your body know when to start and stop growing? Your growth is controlled by hormones. **Hormones** are chemicals that control growth and some of your body's other processes. You might think of hormones as chemical messengers that travel throughout your body.

Hormones are made in body parts called *glands*. Glands are located in different places in your body. They secrete hormones directly into your bloodstream. Each gland makes one or more hormones that each do a specific job. Glands and hormones make up the *endocrine system*.

The *pituitary gland* is found at the base of your brain. It makes the hormone that controls growth. When the pituitary gland produces the growth hormone, your bones and other body tissues grow. When the growth hormone isn't being produced, your body doesn't grow.

Other hormones cause many of the body changes that occur during puberty. These changes prepare the body for reproduction.

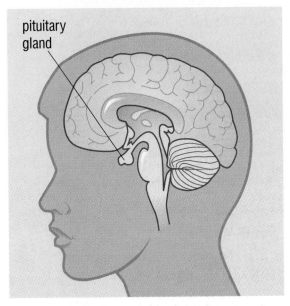

pituitary gland

In an adult male, the pituitary gland is a bit smaller than the tip of the little finger.

LESSON WRAP UP

Show What You Know

1. Name four stages of the life cycle after birth.

2. How does your body control your growth?

3. **THINK CRITICALLY** Your older brother lends you his shirt, which is too small for you. How can that be? Shouldn't your older brother be taller and bigger than you?

Show What You Can Do

4. **APPLY HEALTH ACTIVITY**
   Science Connection
   List two inherited traits. Poll your family to see which members have these traits.

5. **PRACTICE LIFE SKILLS**
   Resolve Conflicts Write a story about four characters who resolve a conflict. Each character should be in a different stage of the life cycle. How might your characters act toward each other?

In this lesson, you will learn:

▶ what cells are.

▶ how cells, tissues, and organs form body systems.

VOCABULARY

cell (sel) the basic structural unit of life

tissue (tish′ü) a group of cells, usually of the same type, that work together to do a certain job

organ (ôr′gən) a structure, made of two or more tissues, that has a job

body system (bod′ē sis′təm) a group of organs that work together to perform a particular job for the body

QUICK START Have you ever watched a home being built? What went into making it?

Think about the different parts of a home. The walls support the roof. The roof protects what's inside. The plumbing system provides water. The electrical system powers lights and appliances. The heating system keeps the inside warm. All these home systems work together to make a comfortable place to live. Your body, like a home, is made of many systems. These systems work together inside a marvelous machine—your body.

The systems in a home work together, just like all the parts of a person's body work together.

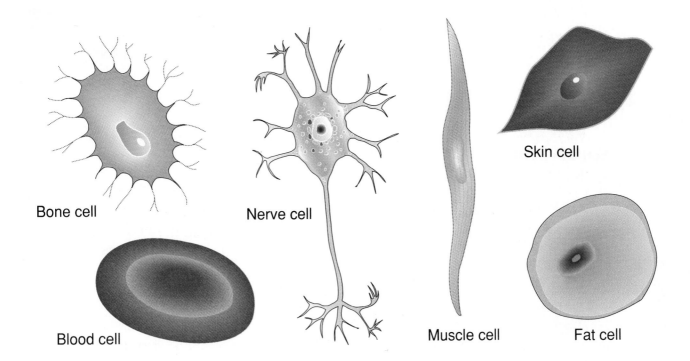

Bone cell

Nerve cell

Skin cell

Blood cell

Muscle cell

Fat cell

Cells—Your Body's Building Blocks

A home is made of many small parts, such as bricks and pieces of wood. Your body is also made up of many small parts. But the "bricks and wood" in your body are cells.

A **cell** is the basic structural unit of life. All living things are made of cells. Cells in your body make new cells by dividing. You grow and develop because of these dividing cells.

Your body is made of a number of different kinds of cells. Each kind of cell has a different job. Each kind of cell also has a certain shape and size that helps it do its work. Red blood cells are flexible, which lets them squeeze through tiny spaces. Muscle cells can become shorter and thicker to move bones. Nerve cells have long, thin, arm-like structures that help them send nerve signals. You will read about each of these kinds of cells later in the chapter.

Most cells have some basic parts in common. A *membrane* surrounds the outside of the cell. The *nucleus* is the control center, or "brain," of the cell. Cytoplasm surrounds the nucleus.

Tissues and Organs

One cell can't work alone to keep your body alive. Groups of similar cells work together to do a certain job. These groups of cells form **tissues**. For example, the muscle that helps you bend your arm is actually a group of cells working together to form muscle tissue. *Nerve tissues* are made up of groups of nerve cells.

Like cells, tissues don't work alone. Different tissues that work together to do a certain job form **organs**. For example, your heart is made of several kinds of tissue, including muscle tissue and nerve tissue. Your *heart* is an organ that pumps blood throughout your body. Some other body organs are your brain, skin, liver, and lungs.

HEALTH ACTIVITY
What's That Organ?

You will need: an encyclopedia, a variety of construction materials such as boxes, balloons, glue, markers, paint, scissors

1 Work with a group to design and build a model of an organ. You might choose the heart, the lungs, the brain, the eyes, the ears, or the stomach.

2 Find out more about the organ. What is its shape? What types of cells and tissues make up the organ? Where is it located? What is its job?

3 Create a model of the organ. Write clear, informative sentences to label your model.

Better Safe Than Sorry

Organs like your brain, heart, and lungs are made of soft tissue. They are protected by bones like your skull and ribs. But bones can be broken. That's why it's important to use safety equipment.

RESOLVE CONFLICTS
What Would You Do?

A friend wants to ride your bike, but he doesn't want to wear a safety helmet. What would you tell him?

HEALTHWISE CONSUMER

Use Your Head!

Do you like bicycling, skateboarding, or in-line skating? Wearing a safety helmet during these activities is the most important thing you can do to protect your head. Most safety helmets offer good protection if they fit your head properly. Ask an adult to help you try on several kinds of helmets. Compare the fit, safety features, and price. Then decide which safety helmet seems best for you.

Body Systems—Organs Working Together

You know that your heart is an organ that pumps blood throughout your body. But your heart can't do that by itself. The blood is actually pumped through tubes called *blood vessels*.

Organs and tissues work together in groups called **body systems**. Each system has a specific group of jobs. In Lesson 1, you learned about the job of the endocrine system. The endocrine system makes hormones to control your body's growth and other processes.

As you continue to read this chapter, look for information about the following body systems.

- The *skeletal system* gives your body shape and protects many of your organs.

- The *muscular system* helps your body move.

- The *circulatory system* transports blood throughout your body. Blood delivers oxygen and food to your cells and takes away the cells' wastes.

- The *respiratory system* takes in oxygen from the air and gets rid of waste gases. This is how you breathe.

- The *digestive system* breaks down food for your cells to use.

- The *nervous system* controls most body functions, including movement.

Some body systems work together to do a job. For example, the skeletal, nervous, and muscular systems work together to help you move. The respiratory and circulatory systems work together to take in oxygen from the air and get it to your cells.

LESSON WRAP UP

Show What You Know

1. Name three different types of cells in your body.

2. In what ways are cells, tissues, organs, and body systems alike? In what ways are they different?

3. **THINK CRITICALLY** You can't protect every part of your body when you skate or ride a bike. Which parts do you think are most important to protect? How can you protect them?

Show What You Can Do

4. PORTFOLIO **APPLY HEALTH ACTIVITY**
   Science Connection Draw a diagram of a body organ. Label all its parts. On the back, explain the job that the organ does.

5. **PRACTICE LIFE SKILLS**
   Obtain Help Find out if your community offers bicycle safety classes. Obtain help from a librarian or other adult. How often are classes held? What topics do the classes cover? Share your findings with other students.

3 YOUR BONES AND MUSCLES

In this lesson, you will learn:

▶ the parts of the skeletal and muscular systems.

▶ how these systems work together.

▶ how to care for your skeletal and muscular systems.

VOCABULARY

joint (joint) where two bones meet

cartilage (kär′tə lij) flexible tissue that covers and protects the ends of some bones

ligament (lig′ə mənt) a tough band of tissue that holds two bones together at a joint

muscles (mus′əlz) the tissues that make your body move

⏱ **QUICK START** Compare a cat to a worm. How are they alike? How are they different?

A cat looks very different from a worm. However, they do share one important characteristic—they are both living things. They can both move, grow, change, and make more of their own kind.

In other ways, a cat and a worm are very different from each other. A cat has fur, legs, and a tail. A worm feels smooth and has no legs. But the most important difference is that a cat has bones and a worm does not. In this lesson, you will learn about the bones that give a cat—and you— structure and shape.

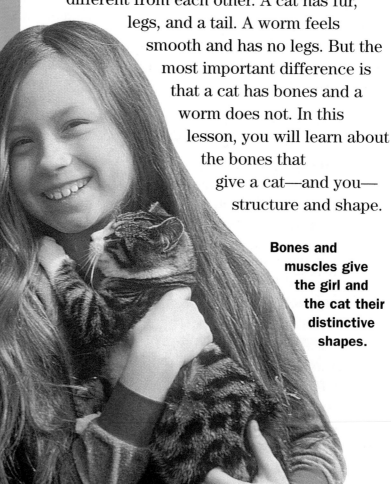

Bones and muscles give the girl and the cat their distinctive shapes.

The Skeleton— Your Body's Super Structure

Like the beams of a house, bones form the framework of the human body. Did you know that you have more than 200 bones in your body? Bones work together to form your *skeletal system.* Your skeletal system gives your body shape. It also helps you walk, sit, and stand.

Your Bones—The Inside Story

Each bone in your body has a certain shape and job. As you know, many bones protect delicate body parts. For example, the hard bones of your skull protect your brain and your eyes. Ribs form a curved cage that protects your heart and lungs.

The bones of the spine support the body, but they also protect the spinal cord. The *spinal cord* is the bundle of nerve tissue that is the main pathway for messages between the brain and the rest of the body.

Some bones make red blood cells. Red blood cells carry oxygen to all your body cells and carry away cell wastes. Most blood cells form in a tissue called *marrow.* Marrow is found in the center of long bones, such as those in your arms and legs.

Regular physical activity helps bones grow properly. You can also keep your bones healthy and growing by eating foods that are rich in a mineral called calcium. Calcium makes bones and teeth hard and strong. Milk products, leafy green vegetables, fruits, and tofu (which is made from soy beans) all contain calcium.

The Skeletal System

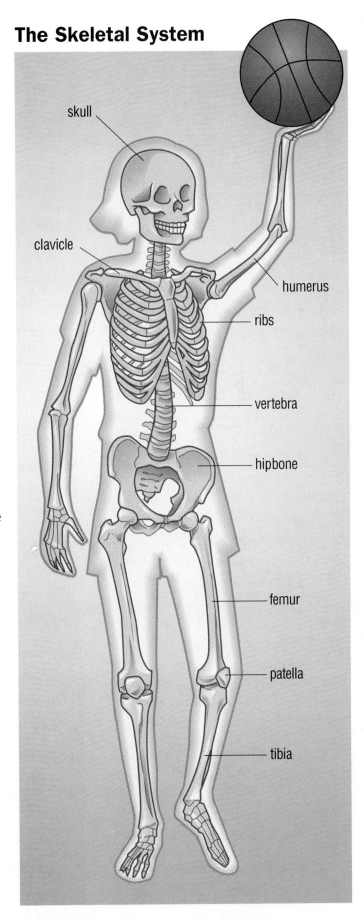

skull

clavicle

humerus

ribs

vertebra

hipbone

femur

patella

tibia

Your Joints

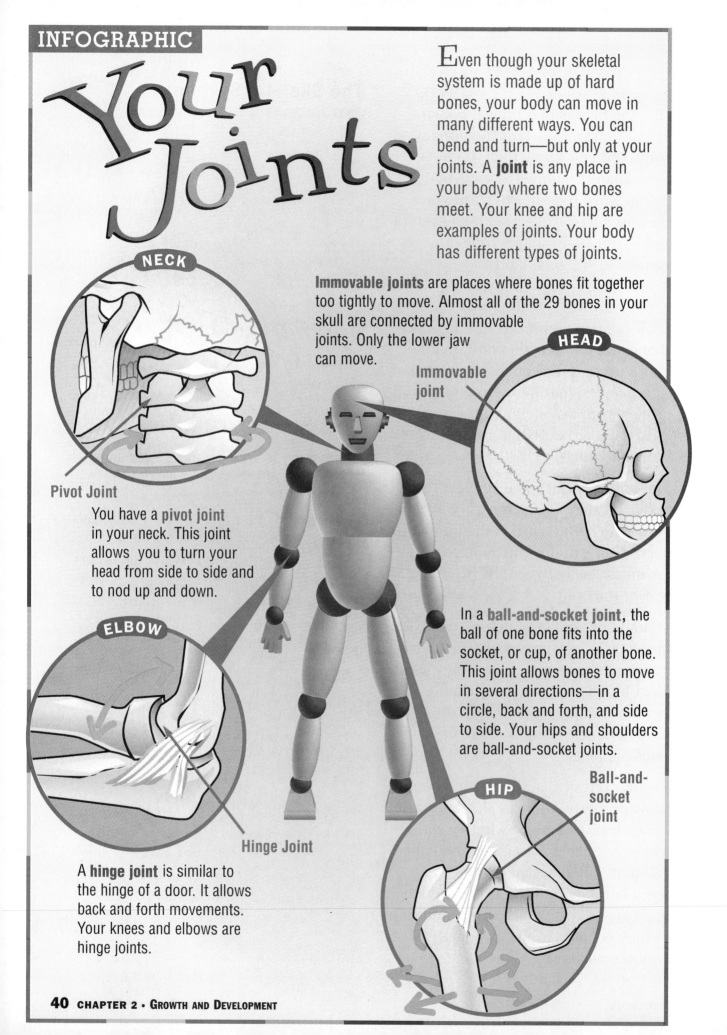

Even though your skeletal system is made up of hard bones, your body can move in many different ways. You can bend and turn—but only at your joints. A **joint** is any place in your body where two bones meet. Your knee and hip are examples of joints. Your body has different types of joints.

Immovable joints are places where bones fit together too tightly to move. Almost all of the 29 bones in your skull are connected by immovable joints. Only the lower jaw can move.

Immovable joint

NECK

HEAD

Pivot Joint

You have a **pivot joint** in your neck. This joint allows you to turn your head from side to side and to nod up and down.

In a **ball-and-socket joint**, the ball of one bone fits into the socket, or cup, of another bone. This joint allows bones to move in several directions—in a circle, back and forth, and side to side. Your hips and shoulders are ball-and-socket joints.

ELBOW

Ball-and-socket joint

HIP

Hinge Joint

A **hinge joint** is similar to the hinge of a door. It allows back and forth movements. Your knees and elbows are hinge joints.

" **No one is actually double-jointed.** "

This is true. There are people who can bend their elbows "backwards" or almost touch their thumb to the inside of their arm. But they aren't really double-jointed. There's no such thing as having two joints in the same location. These people have very flexible ligaments. That gives their joints a wider range of movement than the average person.

Beyond Bones

Your skeletal system is made of more than just bones. Touch the tip of your nose or the edge of your ears. Do you feel flexible tissue? This tissue is called cartilage.

Cartilage is flexible tissue that covers the ends of some bones. Cartilage protects bones from scraping against each other. It absorbs the force of your movements, such as walking and jumping. Cartilage also holds some bones together. It joins your ribs to your breastbone, the flat bone in the center of your chest. The cartilage allows your ribs to move as you breathe in and out.

Ligaments are another part of the skeletal system. A **ligament** is a tough band of tissue that holds two bones together where they meet. For example, ligaments hold the bones of your arm together at the elbow. When you bend your elbow, the ligaments stretch but continue to hold the moving bones together.

How Do You Grow Taller?

Cells in the ends of your bones divide to make more bone cells. In this way, your bones become longer, and you grow taller. Your bones will continue to grow until you are about 17 if you're a girl and about 20 if you're a boy. Even though you will stop growing taller, your bones will still be able to make new bone tissue to heal themselves if they ever break.

SET GOALS

What Would You Do?

Your brother doesn't like milk, so he usually drinks juice or water instead. You're worried that he may not be getting enough calcium. How can you help him set a goal to eat more foods with calcium?

Increase Your Muscle Power

Physical Activities	Muscles Strengthened
Running	leg muscles
Swimming	
Baseball	

1 Work with a partner. Make a list of fun physical activities that you both enjoy.

2 Next to each activity, identify the muscles that it helps strengthen.

3 Look over your list. Decide if there are some muscles that you wish to strengthen more. Set a goal to do the activities that strengthen these muscles.

4 After two weeks, report back to your partner. Discuss how often you worked at these activities and how they affected your muscles.

Your Muscles

You've learned how joints allow different kinds of movement. But what moves the bones?

Muscles are the tissues that make your body move. You have about 650 muscles. Together these muscles make up your *muscular system*. Muscles are attached to bones by *tendons*, tough cords of tissue. Can you find the hard cord above the back of your heel? That's a tendon.

Many of your muscles move because you decide to move them. Muscles that you can control by thinking about them are called *voluntary muscles*. Voluntary muscles are attached to your bones. You use these muscles whenever you smile, walk, run, or play a video game.

Involuntary muscles cannot be controlled by thinking about them. Usually you don't even know they are working. Your heart is an involuntary muscle. It beats without you thinking about it. Muscles lining the walls of your blood vessels and the muscles of your stomach and intestines are involuntary muscles.

Muscles Move You

Hold your arm straight out in front of you. Now bend it up. You can bend your arm because a muscle in your upper arm, called the *biceps*, contracts. When a muscle *contracts*, it gets shorter and thicker. As the muscle gets shorter, it pulls on the bone it is attached to and the bone moves.

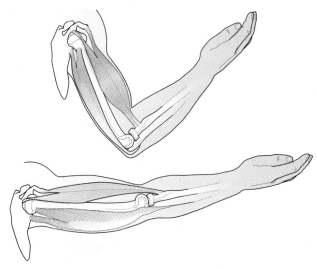

Muscles work in pairs to move bones. When one muscle in a pair contracts, the other muscle relaxes.

Now straighten your arm again. Do you think the biceps pushed your forearm down? If you said no, you're right—muscles can pull but not push.

A different muscle on the outside of your upper arm pulls your arm down. This muscle, called the *triceps*, contracts to straighten the arm. At the same time, the biceps muscle *relaxes*, becoming longer and thinner. Try to feel the change in shape of these two muscles as they contract and relax.

Caring for Your Skeletal and Muscular Systems

Good nutrition and regular physical activity will help keep your muscular and skeletal systems strong and healthy throughout your life. You explored some of the ways exercise can help you. You can read more about the benefits of physical activity in Chapter 6.

LESSON WRAP UP

Show What You Know

1. Briefly describe the skeletal system and its functions.

2. How do muscles help move your arm?

3. **THINK CRITICALLY** Compare how three different kinds of movable joints work.

Show What You Can Do

4. **APPLY HEALTH ACTIVITY**
   Set Goals Write a letter to a friend. Tell what muscles you want to strengthen and what physical activities might help you.

5. **PRACTICE LIFE SKILLS**
   Obtain Help Find out about foods that contain calcium. Obtain help from a librarian or teacher. Create a collage of photos to explain why eating foods with calcium is important.

In this lesson, you will learn:

▶ the parts of the circulatory and respiratory systems.

▶ how these systems work together.

▶ how to care for your circulatory and respiratory systems.

VOCABULARY

artery (är′tə rē) a blood vessel that carries blood away from the heart

capillary (kap′ə ler′ē) a narrow blood vessel that connects an artery and a vein

vein (vān) a blood vessel that carries blood back to the heart

lungs (lungz) two large respiratory organs inside the chest where blood picks up oxygen and loses carbon dioxide

alveoli (al vē′ə lī) small air sacs in the lungs

QUICK START A person can live for weeks without food and for days without water. But how long can a person live without air?

When you are very active, like the swimmer below, you can feel your heart pumping as you breathe heavily. Most of the time, you are probably unaware of your breathing. But during your lifetime, you may breathe more than 600 million times. And your heart may beat more than 2 billion times! In this lesson, you will learn how the heart and lungs work together.

Red Blood Cells	White Blood Cells	Platelets

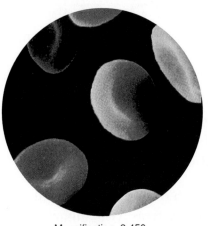
Magnification: 3,450×

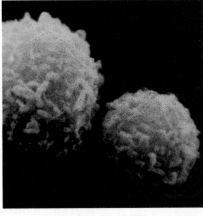
Magnification: 5,750×

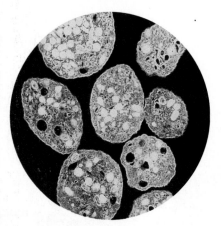
Magnification: 9,200×

About half the blood in your body is a liquid called plasma, most of which is water. The other half of your blood is made up of red blood cells, white blood cells, and platelets.

Your Heart—The Body Pump

The *circulatory system* delivers food and oxygen to cells. It also picks up wastes from the cells. The circulatory system has three main parts. They are the heart, blood, and blood vessels. The heart is a hollow, muscular organ that pumps blood through the body. It is about the size of your fist and has four parts, or chambers.

Think about what happens when you squeeze a plastic bottle full of liquid. The liquid is pushed out. The pumping action of the heart is similar. The heart fills with blood. Then it squeezes to push the blood out with enough force to move it through your body.

You can feel your heartbeat by placing your fingers on your wrist. What you feel is your *pulse*. Your heart beats about 70 to 100 times each minute. When you exercise, your heart beats faster so that it can send more oxygen to body cells and remove more wastes.

What Is Blood?

Blood is a liquid with special cells and other materials in it. Blood is like a moving pickup and delivery system. It delivers oxygen and nutrients to your body cells. It picks up wastes from body cells.

Water makes up more than half of all your blood. This watery part carries nutrients from food to body cells. The rest of your blood is made up of different kinds of special cells.

Red blood cells carry oxygen to other body cells. Your body cells need oxygen in order to use nutrients for energy. Red blood cells also pick up carbon dioxide, a waste gas produced when cells use nutrients.

White blood cells help the body fight disease. White blood cells are larger than red blood cells. There are fewer white cells than red cells in your blood.

Platelets are blood cell fragments. They are not whole cells. Platelets help you stop bleeding.

The Circulatory System

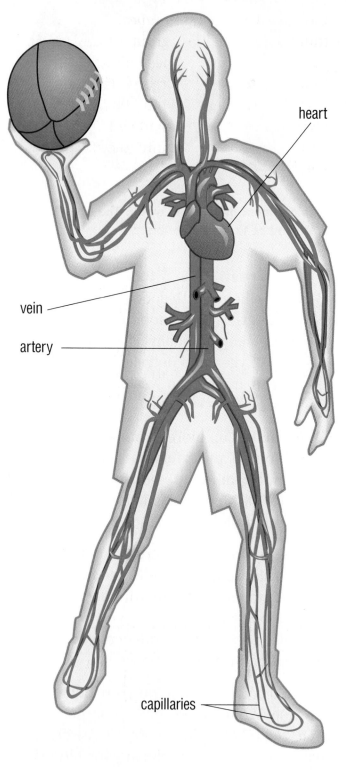

heart

vein

artery

capillaries

Blood Vessels—
The Roads of Circulation

Long connecting tubes that carry blood are called *blood vessels*. Your blood travels to and from the heart through blood vessels. An adult's circulatory system has more than 80,000 miles of blood vessels! There are three main kinds of blood vessels.

An **artery** is a large blood vessel that carries blood away from your heart. The blood in arteries has oxygen and nutrients. Arteries lead to all parts of your body. Arteries are red in the picture. You can see how arteries branch again and again until they become very small.

Blood flows from the small arteries into the capillaries. A **capillary** is a narrow blood vessel that connects an artery and a vein. Capillaries are so small that blood cells move through them one at a time. Oxygen and nutrients pass through the thin capillary walls into the body cells. Blood also picks up cell wastes at this time.

Now the blood leaves the capillaries and enters the smallest veins. A **vein** is a blood vessel that carries blood back to the heart. Veins are blue in the picture.

The further veins are from the heart, the thinner they become. Veins help to regulate the flow of blood back to the heart. Controlling the flow of blood in your legs and feet is very important. The blood in these organs must flow against gravity to get to your heart.

The Respiratory System at Work

You have just learned how your blood delivers oxygen to body cells. You also read how blood picks up the waste gas carbon dioxide. How does your circulatory system get the oxygen for this exchange of gases?

Your *respiratory system* is a group of organs that bring oxygen into your body. Your respiratory system also removes carbon dioxide from your body. Humans can live for only a few minutes without breathing. When you breathe in, air moves through your nose or mouth. The air travels through your throat to the *trachea*, or windpipe.

Your trachea divides into two *bronchi*. The bronchi carry air into your lungs. Your **lungs** are two large respiratory organs located in your chest where blood picks up oxygen and loses carbon dioxide. They are the main organs of your respiratory system.

Inside your lungs, the bronchi divide into smaller *bronchial tubes*. Each thin tube leads into a group of tiny air sacs called **alveoli**. These air sacs look like bunches of grapes. The average person has about 300 million alveoli. The alveoli provide a large area for gases to pass into and out of your blood.

Alveoli are an important link between your respiratory and circulatory systems. The alveoli are surrounded by capillaries. When air enters your lungs, it fills the alveoli. Oxygen moves from the alveoli into the blood in the capillaries. At the same time, carbon dioxide from the blood moves into the alveoli. When you breathe out, this carbon dioxide leaves your body.

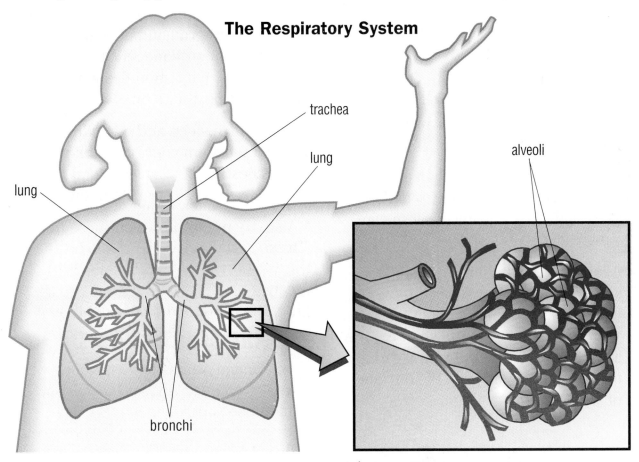

The Respiratory System

trachea

lung

alveoli

lung

bronchi

HEALTH ACTIVITY
Find Your Pulse

You will need: clock or watch with a second hand

1 Work with a group. Design an activity to compare your pulse at rest and after an activity such as jumping jacks.

2 Brainstorm ideas. Then write down the plan for your activity.

3 Carry out your activity. What did you discover? How does such an activity help you care for your circulatory and respiratory systems?

Caring for Your Circulatory and Respiratory Systems

Taking care of your heart and lungs will help you make sure your body cells get the oxygen they need. Following are some actions you can take.

- Don't smoke! Smoking damages your lungs. It causes lung cancer and other serious diseases. Many of these can cause death.

- Avoid places with dirty, polluted, or smoke-filled air. If you need to work in a dusty room or in a room filled with someone's cigarette smoke, open a window to let fresh air in. Wearing a mask can help you keep the dirt out of your lungs.

- Get moving—run, jump, walk, bike, skate, swim, or dance. Regular physical activity improves your lung and heart power.

- Get enough sleep and rest. When you are well-rested, your body can work at its best.

- Don't hold back a sneeze or cough. Also, try not to blow your nose too hard.

LIFE SKILL

PRACTICE REFUSAL SKILLS
What Would You Do?
Your friend wants you to try "just one" cigarette. What would you say to refuse your friend?

Lung Power at Work

It is difficult for most people to breathe at the top of a mountain, because there is less oxygen at higher altitudes. Some people, such as the Quechua Indians in Ecuador, live their whole lives at high altitudes. They have strong lungs and large chests that help them take in great quantities of air. They also have more red blood cells than people who live at lower altitudes. This is how they can get enough oxygen from the thin air where they live.

LESSON WRAP UP

Show What You Know

1. What is the job of the circulatory system?

2. How do alveoli help your body exchange oxygen and carbon dioxide?

3. **THINK CRITICALLY** What are two questions you could ask people to see whether they are taking care of their circulatory and respiratory systems?

Show What You Can Do

4. PORTFOLIO **APPLY HEALTH ACTIVITY**
   Science Connection
   Make a chart showing your pulse after different physical activities. What conclusions can you draw about your pulse and the level of physical activity?

5. **PRACTICE LIFE SKILLS**
   Obtain Help A friend is knocked down while playing a sport. She appears to have stopped breathing. What should you do to get help right away?

In this lesson, you will learn:

▶ **about the digestive system and how it breaks down food.**

▶ **how nutrients from food reach body cells.**

▶ **how to care for your digestive system.**

VOCABULARY

digestion (di jes′chən) a process that turns food into a form body cells can use

stomach (stum′ək) a muscular organ where food is broken down and mixed with digestive juices

small intestine (smôl in tes′tin) an organ that finishes breaking down food after it leaves the stomach

large intestine (lärj in tes′tin) an organ that absorbs water from undigested food and stores the wastes

QUICK START "That pizza makes my mouth water!" Have you ever said something like that? Why does your mouth water when you see, smell, or taste food?

A watering mouth is one of the first steps in an essential body process known as digestion. **Digestion** turns food into a form your body cells can use for energy, growth, and development. In this lesson, you will learn how digestion works.

Digestion—The First Steps

Every cell in your body needs energy. The energy comes from *nutrients*, the parts of food that your body needs to stay healthy. But a slice of pizza is not in a form that your tiny body cells can use. How do your cells get the nutrients from food? Your *digestive system* breaks the food down first. Then your body can absorb the nutrients.

Digestion begins in the mouth. Your teeth tear and grind food into tiny pieces. Food must be chewed into small bits before it can move through the rest of the digestive system.

As you chew, the food pieces are mixed with saliva. *Saliva* is a mixture of water, a slippery substance called *mucus*, and certain chemicals. Saliva is made by three pairs of *salivary glands* in your mouth.

Saliva has two roles. The water and mucus moisten food, making it easy to chew and swallow. The chemicals in saliva begin to break down starchy foods such as potatoes, rice, bread—and pizza crust.

"Down the Hatch!"

As you swallow, chewed food moves into the esophagus. The *esophagus* is a tube that connects your mouth and stomach. Muscles in your esophagus push the food toward your stomach. The **stomach** is a muscular, baglike organ that breaks down food even more. Strong stomach muscles mash the food and mix it with digestive juices. These juices begin to break down any proteins in the food, such as those in the cheese on pizza.

The Digestive System

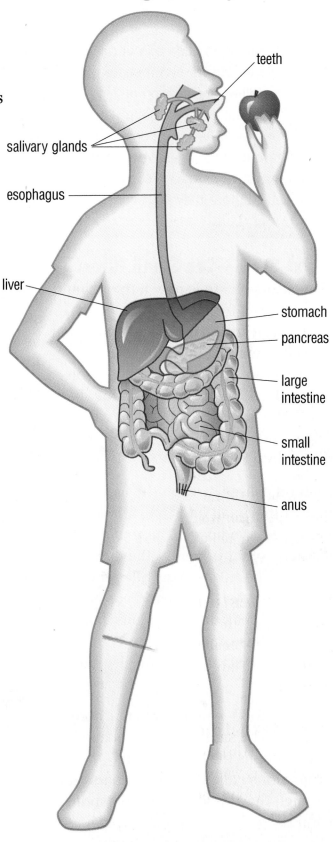

teeth

salivary glands

esophagus

liver

stomach

pancreas

large intestine

small intestine

anus

Tummy Troubles

Americans spend hundreds of millions of dollars each year on products that claim to relieve indigestion or heartburn. But most of this money could be saved. Why? If people took good care of their digestive systems, most digestive problems could be stopped—before they start!

Next Stop—The Small Intestine

The pizza you ate is now a thick liquid. It is squirted from your stomach into your **small intestine**. This organ then finishes breaking down food and absorbs its nutrients. Most digestion takes place in the small intestine. In an adult, the small intestine is as wide as a finger and about 23 feet long. It is folded into big loops.

As food passes through the upper part of the small intestine, it is mixed with digestive juices. These juices are made by other organs in the digestive system. The *liver* makes bile to help break down fats. The *pancreas* adds juices to break down proteins, fats, and starches. Juices produced by the walls of the small intestine also break down foods.

Now the food is in a form your body can use. The small intestine is lined with millions of tiny, fingerlike projections called *villi*. Nutrients pass through the villi and into surrounding capillaries. This process is known as absorption. Your blood then carries the nutrients to your cells.

Last Stop—The Large Intestine

Any food still left that is not digested moves from the small intestine to the large intestine. The **large intestine** is about 2 inches wide and 5 feet long. Its job is to "recycle" the water from the undigested food back into the blood. The remaining waste is stored in the large intestine until it leaves the body through the *anus*.

Caring for Your Digestive System

Following are some guidelines to help you have a healthy digestive system.

- Eat slowly and chew thoroughly.

- Eat a balanced diet. Limit fried foods.

- Drink 6 to 8 glasses of water a day.

- Limit soda or carbonated beverages.

- Get plenty of exercise and rest.

MAKE DECISIONS
What Would You Do?

Before soccer practice, your friend usually has a quick bite to eat. It looks like he hardly even chews! What would you tell him?

Love Your Stomach!

SET GOALS

You will need: cardboard, crayons, paint, tape, glue

1 Work in groups. Research facts about how exercise, rest, and a good diet can keep your digestive system healthy. You might start by looking at the guidelines on page 52 and in Chapters 5 and 6.

2 Set goals to keep your digestive system healthy. For example, one goal might be to eat lots of food with fiber, such as grains, vegetables, and fruits.

3 Create a poster for each of your goals. Tell what the goal is and why it is important. Draw a picture of your goal.

LESSON WRAP UP

Show What You Know

1. How does the digestive system work to break down food?

2. What do the villi in the small intestine do?

3. **THINK CRITICALLY** You want to know whether people are taking care of their digestive systems. Write three questions you might ask on a survey.

Show What You Can Do

4. **PORTFOLIO** **APPLY HEALTH ACTIVITY**
Set Goals Choose one goal you would like to set that would help your digestive system. Write the steps you would take to reach this goal.

5. **PRACTICE LIFE SKILLS**
Practice Refusal Skills
You have an upset stomach. One of your classmates offers you a pink pill and says that it will help your stomach feel better. Write what you would say to your classmate to refuse the pill.

LESSON 6 — YOUR NERVES AND SENSE ORGANS

In this lesson, you will learn:

▶ the parts of the nervous system.

▶ the roles of sensory nerves, motor nerves, and reflexes.

▶ how to care for your nervous system.

VOCABULARY

brain (brān) organ that controls your body's systems and coordinates your actions, emotions, and thoughts

spinal cord (spī′nəl kôrd) the long bundle of nerves that extends down your back from your brain

sensory nerve cell (sen′sə rē nûrv sel) a nerve cell that carries messages from your sense organs to your spinal cord or brain

motor nerve cell (mō′tər nûrv sel) a nerve cell that carries messages from your brain or spinal cord to other parts of your body

QUICK START "Ouch! That's hot!" What happens when you touch something that is very hot?

You touch something hot then pull your hand away. It happens so quickly that you don't even think about it. How does your body know the surface is hot? How can you pull away so fast?

This reaction—and every other movement you make—is controlled by the nervous system. The *nervous system* is made up of the brain, the spinal cord, the nerves, and the sense organs. It is the body's control system. You couldn't make a move without it. The nervous system protects the body from harm. It tells the body when fuel is needed and when to take a rest.

The Parts of Your Nervous System

Your nervous system controls everything your body does. That includes things you think about, such as speaking or moving your arm. It also includes things you do not think about, such as breathing or digesting food.

THE BRAIN

Your **brain** is an organ that controls all your body's systems. It coordinates your actions, emotions, and thoughts. The brain also interprets messages that it receives from your body. Your brain contains billions of nerve cells.

THE SENSE ORGANS

You have five *sense organs* that help gather information about the world for you. These sense organs are your eyes (vision), ears (hearing), nose (smell), tongue (taste), and skin (touch). Each sense organ sends messages to a different part of the brain to be interpreted.

Smell

Taste

Touch

Hearing

Vision

THE SPINAL CORD

Your **spinal cord** is a long bundle of nerves that extends down your back from your brain. Messages to and from your brain travel along your spinal cord. Your spinal cord is protected by your *spine*, or backbone.

THE NERVES

Signals travel along *nerves*, which are long, thin bundles of *nerve cells*. A nerve cell consists of a cell body with nerve fibers extending out from it. Nerve cells carry messages to and from different parts of the body. Some nerves are connected directly to the brain. However, most messages travel to and from the brain along nerves that branch out from the spinal cord.

Your Nervous System at Work

Millions of signals flash through your brain at any moment. They carry a lot of information. They bring news about your body and how it's working. They tell you about the things going on in your environment. How messages travel to and from different parts of your body is the story of your nervous system at work.

Even doing something as simple as eating popcorn uses all of your sense organs. Your eyes see the light yellow kernels. Your hand feels the warmth of the freshly popped corn. Your nose picks up the smell of popcorn in the air. The taste buds on your tongue enjoy the delicious flavor. And your ears hear the crunch of the popcorn as you chew it.

What happens when you touch warm popcorn?

1. **Signals travel from the skin of your finger along sensory nerves in your arm.**

2. **These signals go to your spinal cord, and from there to your brain.**

3. **Your brain interprets the signal, which tells you the popcorn is warm.**

Sensory and Motor Nerves

Each of your sense organs, in turn, sends messages to the brain. **Sensory nerve cells** carry these messages from your sense organs to your spinal cord or brain. The signals reach the spinal cord faster than you can imagine. Then they travel along the spinal cord to the brain. Your brain interprets the signals.

The brain usually sends messages back to the body through the spinal cord. **Motor nerve cells** carry the messages from your brain or spinal cord to other parts of your body. For example, after seeing the popcorn, your brain sent messages to your arm and hand to pick up a piece.

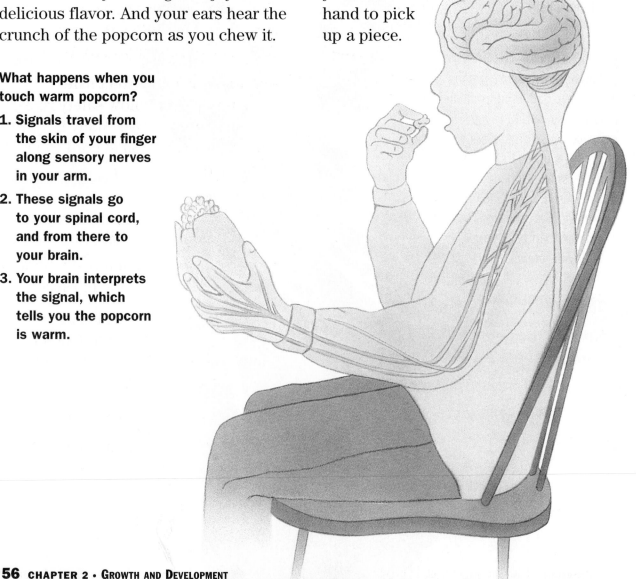

"The bigger your brain is, the smarter you are."

This is not true. The average human brain weighs about 3 pounds. Although larger human brains have been recorded, the people who had them weren't necessarily smarter than others. In fact Neanderthals, who lived about 50,000 years ago, had larger brains than modern people. But people today are a lot smarter than the Neanderthals were.

Reflexes—Automatic Protection

What's the difference between feeling a piece of warm popcorn and touching a very hot pot? The difference is in the way your nervous system deals with the messages it receives.

When your finger touches something very hot, your hand pulls away instantly and automatically. It all happens before your brain even realizes the danger. This quick, automatic action is called a *reflex*. You cannot control your reflexes. This is one of the ways the nervous system protects your body.

LIFE SKILL

MAKE DECISIONS

What Would You Do?

You want to take a cup of hot cocoa off the counter. But you're not sure how hot the cocoa is and you don't want to burn your tongue. What would you do?

Caring for Your Nervous System

Taking care of your nervous system is important to your health. Here are some guidelines for you to follow.

- Always use the correct safety equipment and follow safety rules when you are active. Many injuries to the head and spinal cord can be prevented.

- Eat a balanced diet.

- Get plenty of exercise.

- Find time to relax and rest your body. Make sure you get enough sleep.

- Avoid getting too much sensory information at once. For example, loud noises can damage your hearing.

- Only use drugs given to you by a doctor or other trusted adult.

- Avoid drinking alcoholic beverages. They can damage your nervous system.

Block It Out

MANAGE STRESS

1 Too much sensory information can cause stress. Work with a partner to find out how messages from your environment affect your stress level.

2 Take turns. Place your hands over your ears and close your eyes.

3 Did blocking out the sights and sounds make you feel more calm or more upset? Remember, people are different. Write down your thoughts.

4 Discuss your results with others. Can you use what you learned to help you feel better?

LESSON WRAP UP

Show What You Know

1. What are the main parts of your nervous system?

2. What happens in the nervous system if you touch a very hot iron?

3. **THINK CRITICALLY** Brainstorm. Give two examples of safety equipment and two examples of safety rules that help protect the nervous system.

Show What You Can Do

4. PORTFOLIO **APPLY HEALTH ACTIVITY**
Manage Stress How can you avoid getting too much sensory information? Draw a picture to show one way. Write a caption to explain your picture.

5. **PRACTICE LIFE SKILLS**
Obtain Help How do people unwind after a busy day? Ask five people, including some adults, what they do to relax. Share your results with the rest of your class.

Run Faster, Jump Higher!

What's in a sneaker?

At the rate you're growing, you probably need a new pair of sneakers twice a year or more. Shop around before you buy. New advances in sneaker shock absorbers can make your slam dunk less rattling.

Some shoes now come with plastic heel inserts. The inserts distribute the impact of a foot landing on the ground. In other words, you don't get that horrible, bone-jarring crunch in one part of your heel when you land. That's because your whole heel takes the force of impact.

Other sneaker heels contain disks filled with thick liquid. The liquid also distributes the force of impact evenly. Some sneakers use pouches filled with air to do the same thing. Still others include pads with compartments that contain gel.

The kind of cushioning system you choose depends on the sports you play. Different sports put stress on different parts of the foot.

LIFE SKILL

RESOLVE CONFLICTS

REFEREE AN ARGUMENT

Suppose that you and two friends are playing. One friend has brand-new, expensive sneakers. He is making fun of the other friend, who has old-fashioned, inexpensive sneakers. Write a conversation that shows how you would referee the problem and keep it from becoming a real argument.

VOCABULARY

Write the word or words from the box that best completes each sentence.

arteries

cell

heredity

joint

lungs

digestion

puberty

spinal cord

1. The time of life when a person first becomes able to reproduce is ___?___. (Lesson 1)

2. The basic unit of life is the ___?___. (Lesson 2)

3. The place where two bones meet is a(n) ___?___. (Lesson 3)

4. The two large organs inside your chest where blood picks up oxygen and loses carbon dioxide are the ___?___. (Lesson 4)

5. Food is broken down in the body during the process of ___?___. (Lesson 5)

REVIEW HEALTH IDEAS

Use your knowledge of growth and development from Chapter 2 to answer these questions.

1. How does the growth rate differ at each stage of the life cycle? (Lesson 1)

2. What are some traits that can be inherited? (Lesson 1)

3. Why does your body have different kinds of cells? (Lesson 2)

4. What is an organ? (Lesson 2)

5. How do your skeletal and muscular systems work together? (Lesson 3)

6. How does oxygen from the air you breathe get to the cells in your body? (Lesson 4)

7. What is the main difference between an artery and a vein? (Lesson 4)

8. Why does your body need to digest food? (Lesson 5)

9. How does saliva help digest food? (Lesson 5)

10. Why does your body need both motor and sensory nerves? (Lesson 6)

APPLY HEALTH IDEAS

1. Knowing that people grow at different rates can help you get along with others. Describe one way. (Lesson 1)

2. Explain the statement, "You are what you eat." (Lesson 5)

3. Describe one action, such as throwing a ball. Tell how some of your body systems work together to produce this action. (Lessons 2–6)

4.  **MAKE DECISIONS** Write a factual, entertaining "Owner's Guide for the Human Body." Suggest some good decisions for keeping your body systems healthy. (Lessons 2–6)

5. **PRACTICE REFUSAL SKILLS** Work with a partner. Act out a situation where one friend wants the other to turn music up very loud. (Lesson 6)

YOUR HEALTH AT HOME

How do your decisions and actions at home affect your body systems?

Pay attention to the activities you do in one evening. On a sheet of paper, start a journal. In your journal, note the major body systems involved in each activity.

The next day, look over your notes. Were all your activities healthful? Why or why not? What changes would you make?

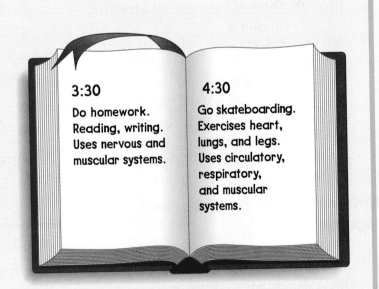

3:30
Do homework.
Reading, writing.
Uses nervous and muscular systems.

4:30
Go skateboarding.
Exercises heart, lungs, and legs.
Uses circulatory, respiratory, and muscular systems.

Write True or False for each statement. If false, change the underlined word or phrase to make it true.

1. Puberty marks the beginning of <u>adulthood</u>.

2. <u>Respiration</u> is the passing of traits from parents to children.

3. A cell is to a <u>tissue</u> as a tissue is to an organ.

4. All body cells <u>have the same shape</u>.

5. A joint that does not move is called <u>a ball-and-socket joint</u>.

6. When a muscle contracts, it <u>pushes</u> on a bone to create movement.

7. A <u>capillary</u> is a narrow blood vessel that connects an artery and a vein.

8. Oxygen passes from your lungs into your blood by traveling through <u>tiny air sacs called alveoli</u>.

9. Most digestion takes place in your <u>stomach</u>.

10. A long bundle of nerves that carries messages between your brain and other parts of your body is your <u>pituitary gland</u>.

Write a sentence to answer each question.

11. Why do some parts of the body need extra protection?

12. What do hormones do?

13. How does environment affect growth and development?

14. What is a reflex?

15. Describe the main functions of your skeletal system.

16. How does blood flow to all parts of your body?

17. Why is physical activity important to the health of your heart and lungs?

18. Choose two senses. What are their roles?

19. How do nutrients pass from your digestive system into your bloodstream?

20. Why is safety equipment important to the care of your nervous system?

Performance Assessment

 Imagine that you are biting into a sweet, ripe strawberry. (Or choose another food if you don't like strawberries!) Describe how your body systems work together as you eat.

EMOTIONAL AND INTELLECTUAL HEALTH

Being emotionally and intellectually healthy includes:

- feeling good about yourself.

- getting along with others.

- learning to deal with conflict and stress.

1 LEARNING ABOUT YOURSELF

In this lesson, you will learn:

▶ how the way you feel about yourself affects your health.

▶ about your personal strengths, weaknesses, and needs.

VOCABULARY

self-concept
(self′kon′sept) the thoughts that you have about yourself

personality
(pûr′sə nal′i tē) all of the ways you feel, think, and act

self-esteem
(self′e stēm′) the level of respect you have for yourself

need (nēd) something that you must have to stay alive or to be healthy

QUICK START You are part of a soccer team. If your team became champions, how would you feel about the win? How would you feel about yourself?

Good things happen every day. Things that are not so good also happen every day. When they happen to you, how do you feel? How do you react? Your reaction to everyday events is influenced by the way you feel about yourself. And the way you feel about yourself affects your health.

Being part of a team effort can help all parts of your health—physical, emotional, intellectual, and social.

Your Self-Concept

If you were asked to tell three things about yourself, what would you say? Would you tell things that you like about yourself? Would you tell things that you don't like? The thoughts that you have about yourself make up your **self-concept**.

Part of your self-concept is based on your personality. Your **personality** is a combination of all of the ways you feel, think, and act. It includes those special things you like—and don't like. For example, your personality might include the following.

- You are easy to get along with.

- You are trustworthy and responsible.

- You like spiders.

- You love stories about outer space.

- You like to read about faraway places, where people do things in different ways.

- You don't like the color yellow.

- You tap your foot impatiently when your brother keeps you waiting.

- You want to be a doctor or veterinarian someday.

Do any of these descriptions match your personality? What might you write about yourself in your own list?

All of the items on your list make a picture of how you see yourself—who and what you think you are. This is part of your self-concept. How you feel about yourself is something different. Your **self-esteem** is the level of respect you have for yourself.

Your self-concept is like a mirror in your mind. It is what you "see" when you think about yourself.

Self-Esteem and Your Health

Self-esteem is an important part of your emotional health. It affects other parts of your health, too. If you have high self-esteem, you probably like other people and get along with them. You probably care enough about yourself to make good choices about your physical health.

If you have low self-esteem, you are more likely to feel anger, worry, or fear. Scientists have learned that these feelings tire you out. They make your heart work too hard.

You can set goals to raise your self-esteem. Building friendships and being close to your family can help your self-esteem. So can working hard on a project you care about. When you have high self-esteem, you take better care of yourself. High self-esteem is better for your health.

Step by Step

LIFE SKILL

SET GOALS

You will need: index card

1 List a few of your strengths on one side of an index card. On the other side, list some things you think you could improve. Choose things you can work at, such as a sport or a school subject.

2 Circle one of the things that you'd like to improve. Set a goal to make that improvement. Think of and describe three steps you could take to help reach your goal. Either write them in words or draw pictures.

3 Do your best to carry out the steps you described. Keep a record of the progress you make in reaching your goal.

Strengths

• Try to be nice to everyone.
• Work well with others.
• Never an

Things to Improve

• Watch less TV.
• Clean my room.
• Help with chores at home.

HEALTH FALLACY

"The clothes you wear can change your personality."

This is not true. Some people think they need special clothes—the "right" clothes—to like themselves. These clothes may have a fancy label or come from a special store. But clothes can't change who you are. Your self-esteem comes from inside.

Your Strengths and Weaknesses

Things you do well are *strengths*. You may be born with some strengths, such as a good singing voice. Other strengths, such as being a good swimmer, you may have to work on. It's important to know your strengths and feel good about them.

Like everyone, you also have some *weaknesses*—things you wish you did better. Be honest with yourself about your weaknesses. Also know what you can and can't change. If you can make a change, try. Sometimes just trying to do better can help you feel good about yourself.

Your Needs

A **need** is something you must have to stay alive or to be healthy. A *want*, on the other hand, is something you would like to have. You may want a new bicycle, but you need to eat food. Everyone has needs.

No one can live without the following physical needs.

- water to drink
- healthful food
- clothing and shelter

Emotional and intellectual needs like these are also important.

- love
- friendship
- feeling safe
- self-esteem
- knowing how to solve problems

Your actions are often based on your needs. For example, you might eat a snack if you are hungry. You might call a friend if you are lonely.

If one of your needs is not being met, you will feel it. You may feel unhappy. You may get angry easily. A need that is not met is damaging to your health. But if your needs are being met, you will feel good about yourself and about life. You will feel healthy.

MANAGE STRESS

What Would You Do?

It's your first day at a new school. You will meet many new people for the first time. You're a little nervous. You need to calm yourself down. What could you do to feel better?

LESSON WRAP UP

Show What You Know

1. What is self-esteem?

2. Name three needs that everyone has.

3. **THINK CRITICALLY** Suppose that you work hard to become better at spelling. How might working on this help your self-esteem? How might it improve your health?

Show What You Can Do

4. **APPLY HEALTH ACTIVITY** PORTFOLIO **Set Goals** List four of your weaknesses. Circle the weaknesses you think you can improve. Set a goal for improving each weakness you circled.

5. **PRACTICE LIFE SKILLS** **Make Decisions** Suppose one of your friends has low self-esteem. Work with a partner. Suggest decisions that your friend could make that would improve his or her self-esteem.

In this lesson, you will learn:

▶ appropriate ways to treat people.

▶ some of the good and bad effects people have on each other.

▶ when and how to say "no" to people.

VOCABULARY

appreciate (ə prē′shē āt′) to understand the value of someone or something

consideration (kən sid′ə rā′shən) thoughtfulness toward other people and their feelings

cooperation (kō op′ə rā′shən) working together for the same purpose or goal

influence (in′flü ənts) to have either a positive or a negative effect on people

QUICK START You've moved to a new town and miss having friends nearby. You need to make new friends. What decisions would you make to help meet this need?

You will meet many different people in your lifetime. As family members marry, new relatives will join your family. In school and at work, you will deal with people in all kinds of situations. Some of these people will become good friends. Others will not. But getting along with many different kinds of people is an important part of being a healthy person.

Getting along with other people helps you feel good about yourself.

What can you learn from an older person? What can you teach an older person?

Appreciating Others

Think about three people you know. How would you describe their personalities? Your personality might be like theirs in some ways and different in others. Either way, you appreciate them. When you **appreciate** people or things, you understand their value.

You appreciate how important other members of your family are to you. You care about them and they care about you. They give you a home, and they help you when you need it.

You probably appreciate people who are similar to you. You like what you have in common. You may appreciate people who play basketball with you, who take dance class with you, or who enjoy animal stories as you do.

You can also appreciate people who are different. You may appreciate people who grew up in another country or who are much older than you. People

who are different from you can show you new ways of doing things. Knowing them can give you the chance to discover new ideas.

Consideration for Others

You can show appreciation for others by treating them with consideration. **Consideration** means showing thoughtfulness toward people and their feelings. It means acting in a way that says, "I'm thinking about you." Here are just a few ways to show consideration for others.

- Remember that all people are good at some things and not good at others.

- Listen to what other people have to say.

- Share your thoughts, feelings, and activities with others.

- Appreciate the differences that make each person special—and interesting.

Cooperating With Others

On a basketball team, not everyone can shoot the ball at the same time. Different people are good at playing different positions.

On a good team, the players remember their common goals—to have fun and to try to win the game. **Cooperation** means working together for the same purpose or goal. Cooperation helps a team reach its goals.

Cooperation is very important in your classroom. Think about a group project. Maybe one person in the group draws well. Another person writes well. Someone else is very good at finding information or speaking in front of the class. With cooperation, your project will be a success.

Whenever people work together, cooperation is important. Here are some ways to make working in a group more successful.

- Decide on your goal as a group. List all of the jobs that need to be done to reach that goal. Decide when and how certain jobs will be done.

- Let everyone in the group contribute. Not everyone can do the same thing, but each of you can do something.

- When you have a group discussion, give everyone a chance to speak. When one member is talking, others should listen respectfully.

- Be aware that different views may lead to different solutions. Often there are many possible solutions to a problem.

- When you discuss ideas, focus on important things. If you don't like an idea, don't make fun of the person who suggested it. Instead, explain what you think the problem is. And if you like an idea, tell why. Suggest ways to make good ideas work.

LIFE SKILL

RESOLVE CONFLICTS

What Would You Do?

A classmate is working with you to design a class flag. You think that you can draw better than she can. But she wants to be the one who does the artwork. Your goal is to resolve the conflict and to cooperate on this project. How can you do it?

People Influence Each Other

Your attitude about cooperation can influence other people. To **influence** means to have either a positive or a negative effect on people. For example, if you often complain, then the other people in the group may become unhappy or uncooperative. It will be hard to get things done. But if you are excited about what you are doing, you may influence other group members to be interested, too.

Who has an influence on you? Think about people you admire—parents, older brothers or sisters, teachers, and neighbors. Perhaps they influence you by giving you advice. Or they might influence you by their actions— actions that you want to imitate, or copy.

What health benefits does working cooperatively bring?

Your friends and classmates can also influence you. A friend may convince you to go hiking instead of watching TV. Seeing other students studying for a test may influence you to study, too. These are positive influences.

But some influences can be negative. Classmates or friends may use peer pressure to get you to do something you don't want to do. If you feel forced to go along with the crowd, you are feeling peer pressure.

For example, someone may try to talk you into doing something dangerous, such as swimming without a lifeguard or smoking a cigarette. When this happens, you need to be strong. You should do what you believe is right, even if you think you might lose a friend. A real friend wouldn't try to make you do things that you think are wrong.

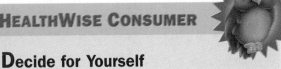

HEALTHWISE CONSUMER

Decide for Yourself

A friend says to you, "You should buy the backpack I have." or "The kind of bike I have is the best." The backpack and the bike may be right for your friend, but they may not be right for you.

Perhaps you already have a good backpack. Maybe the price of the bike doesn't fit into your family's budget. Before purchasing an item, you need to consider what's best for you and your family—not what's best for someone else.

Dealing with Negative Influences

Saying "no" might not be easy—but sometimes it's a smart health choice. Following are some ways to handle negative influences. Think about which ones would work best for you.

Think about the possible results. Think about what might happen if you let yourself be influenced in a negative way. Some questions you might ask yourself include "Might I, or someone else, get sick or hurt if I do this? Might I hurt someone's feelings? The answers will help you decide what to do.

Think about your options. Saying "yes" or saying "no" may seem to be your only choices. But there may be other options. For example, suppose a friend wants you to climb up a dangerous hill. You might suggest a safer hill to climb. Or you might suggest playing a game or working on a hobby instead.

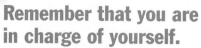

Know your values. Know what's important to you. Think about how you feel about honesty and responsibility. Make choices according to what you think is right—not what other people say is right.

Remember that you are in charge of yourself. People may try to influence you by saying that you "have to" do something that you feel is unsafe or wrong. But you are in charge of yourself! Don't rush into things. If you have to, just walk away from the situation at that moment.

I "No" You

1 Work with a partner. Write about a situation in which someone tries to influence one of you in a negative way.

2 Together, write a skit that shows how to refuse to be influenced in this situation.

3 Act out the skit for the class. Do your classmates agree with the way the situation is handled? What other ways might someone say "no" in a similar situation? Share your ideas.

LESSON WRAP UP

Show What You Know

1. Why should people appreciate differences in one another?

2. Give examples of positive and negative influences.

3. **THINK CRITICALLY** Think of a time when someone's actions have bothered you. How did you react? What are some other choices you could have made?

Show What You Can Do

4. **PORTFOLIO** **APPLY HEALTH ACTIVITY**
   Practice Refusal Skills
   Suppose one of your classmates tries to get you to steal a candy bar from a store. Write a skit showing what your classmate says and how you would refuse.

5. **LIFE SKILL** **PRACTICE LIFE SKILLS**
   Set Goals List six goals for how people can cooperate. Turn them into a poem. Begin with, "We cooperate when. . . ." Share your poem with the class.

3 EMOTIONS AND CONFLICTS

In this lesson, you will learn:

▶ about emotions and what causes them.

▶ about ways to deal with emotions.

▶ about ways to resolve conflicts.

VOCABULARY

emotion (i mō′shən) a strong feeling, such as love, sadness, or anger

conflict (kon′flikt) a struggle or disagreement between two or more people or points of view

resolve (ri zolv′) to settle a problem

compromise (kom′prə mīz′) to settle an argument or reach an agreement by give and take

QUICK START "How nice!" your grandmother says. "I really enjoyed that hug." Why might you want to hug your grandmother? What does the hug say to her?

You hug your grandmother because you have a strong feeling of love for her. She can't see your love, but the hug is a good sign that you feel it. And it makes her feel happy.

Love and happiness are just two of the feelings you have. Think about some others. Feelings may be "invisible," but you show them through your words and actions.

Your feelings sometimes show in your face. What feelings do you think are shown here?

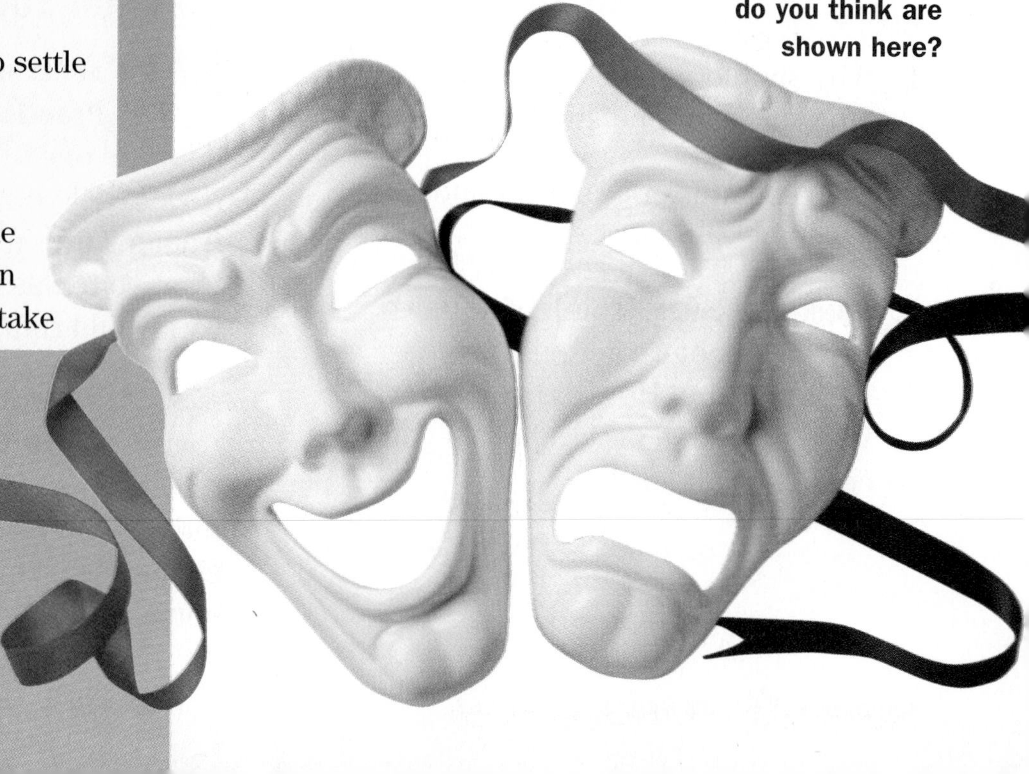

Talking things over with another person can be helpful.

Your Emotions

"That's terrific!" "I'm scared!" Statements like these express emotions. **Emotions** are strong feelings.

Often, emotions are reactions to people or events. For example, happiness may be a reaction to pleasant events. Good news and celebrations usually make you feel happy. Anger, jealousy, guilt, sadness, and fear may be some reactions to unpleasant events. Think of times when you've felt these emotions.

CULTURAL PERSPECTIVES

Showing Your Feelings

How people show—or don't show—their emotions often depends on their culture. In Italy or Mexico, for example, it is common for two people to greet each other with hugs. In Japan, two people might bow to each other instead.

Different groups of people have different ideas about emotions. Some people may show their emotions more openly than others.

Dealing with Your Emotions

Many of the ways in which you deal with emotions are learned from your family. Remember, however, that you have a choice about how to react to some situations.

Sometimes you can control your emotions by controlling your behavior. For example, telling secrets might make you feel guilty. If you stop telling secrets, you will not feel guilty.

Sometimes emotions are reactions to things that you cannot control. For example, if your pet died, you would feel sad. It's all right to feel sad. But people who are sad for too long should talk to someone who can help them. Talking to the right person about your feelings is a good way to feel better. The right person may be a parent, a teacher, a counselor, or a coach.

LIFE SKILL

OBTAIN HELP

What Would You Do?

Your best friend's dog ran away. Weeks later, your friend is still very sad and avoids people. What advice could you offer to help your friend?

Dealing With Conflict

When problems between people are not solved, conflicts may begin. A **conflict** is a struggle or disagreement between two or more people or points of view. Sometimes a conflict can lead to anger. There are many ways to deal with conflict.

- Don't keep your anger inside. If you keep your anger to yourself, the feeling may not go away. It might cause you to behave badly, even toward someone who is not part of the conflict. Sometimes people get physically or emotionally hurt when anger is not handled in healthful ways.

- Don't yell at the other person. If you yell, you might feel a little better for a while. But the other person might not listen to what you say. He or she might yell back. That could make things worse.

- Try to calm down. Take a deep breath. Count to ten, or go for a short walk. Do something that will help you relax. Relaxing can help you feel better. You will then be more able to think calmly and find an answer to the problem.

- Understand the problem. Tell the other person how you feel. Maybe he or she doesn't know that you are upset. Maybe there has been a simple misunderstanding. Maybe neither one of you was considering the other's point of view.

- Communicate carefully. Say something like "I'm angry because you took my book" instead of "You make me so mad!" The look on your face should give the same message as your words. Listen carefully when the other person talks. Try to understand each other's feelings.

- Work with the other person. Together, list some ways to **resolve**, or settle, the problem. Think about trying to compromise. When you **compromise**, you reach an agreement or settle an argument by give and take.

- Share the problem. Tell a friend or family member how you feel. That person might have an idea about how to resolve the conflict.

- It's important to resolve conflicts. But once you have done that, it's important to move on. Don't keep thinking about it.

A handshake is a good way to signal the resolution of a conflict.

Act It Out

RESOLVE CONFLICTS

You will need: index cards

1 Work in a small group. Each person should choose a conflict that could happen between two people. Write your conflict on one side of a card and how to resolve it on the other side.

2 Exchange and read the cards. Mark "+" for resolutions that you think will work. Mark "−" for those that you think won't work. Pass the cards around so all group members have a chance to read and mark each resolution.

3 Two volunteers from the group should act out the conflict and resolution with the most +'s.

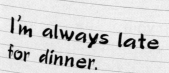

I'm always late for dinner.

Check my watch more often.

+ + + −

LESSON WRAP UP

Show What You Know

1. Describe one emotion that could be caused by good news and one that could be caused by bad news.

2. Dana is very angry with her friend. She screams at her friend and runs out of the room. What are some healthier ways Dana could react?

3. **THINK CRITICALLY** You and your sister always fight about what program to watch on television. How can you resolve this conflict?

Show What You Can Do

4. **APPLY HEALTH ACTIVITY**
   Resolve Conflicts Work in a group of four to write a skit. In the skit, have one pair deal with a conflict in an unhealthful way. Have the other pair resolve the same conflict in a healthful way.

5. **PRACTICE LIFE SKILLS**
   Manage Stress Anger makes you feel stress. Try writing about something that has made you angry. Does writing help you handle your feelings?

4 MANAGING STRESS

In this lesson, you will learn:

▶ **about stress and how it can affect your body.**

▶ **about ways to manage stress.**

VOCABULARY

stress (stres) emotional or intellectual pressure or strain

stressor (stre′sər) something that causes stress

QUICK START You've been taking piano lessons for a year. Tonight, you will be part of a piano recital. Some students in the recital have been playing for many years. How do you feel about being in the recital?

You are taking a test tomorrow. Or you are up at bat in a baseball game. Or your birthday party is about to start. At times like these you might feel pressure.

Just about everyone has this feeling from time to time. If you understand this feeling and handle it well, you can help your health in many ways.

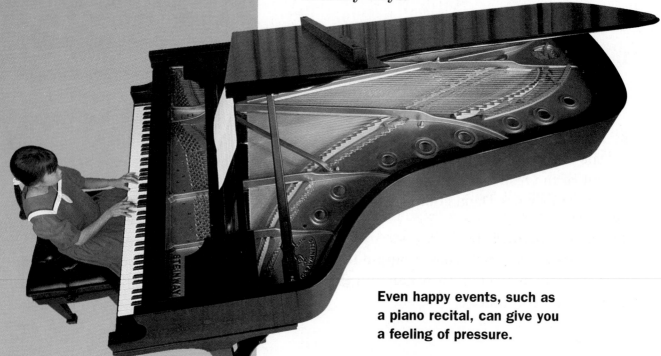

Even happy events, such as a piano recital, can give you a feeling of pressure.

Stress and Your Body

Stress is the name for emotional or intellectual pressure or strain. Some stress passes quickly—for example, the stress you feel about getting to a bus on time. Other stress may go on for a long time—for example, the stress you feel when a loved one is ill.

You feel stress in your mind and emotions. But your body feels it, too. Here are some of the ways in which stress can affect your body.

- Your heart may beat faster.

- You may sweat.

- You may feel cold all over.

- Your stomach or head may hurt.

- You may have trouble sleeping.

You can probably think of several times when you have felt stress. How did the stress affect your body?

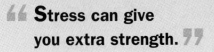

HEALTH FACT

❝ Stress can give you extra strength. ❞

This is true. Under stress, your body releases a chemical called *adrenaline*. Adrenaline makes your lungs and heart work harder. That way, your body gets more oxygen. Blood is sent to your brain and muscles. That's why you may become pale or get goose bumps. With the help of adrenaline, you may also have extra energy and strength for a short time. In some emergencies, people have even been able to lift cars to help other people in trouble!

Responding to Stress

A **stressor** is something that causes stress. One of the best ways to control stress is to steer clear of stressors. Of course, you can't always avoid stressful situations. Here are some ways to handle them.

- Don't panic. Take a few deep breaths.

- Talk to a friend or relative about it.

- Relax. Try to find a quiet place to lie down. Try playing some soft music.

- Do a physical activity.

- Always be sure to eat right, stay active, and get enough sleep. If your physical health is good, you will be better able to deal with stress.

LIFE SKILL

SET GOALS

What Would You Do?

You have to give an oral book report in class. But talking in front of everyone makes you feel stress. What goals can you set that will help you give your report successfully?

HEALTH ACTIVITY
Poster Power

MANAGE STRESS

STRESSOR:
Talking at School Assembly

um...
um...

STRESS BUSTER TIP #1:
Take some deep breaths.
STRESS BUSTER TIP #2:
Get enough sleep the
night before speech.

You will need: markers, poster paper

1 Work in small groups. Think about different events that might cause stress. Choose one event.

2 Together, create a poster about managing stress. Show the event that you chose. Then show at least one thing a person could do to react to the stress in a healthful way.

3 Display the finished poster in your classroom.

LESSON WRAP UP

Show What You Know

1. What are two ways that stress affects your body?

2. What are three things you can do to avoid stress?

3. **THINK CRITICALLY** Do all people manage stress in the same way? Which ways of dealing with stress are best for you?

Show What You Can Do

4. PORTFOLIO **APPLY HEALTH ACTIVITY**
Manage Stress It helps to understand what makes you feel stress. Make a chart. Show stressors in one column. In a second column, write how these stressors make you feel. In a third column, suggest how to deal with each one.

5. LIFE SKILL **PRACTICE LIFE SKILLS**
Obtain Help Work with a partner. List three possible stressors. Describe ways to obtain help in dealing with them.

YOU CAN MAKE A DIFFERENCE

Stop the Violence

Mia Robinson

Washington, like many big cities across the United States, is troubled by violence. In neighborhoods throughout the city, children live in stress caused by fear of violence.

When she was only ten years old, Mia Robinson joined a group called the Youth Task Force to Stop the Violence. Mia was angry and concerned about the violence that young people see every day. She wanted to help others her age to deal with the fear and stress violence can cause.

Mia found that she liked speaking to groups about avoiding violence. She visited children in their own neighborhoods. She encouraged them to talk about their fears. Just speaking out helped the children feel less afraid.

Mia has made a heroic effort to help others deal with violence in their lives. She has appeared on many radio and television shows to talk about her work. By helping others to voice and handle their fears, Mia has really made a difference.

LIFE SKILL
OBTAIN HELP

STOP THE VIOLENCE

Many police departments have community relations officers who can help people in the community deal with fears of violence. Find the address of your local or state police department. Write to the Community Relations Officer to find out what is being done about violence prevention in your community.

VOCABULARY

Write the word from the box that best completes each sentence.

compromise
conflict
consideration
cooperation
influence
need
self-concept
stressor

1. Your thoughts about yourself make up your ___?___. (Lesson 1)

2. Your behavior can ___?___ others to act the same way. (Lesson 2)

3. A disagreement between friends is an example of a(n) ___?___. (Lesson 3)

4. If both sides in an argument give up a little, the result is a(n) ___?___. (Lesson 3)

5. An event or situation that makes you feel emotional or intellectual pressure is a(n) ___?___. (Lesson 4)

REVIEW HEALTH IDEAS

Use your knowledge of emotional and intellectual health from Chapter 3 to answer these questions.

1. How can you improve your self-esteem? (Lesson 1)

2. What can happen if one of your needs is not met? (Lesson 1)

3. What are three ways to show consideration for others? (Lesson 2)

4. What are some ways to help make working in a group more successful? (Lesson 2)

5. How can knowing your own values help you make the right choices? (Lesson 2)

6. Give three examples of emotional reactions to unpleasant events. (Lesson 3)

7. What might happen if a person keeps anger inside? (Lesson 3)

8. When you are trying to resolve a conflict, why might you want to talk to a friend or family member? (Lesson 3)

9. How can you avoid some stressors? (Lesson 4)

10. How can physical activity help you handle stress? (Lesson 4)

APPLY HEALTH IDEAS

1. A friend says, "I hate the way I look!" What might you say to help your friend's self-esteem? (Lesson 1)

2. Your new neighbors have just come from another country. Why might you want to get to know them? (Lesson 2)

3. You are in a school play and feel anxious. What can you do to handle the stress? (Lesson 4)

4. **PORTFOLIO** **RESOLVE CONFLICTS** Write about resolving a conflict through compromise. Use your own experience or something you read or saw. What did people give up? What did they gain? (Lesson 3)

5. **LIFE SKILL** **PRACTICE REFUSAL SKILLS** List three questions you could ask yourself to help deal with some negative influences that you might face. (Lesson 2)

YOUR HEALTH AT HOME

How do you communicate at home? For the next two days, keep track of some of the times you communicate with your family. Record answers to these questions.

Did each person understand the other?

Sis and I had a misunderstanding about who was going to walk the dog.

Did each person show appreciation for the other?

Sis said she knew practice was important for me, but I had to tell her in advance about walking the dog.

- Did each person understand the other?

- Did each person show appreciation for the other?

- Was there a conflict? If so, what was done about it?

After two days, look over your notes. Write any ideas you have about improving communication at home.

Write True or False for each statement. If false, change the underlined word or phrase to make it true.

1. Personality is <u>a combination of all the ways you feel, think, and act.</u>

2. Your personal strengths are <u>only the abilities that you were born with.</u>

3. To show people consideration, <u>let them know that your ideas are better than anyone else's.</u>

4. People who cooperate <u>work together to get something done that is important to all of them.</u>

5. When a friend tries to get you to do something that you think is wrong, <u>do what she says so she'll keep being your friend.</u>

6. You can't control all the events in your life, but <u>you can control how you will react to them.</u>

7. A very common emotional reaction to conflict is <u>anger.</u>

8. If you're in a conflict, yelling <u>helps</u> because it makes you feel better.

9. Some kinds of stress <u>last for a long time.</u>

10. If you can't avoid the cause of stress, then <u>there is nothing you can do about it.</u>

Write a sentence to answer each question.

11. How does your self-esteem affect the way you get along with others?

12. What is a healthful way to deal with personal weaknesses?

13–15. Give three examples of negative influences that you might face at school.

16. When you work in a group, why is cooperation important?

17. Why is it important to stay calm during a conflict?

18. Why might a compromise help resolve conflict?

19. What is one way that stress can affect your body?

20. Name one healthful way to deal with stress.

✓ Performance Assessment

 Think about a conflict you had with a friend that was successfully resolved. Write a paragraph describing the methods you used for resolving the conflict.

FAMILY AND SOCIAL HEALTH

THE BIG IDEA

Your physical, emotional and intellectual, and social health are affected by the way you get along with:

■ family members.

■ classmates.

■ friends.

In this lesson, you will learn:

▶ about different kinds of families.

▶ how family actions and health habits affect your health.

▶ about the responsibilities, rights, and privileges of family members.

VOCABULARY

family (fam′ə lē) a group of people, usually made up of parents, children, and other relatives

responsibilities (ri spon′sə bil′i tēz) jobs or duties

right (rīt) something a person needs and deserves because it is fair, moral, or lawful

privilege (priv′ə lij) a special favor granted to a person or group

QUICK START Suppose you want to stay up late on a school night. Your parent tells you to go to bed at your usual bedtime. Why do you think your parent is telling you what to do?

You may not always agree with members of your family about rules. However, part of what your family does is help and protect you. Your family is an important part of your life. The way you get along with your family can affect your physical, emotional, intellectual, and social health.

Family rules about bedtime change as you grow older.

Different Kinds of Families

Type of Family	Description	Type of Family	Description
Nuclear	Two parents raise one or more children.	Blended	When one or both parents have been married before; may include children from a previous marriage.
Single-Parent	One parent raises one or more children.	Adoptive	A family adopts and raises one or more children born to others.
Extended	Family includes other relatives, such as grandparents, aunts, and uncles, who might act as parents in some cases.	Foster	A family cares temporarily for one or more children who are not birth children of the parents.

Families

A **family** is a group of people, usually one or two adults and any children they have. Other relatives are also part of a family. But family members might not live together. Families may change over time because of births, deaths, marriages, or divorces. The chart above shows some of the many kinds of families people might have.

Your Family and You

Following are some things for which you depend on your family.

- Security—for example, your family provides food, clothing, and shelter. When you're hurt or sick, your family takes care of you.

- Education—your family has taught you how to walk, talk, and eat. Your family also teaches you how to act, deal with others, and be responsible.

- Support—your family loves you. They help you build your self-esteem. They encourage you when you do well and help when you have problems.

CULTURAL PERSPECTIVES

Families Around the World

You can find every type of family in the United States and in other countries. In some parts of the world, the extended family is most common. For example, some villages in Africa are made up of single extended families. Many of the people of Western Samoa also live in extended families. Often, they elect one member to be the head of the family. What types of families are represented by the students of your class?

Your Family and Your Health

Your family influences your health in many ways. For example, family rules such as eating right and wearing seat belts affect your physical health.

Your emotional and intellectual health is affected by how family members *cooperate*, or work together for the same purpose or goal. Helping with chores and following family rules are some ways family members cooperate.

If you cooperate with your family members, you are likely to behave this way with others, too. Thus, your family affects your social health.

Family problems, such as death and divorce, can also affect your emotional and intellectual health. It helps if family members can *communicate*, or talk with and listen to each other. Being able to communicate helps family members feel safer and more secure.

Family Responsibilities, Rights, and Privileges

Each member of your family has **responsibilities**—jobs or duties—to perform. If a responsibility is not carried out, someone else must do the job.

A **right** is something you need and deserve because it is fair, moral, or lawful. Food and shelter are rights that help you maintain your physical health. Consideration from others is a right that helps protect your emotional and intellectual health.

A **privilege** is a special favor that someone grants. It may be a new bicycle or a later bedtime. Privileges within a family depend on the family and on the individual. Usually, the way to earn privileges is to earn your family's trust.

Earning privileges often depends on carrying out your responsibilities. If you follow your family's rules, your family may trust you enough to give you certain privileges. If you do not take care of your responsibilities, you cannot expect to earn privileges.

SET GOALS

What Would You Do?

You want to join a club that meets after school. But that is when you usually help your parent clean the house. What goals can you set to help you meet your responsibilities and still join the club?

Enjoying activities together strengthens family ties.

Head of the Household

LIFE SKILL

MAKE DECISIONS

1 Work in pairs. Work together to write a list of rules to help keep a family safe and healthy.

2 Work with your partner. Together, decide how you will order the list from most to least important.

3 Compare your ordered list with a list made by another pair of students. Discuss any differences in the order of the rules. Make a group decision about how the rules should be ordered.

LESSON WRAP UP

Show What You Know

1. Describe four types of families.

2. Give one example of how family actions can positively affect your health.

3. **THINK CRITICALLY** Suppose a bully is bothering your younger brother and calling him names. What is your responsibility? What are your brother's rights? Who can help protect these rights?

Show What You Can Do

4. **PORTFOLIO** **APPLY HEALTH ACTIVITY** **Make Decisions** Write an article for the family section of a newspaper. Decide on a list of guidelines for healthful living that will be featured in your article.

5. **LIFE SKILL** **PRACTICE LIFE SKILLS** **Set Goals** Set a goal to earn a privilege you would like to have at home. Write a step-by-step plan for how you will reach your goal through your actions or changes in your behavior.

2 CLASSROOM RELATIONSHIPS

In this lesson, you will learn:

▶ how classroom life compares to family life.

▶ why rules, cooperation, respect, and sharing are important in a healthy class.

▶ the importance of good communication in the classroom.

VOCABULARY

interact (in′tə rakt′) to deal with others

respect (ri spekt′) consideration or esteem between people

communication (kə mū′ni kā′shən) exchanging or sharing feelings, thoughts, or information

QUICK START There is a group of people you spend time with almost every day. You have rules you all follow. You help each other. You eat some meals together. But they are not your family! Who are they?

You belong to a number of different *social groups*. A social group involves two or more people. People in a social group **interact**. In other words, they deal with each other. Your family is the first and most important social group to which you belong. Another important social group in your life is your class at school. Can you think of other social groups you belong to?

These students asked their teacher for help. Together they are all solving a problem at the computer.

SOME CLASSROOM RULES, RESPONSIBILITIES, RIGHTS, AND PRIVILEGES

RULES	LINE UP, RAISE YOUR HAND
RESPONSIBILITIES	DO YOUR HOMEWORK, PAY ATTENTION
RIGHTS	RESPECT, NONVIOLENT CLASSROOM
PRIVILEGES	RECESS, TAKE BOOKS OUT OF LIBRARY

The Classroom

Just as with a healthy family, a healthy class depends on each member's cooperation. Also, as in a family, there are rules, responsibilities, rights, and privileges in a classroom.

One rule your class might have is to raise your hand before speaking. What are some other rules in your classroom? What are some rights and privileges?

A classroom in which the teacher and students work well together is more effective and more enjoyable than a classroom in which they do not. Teachers can teach more and students can learn more in a healthy class.

HEALTHWISE CONSUMER

Classroom Consumers

Outside of the cafeteria, you probably don't spend money while you're at school. But you are still a consumer, using paper, pens, books, and other products.

One way you can be a responsible consumer—at home and at school— is by recycling. Your school may have some special containers for cans, bottles, and papers. If your school does not have a recycling program, you might be able to help start one. Wherever you are, you can work to keep your environment healthy.

Working It Out

LIFE SKILL

RESOLVE
CONFLICTS

ACT I
RESOLVE
PROBLEMS

1 Work in small groups. Choose a problem or conflict that might come up in the classroom.

2 Write a scene that shows the problem or conflict. Also show one poor way and one better way to resolve it.

3 Act out your scene for the class. Ask if anyone in the class can explain why the good solution works better than the poor solution. Ask if anyone can think of another good solution.

A Healthy Classroom

The members of a healthy class care about how they interact with each other. In a healthy class, people share some characteristics, or qualities.

- They follow *classroom rules*— guidelines that keep a classroom safe, fair, and quiet.

- They *cooperate* by working together toward a common goal.

- Members of a healthy class have *respect* for their teacher and for one another. **Respect** is consideration or esteem between people.

- They *share* ideas, time, and materials. For example, each person is given a chance to contribute to the class.

When people share ideas, they are communicating. **Communication** involves exchanging or sharing feelings, thoughts, or information. Good communication includes listening without interrupting, taking turns talking, and keeping an open mind.

Good communication can help you avoid disagreements. It can also help you settle disagreements if they do happen. Good communication involves explaining how you feel instead of blaming the other person. Don't say, "You aren't making any sense." Instead use an "I" statement, such as "I don't understand what you're saying." It will be easier to solve the problem if neither of you is hurt or upset.

Classroom Responsibilities

Each class member has rights and responsibilities. For example, every student has a right to an education and to fair treatment.

Some classroom responsibilities are jobs for certain students, such as being hall monitor or chalkboard cleaner. But there are other responsibilities that are shared among all the students in a classroom. They include the following.

- Obey class rules.

- Show respect toward others.

- Contribute your work and ideas to the class.

- Cooperate with others.

- Show consideration for students who have difficulty hearing or speaking.

It is the teacher's responsibility to teach, and it is your responsibility to learn. It is also your responsibility to help create a class where learning can happen. If you do not accept these responsibilities, you prevent the teacher from teaching and the other students from learning. If you do accept these responsibilities, you help support your right and your classmates' rights to an education.

LIFE SKILL

RESOLVE CONFLICTS

What Would You Do?

A classmate is disrupting the class by being loud. What steps could you take to help protect your right to an education?

LESSON WRAP UP

Show What You Know

1. In what ways is a class at school like a family?

2. What are the most important characteristics of a healthy class?

3. **THINK CRITICALLY** What is the most important thing to do to make sure good communication happens in your classroom?

Show What You Can Do

4. **PORTFOLIO** **APPLY HEALTH ACTIVITY** **Resolve Conflicts** Write a short paragraph describing a conflict that might come up in the classroom. Then write about how the conflict could be resolved by good communication.

5. **LIFE SKILL** **PRACTICE LIFE SKILLS** **Make Decisions** Describe a decision made in your classroom that involved several students. Explain how good communication was part of making the decision.

RELATIONSHIPS WITH FRIENDS

In this lesson, you will learn:

▶ why friends are important.

▶ about what a healthy friendship involves.

▶ how to make and keep good friends.

VOCABULARY

trustworthy
(trust′wûr′thē) honest and truthful; able to be trusted

QUICK START Suppose you see someone new at school. What can you do to meet and find out more about this person?

Friendship is very important to your emotional, intellectual, and social health. Good friends care about each other. Your friends share with you, and they're around when you need them. The best way to have good friends is to be a good friend. If you are caring and considerate, people will want to be your friend.

A Healthy Friendship

Friendship often grows out of similar interests. But most friendships involve more than just shared interests. A healthy friendship is also based on respect. Each person respects the other person's needs, strengths and weaknesses, beliefs, and family rules.

A healthy friendship is based on trust, too. Good friends are **trustworthy**. You can trust them to tell the truth and not to do anything on purpose to hurt you. To have good friends, you also must be trustworthy.

Sometimes friends have a conflict. A *conflict* is a strong disagreement between two or more people or points of view. Good friends understand that it is okay to have different opinions. They will do their best to end the conflict. They will talk things over. Perhaps they will *compromise*, or reach an agreement by give and take. They may accept the fact that they might never agree on certain subjects.

You and Your Friends

Friends often share a common activity. Some like to read, skate, jump rope, walk, or play games together. Some friends—such as neighbors and classmates—you see every day. Others you see less often. Good friends are all alike in three ways—they are good at sharing, caring, and helping.

To have good friends, you need to be a good friend. To be a good friend, you have to behave like one. Let your friends see that you care about them. Help them when they need it, and share with them.

MAKING NEW FRIENDS

One way to get to know a person is to introduce yourself.
People who are new to your town will be eager to meet their neighbors.

> Hi, my name is Luis. I saw you moving in across the street yesterday. Would you like to take a ride around the neighborhood?

> It is very nice of you to introduce yourself. I was really feeling lonely because I had no one to talk to.

Another way to make new friends is to join a group whose members share your interests. Perhaps a club or a sport would interest you.

A good way to make new friends is to be kind, honest, and friendly. Listening well is also important.

HOW TO FIND GOOD FRIENDS

Look for People Who
- ☆ tell the truth
- ☆ are respectful of you and your family's rules
- ☆ treat others with consideration and respect

Avoid People Who
- ☹ make fun of you or your ideas
- ☹ say negative things about others when they are not present
- ☹ try to persuade you to do things you don't want to do

" Having friends is good for your health. "

It's true. After many studies, scientists believe that having friends is good for your health. People who have an active social life live longer than people who do not. Having close friends, or just people to talk to once in a while, makes you feel better and helps you manage stress.

Unfriendly Times

It's very pleasant when everyone gets along well with everyone else. But that's not the case all the time. Sometimes people aren't careful about each other's feelings.

When people make new friends, they might pay less attention to their old friends. Old friends get upset when this happens. When you make new friends, introduce them to your old ones. It will be fun to include your old friends and your new friends in your activities.

Sometimes people join a group that does not welcome everyone. It can hurt to feel left out. If there's a group that you want to join, find out how to go about it. If you are not welcomed, you are probably not losing out. The people in the group do not respect the feelings of others. They would not make good, trustworthy friends.

Perhaps you already belong to a group. Think about how your group treats new people. Are new people welcomed? Does your group try not to hurt anyone's feelings?

Feeling left out of a group can hurt. Always try to respect the feelings of others.

LIFE SKILL

MANAGE STRESS

What Would You Do?

Suppose your pal makes a new friend over the summer. Your pal starts spending less time with you and more time with the new friend. You feel upset, especially when you see your pal and the new friend together. What would you do to feel better?

Calling All Friends

LIFE SKILL

MAKE DECISIONS

You will need: paste, scissors, magazines, newspapers

1 Work in small groups. Decide on a list of ways friends behave toward each other.

2 Make a Friendship Scrapbook. Look through magazines and newspapers. Cut out pictures of people interacting. Decide which pictures show friendly interaction. Paste these pictures in your scrapbook. Leave room for captions.

3 Write captions that describe the characteristics of friendship shown in the pictures. Share the scrapbooks with all students in the class.

What Friends Do
• Give help to you.
• Encourage you.
• Play with you.
• Laugh at your jokes.

LESSON WRAP UP

Show What You Know

1. Name two reasons why it is important to have friends. Give examples to explain your reasons.

2. Describe three things to look for in a good friend.

3. **THINK CRITICALLY** Why might you decide that someone you met would not make a good friend?

Show What You Can Do

4. **PORTFOLIO** **APPLY HEALTH ACTIVITY**
Make Decisions Without using any names, write a paragraph describing one of your close friends. Decide what characteristics make this person a good friend and describe those characteristics.

5. **LIFE SKILL** **PRACTICE LIFE SKILLS**
Resolve Conflicts Suppose one of your friends feels jealous because you have made new friends. Write your friend a letter. What could you say to resolve the conflict?

TECHNOLOGY

Electronic Friends

A computer can mean access to on-line friends.

Be sure your parents know you want an electronic penpal. Never give <u>anyone</u> your password. Don't even give out your phone number or address. Don't arrange to meet anyone in real life. If someone is pressing you to do so, tell your parents or a trusted adult. Also, remember that time spent on-line costs money!

If you can use a computer, you can make a friend! Ryan Holden, a ten-year-old from North Carolina, has a pen pal in Australia. They talk to each other on-line, with only seconds separating them instead of thousands of miles.

If you want your own on-line friend, you need a computer, a modem, and an on-line service. You can enter a chat room and talk with several people at once, or you can send e-mail that is more private.

There are a few important rules to follow when you're looking for an on-line friend.

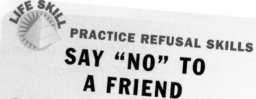

LIFE SKILL
PRACTICE REFUSAL SKILLS
SAY "NO" TO A FRIEND

Suppose an on-line pen pal keeps asking you for your password. You know that giving out your password can give that person access to a lot of information about you and your family. How can you say "no" and mean it? Write an e-mail message to your new friend.

VOCABULARY

Write the word from the box that best completes each sentence. Use each word only once.

communication

compromise

conflict

cooperate

privilege

respect

right

social

1. Being safe and secure is a __?__ that you deserve. (Lesson 1)

2. A special favor that someone grants you is a __?__. (Lesson 1)

3. Listening carefully to what other people say is an important part of __?__. (Lesson 2)

4. Good friends settle a __?__ by talking it over. (Lesson 3)

5. If you have a disagreement with a friend, a good way to settle it is to __?__. (Lesson 3)

REVIEW HEALTH IDEAS

Use your knowledge of family and social health from Chapter 4 to answer these questions.

1. Name three things you depend on your family for. (Lesson 1)

2. What are two ways in which your family affects your physical health? (Lesson 1)

3. What happens if a family member does not carry out his or her responsibility? (Lesson 1)

4. What is one right that helps protect your emotional and intellectual health? (Lesson 1)

5. What are two classroom responsibilities? (Lesson 2)

6. Name two ways in which family life and classroom life are similar. (Lesson 2)

7. What are three characteristics of a healthy class? (Lesson 2)

8. What are two things on which a healthy friendship is based? (Lesson 3)

9. How do friends deal with a conflict? (Lesson 3)

10. What are some good ways to make new friends? (Lesson 3)

APPLY HEALTH IDEAS

1. How could doing a jigsaw puzzle together affect the social health of family members? (Lesson 1)

2. What are some effects of a noisy classroom on learning? (Lesson 2)

3. How can you resolve a conflict with a friend about going to a party? (Lesson 3)

4.  **MAKE DECISIONS** Your best friend has moved away. You feel lonely. What could you do to feel better? (Lesson 3)

5. **PRACTICE REFUSAL SKILLS** You promised your parents you'd be home at 8 P.M. Your friend wants you to stay until 9 P.M. What you would say to refuse your friend? (Lessons 1 and 3)

YOUR HEALTH AT HOME

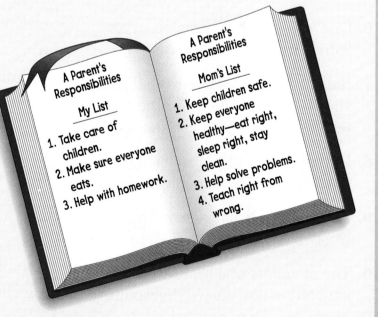

A Parent's Responsibilities

My List

1. Take care of children.
2. Make sure everyone eats.
3. Help with homework.

A Parent's Responsibilities

Mom's List

1. Keep children safe.
2. Keep everyone healthy—eat right, sleep right, stay clean.
3. Help solve problems.
4. Teach right from wrong.

What kinds of responsibilities do parents have?

List all the family responsibilities you think a parent has. Then ask your parent or guardian to list all the responsibilities he or she can think of. Compare the two lists.

- Did your parent or guardian list any responsibilities that you did not list? What are they?

- Did you list any responsibilities that your parent or guardian did not list? What are they?

Discuss these lists with your family.

Write the word in parentheses that makes each sentence true.

1. A family that includes uncles, cousins, and grandparents in the household is a(n) (nuclear, extended) family.

2. A family in which children live temporarily because they cannot live with their own relatives is a (foster, blended) family.

3. Following the family's rules is one way family members (cooperate, compromise).

4. It is your (privilege, responsibility) to learn in the classroom.

5. You have a (right, privilege) to a safe and secure home.

6. One way to gain a (privilege, right) is to earn your family's trust.

7. Raising your hand before speaking shows (trust, respect) for the teacher and for your classmates.

8. Listening carefully is an example of good (conflict, communication).

9. Someone who is honest is (jealous, trustworthy).

10. The members of a healthy class care about how they (compromise, interact) with each other.

Write a sentence to answer each question.

11. What is a blended family?

12. What is a good way for a group of people to reach a common goal?

13. What kinds of guidelines help keep a family healthy?

14. How can a family member's behavior affect the emotional, intellectual, and social health of other family members?

15. How do rules help keep a class healthy?

16. What is one good way to make new friends?

17–19. Name three things to look for in people when making new friends.

20. How can you help keep old friends from feeling jealous of your new friends?

/ **Performance Assessment**

 Make a diagram about family responsibilities. In your diagram, show some responsibilities that parents have, some that children have, and some that are shared.

NUTRITION

THE BIG IDEA

Eating healthful foods will:

- help you stay healthy.

- give you energy.

- help you feel good about yourself.

In this lesson, you will learn:

▶ why the body needs food.

▶ what nutrients and fiber are and why they are necessary for good health.

VOCABULARY

nutrient (nü′trē ənt) a substance in food that the body needs to stay healthy

proteins (prō′tēnz) nutrients needed for growth and to build and repair body cells

carbohydrates (kär′bo hī′drāts) nutrients used by the body as its main source of daily energy

fats (fats) nutrients that provide large amounts of long-lasting energy

vitamins (vī′tə minz) nutrients, found in small amounts in food, needed by the body to grow and function

QUICK START It's nearly lunchtime and your stomach is making loud gurgling sounds. What is it telling you?

When you are very hungry, you simply can't ignore how you feel. It seems as if your body is shouting "I need food!" The feeling in your stomach telling you that your body needs food is called hunger. Why is hunger's message so strong?

Your body tells you when it's hungry.

Hunger—
The Body's Call for Food

All the cells in your body need food. Without food, cells can't work properly, and some may even stop working. So when you haven't eaten in a while, your body sends your brain an important message—"Feed me!"

The message is received in a part of the brain called the *hunger center*. When the hunger center gets that message, your stomach starts tightening and relaxing as if it were digesting food. But your stomach is empty, so you feel hungry.

What if you ignore these hunger signs and don't eat? You may not have enough energy for the day's activities. You may not be able to think clearly. You might even feel shaky or light-headed.

Think about all the things you do every day. You couldn't do them if you didn't eat. That's why your body tells you to eat food. But what is it about food that is so important?

Nutrients—
Essential for a Healthy Life

Food gives your body the nutrients it needs to live, grow, and be active. A **nutrient** is a substance in food that your body needs to stay healthy. No matter what age a person is, everyone needs the same nutrients. A developing child who is not yet born needs the very same nutrients that you and your parents need!

Nutrients make their way to your body's cells through digestion and other body functions. The way your body processes food is discussed in Chapter 2.

Foods have many different types of nutrients. No one food has all the nutrients you need. That's why it's so important to eat a variety of healthful foods. On the following pages, you'll learn about the different nutrients and the foods they can be found in.

**Eating many types of foods is the only way to get all the nutrients your body needs.
Which types of foods have you eaten today?**

NUTRIENTS AND YOUR BODY

Food contains substances called nutrients. Nutrients are used by the cells in your body. Nutrients help give the body energy. Nutrients also help cells to grow and repair themselves. All the different types of nutrients can be classified into 6 groups. You need to eat a variety of types of foods to get all the nutrients your body needs.

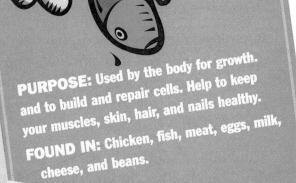

PROTEINS

PURPOSE: Used by the body for growth. and to build and repair cells. Help to keep your muscles, skin, hair, and nails healthy.

FOUND IN: Chicken, fish, meat, eggs, milk, cheese, and beans.

CARBOHYDRATES

PURPOSE: The body's main source of energy. Some carbohydrates, like sugar, give you lots of quick energy. Other carbohydrates, such as starches, give longer-lasting energy.

FOUND IN: Fruits, vegetables, pasta, potatoes, bread, cereal, and rice.

VITAMINS

PURPOSE: Needed to help the body use carbohydrates, fats and proteins and to help body systems function. Many kinds of vitamins are essential.

FOUND IN: Citrus fruits and green vegetables for vitamin C; milk, eggs, and cheeses for vitamin A, vitamin B_{12} and vitamin D.

MINERALS

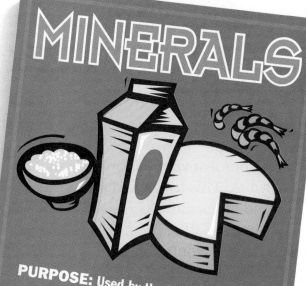

PURPOSE: Used by the body to build new cells and control important body processes. Many minerals are essential to good health.

FOUND IN: Milk and other dairy products contain calcium to build strong bones and teeth; meat, eggs, shellfish are good sources of iron.

FATS

PURPOSE: Used to help the body store vitamins and build tissue to protect important organs.

FOUND IN: Butter, margarine, cooking oils, and some cuts of meat.

WATER

PURPOSE: Dissolves some vitamins and helps bring nutrients to the cells in your body. Also helps keep your body temperature normal. About 2/3 of your body is made of water; most of it is found in your cells and blood.

FOUND IN: Food and drinks, but everyone should drink from 6 to 8 glasses of water a day.

Fiber

Fiber is the part of any plant you eat that can't be digested. Fiber is not considered a nutrient, because it does not provide energy to your body. Fiber is not needed by the body to grow and function.

Still, fiber is a very important part of your diet. This tough and stringy part of food helps move wastes through your body. Eating fiber may also help prevent and control certain types of diseases, especially cancer.

Many Americans do not eat enough fiber. Following are some tips to help you increase the amount of fiber in your diet.

- Eat fruits and vegetables with skins that can be eaten—for example, apples and carrots.

- Eat whole grain foods. Whole wheat bread, pastas, popcorn, bran muffins, and oatmeal are whole grain foods.

These foods are good for you in another way. In addition to fiber, they have carbohydrates, which your body uses for energy. They contain vitamins and minerals, too.

CULTURAL PERSPECTIVES

Kiwis Around the Globe

Modern trade and transportation have helped make certain foods available all around the world. The kiwi fruit, for example, is native to southern China. It was unavailable in other places before the early 1900s.

During this century, New Zealand became the leading producer of kiwi fruit. New Zealand has a mild climate that is perfect for growing this vitamin-rich fruit. In fact, the name *kiwi fruit* comes from its brown fuzzy skin, which looks similar to the kiwi bird of New Zealand.

For many years, kiwi fruit were shipped on airplanes to the United States. Today, more than 38,000 tons of kiwi fruit are grown in the United States, mostly in California.

LIFE SKILL

MANAGE STRESS

What Would You Do?

It's 3:30, time for baseball practice. You feel hungry, but you don't want to get to practice late. What would you do? Why?

Nutrient Name Game

You will need: twelve index cards, scissors, food magazines, glue

1 Work with a partner. Write the name of each of the six nutrient groups on index cards. Paste pictures of foods from each nutrient group on the other cards.

2 Mix up the cards and place them face down in four rows of three cards each. Take turns uncovering pairs of cards.

3 If the pictured foods and the nutrient group match, the player takes the cards. If there's no match, the cards are placed face down again. When all the cards have been matched, the player with more cards wins.

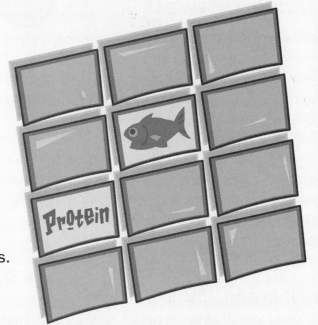

LESSON WRAP UP

Show What You Know

1. Why does the body need food?

2. How do carbohydrates and fats help your body?

3. How do vitamins and minerals help your body?

4. **THINK CRITICALLY** What would happen if you ate only fruit? Would you be healthy? Why or why not?

Show What You Can Do

5. **PORTFOLIO** **APPLY HEALTH ACTIVITY**
   Science Connection
   Make a picture book about foods and nutrients. On the front of each page, paste a picture of a food. On the back, write the major nutrients found in the food. Share your book with other students.

6. **LIFE SKILL** **PRACTICE LIFE SKILLS**
   Set Goals Make a list of healthful snacks that contain carbohydrates and vitamins. Set a goal to add these to your diet.

In this lesson, you will learn:

▶ **about the five basic food groups.**

▶ **about the Food Guide Pyramid.**

▶ **how to maintain a balanced diet.**

VOCABULARY

food group (füd grüp) various foods that are grouped together because they contain the same nutrients

Food Guide Pyramid (füd gīd pir′ə mid′) a chart of the different food groups that helps you understand how to maintain a healthful diet

balanced diet (bal′ənsd dī′it) eating the right variety and amounts of healthful foods every day

serving (sûr′ving) a certain amount of a food

QUICK START "Let's have chocolate cake and soda for lunch," a friend says. Why would you say "no" and choose other foods for lunch?

Knowing about nutrients helps you choose healthful foods. Foods with the same nutrients are placed into one of five **food groups**. All of the food groups are used to form the **Food Guide Pyramid**. The Food Guide Pyramid is a chart that helps you understand how to maintain a healthful diet. It shows you which foods to eat and how much to eat from each food group. Understanding and using the Pyramid can help you stay healthy and full of energy.

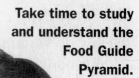

Take time to study and understand the Food Guide Pyramid.

Food Guide Pyramid

Use the Food Guide Pyramid to choose foods rich in different nutrients. You can choose tasty foods from each group. The larger the food group section, the more servings you need daily. The Pyramid also notes foods that you should eat little of—fats, oils, and sweets.

MILK, YOGURT, AND CHEESE GROUP
2–3 Servings
These foods provide calcium and other minerals. Many are also high in protein.

VEGETABLE GROUP
3–5 Servings
Like fruits, vegetables are plant foods. They are naturally low in fat. Vegetables provide vitamins, minerals, and fiber.

FATS, OILS, AND SWEETS
Use sparingly.
You should eat few foods made mostly of fats, oils, or refined (processed) sugar. These are foods with many calories but few nutrients. This category is not considered one of the five food groups. You can find these ingredients in foods from other groups.

MEAT, POULTRY, FISH, DRY BEANS, EGGS, AND NUTS GROUP
2–3 Servings
These foods are high in protein. Most also have vitamins and minerals. These foods help your body grow and stay healthy.

FRUIT GROUP
2–4 Servings
Fruits provide vitamins and minerals. They have natural sugar for quick energy. Fruits also contain fiber and water, both important to your health.

KEY
● Fat (naturally occurring and added)
▲ Sugars (added)
These symbols show fats, oils, and added sugars in foods.

BREAD, CEREAL, RICE, AND PASTA GROUP
6–11 Servings
Foods in this group are made from grains. Grains include wheat, corn, rice, and oats. Grains provide carbohydrates, protein, fiber, vitamins, and minerals.

What's Your Fancy?

What kind of food is your favorite? Do you like Italian, Chinese, or Mexican food best? Perhaps you're a fan of French, Indian, or Thai food. Each culture has its own special way of preparing tasty dishes. But no matter what type of food you eat, it is always possible to create a balanced diet that includes a variety of foods and nutrients.

A Balanced Diet

To get the nutrients your body needs, you must eat a variety of healthful foods. If you have a **balanced diet**, you not only eat the right variety of foods, you also eat the right amount of each food every day. A balanced diet includes foods from all five food groups in the recommended amounts, as shown in the Food Guide Pyramid.

Notice that the sides of the Pyramid tell you how many servings from each food group you should eat in one day. A **serving** is a certain amount of a food. Serving sizes differ from food group to food group.

The size of a food group in the Pyramid tells you how much of that group you should eat. For example, the bread, cereal, rice, and pasta group is bigger than any other in the Pyramid. This tells you that you should eat more grains than any other kind of food.

Fats, oils, and sweets are in the smallest part at the top, and are not really a "food group." You should eat only small amounts of these foods. They don't give your body enough of the nutrients it needs. That's why candy and other foods made up of mostly refined sugar or fat are called "junk food." Instead of junk food, try some fruit, vegetables, or low-fat yogurt. They give your body valuable nutrients—and they taste good, too!

You can maintain a balanced diet by eating meals that have foods from different food groups. A balanced meal is made up of servings from many different food groups. Compare the food group sections in the Food Guide Pyramid. Which foods should you eat most in a balanced diet? Which foods should you eat the least of?

LIFE SKILL
MAKE DECISIONS
What Would You Do?

Your friend's mother makes pasta with vegetables for dinner. She offers you whole milk, soda, or tomato juice to drink. Which drink would you choose to help you have a balanced meal? Why?

Meal Mobiles

LIFE SKILL

MAKE DECISIONS

You will need: magazines, paste, string, cardboard, scissors, hanger, markers

1 Work with a group. Choose a food group. Cut out food pictures from magazines. Collect good examples to show the greatest number of servings per day for your food group.

2 Make a mobile for your food group. Label it and list the nutrients found in the foods.

3 Hang all the groups' mobiles together. Make decisions about which foods you would choose from each mobile to make a balanced diet.

Vegetables

Broccoli

Potato

Carrot

Beets

Cabbage

LESSON WRAP UP

Show What You Know

1. What are the five major food groups shown in the Food Guide Pyramid?

2. The Bread, Cereal, Rice, and Pasta Group is the largest section of the Food Guide Pyramid. How does this help you make decisions about which foods to eat?

3. **THINK CRITICALLY** You have a ham and cheese sandwich and an apple for lunch. Which food group is missing from this lunch? What could be added to make this lunch better balanced?

Show What You Can Do

4. **PORTFOLIO** **APPLY HEALTH ACTIVITY** **Make Decisions** Design a "perfect" lunch menu for you and your classmates. Decide which foods to include to make two or more balanced lunchtime meals.

5. **LIFE SKILL** **PRACTICE LIFE SKILLS** **Obtain Help** Plan a healthful party menu for you and your friends to enjoy. Ask the school nurse or dietitian for help and to check your selections.

3 MAKING FOOD CHOICES

In this lesson, you will learn:

▶ the value of including fresh foods in your diet.

▶ about nutrient information found on food labels.

VOCABULARY

food label (füd lā′bəl) information about the product, including the name and address of the manufacturer, printed on packaging

ingredient (in grē′dē ənt) a substance mixed together with others to make food

additive (ad′i tiv) a substance put in a food to make it more healthful, last longer, look better, or taste better

QUICK START In the supermarket you see five different kinds of cereal that you like. How can you tell which is more healthful?

You've learned about nutrients, food groups, and the suggested number of servings you should eat. But how do you know which nutrients are in the many packaged foods that are available? How do you know how much you should eat? As you'll see, there are many things to consider in making healthful food choices.

There are many things to think about when making healthful food choices.

Food Choices

As you grow older, you'll make more decisions about your life. You'll also make more choices as a consumer. Even today, you often decide for yourself what foods to eat. Perhaps you make your own breakfast. You may decide what lunch to buy or snacks to eat.

Eating fresh foods is one healthy food choice. Fresh foods do not have anything added to them. They have not been heated or frozen. Heating or freezing foods may destroy or break down some nutrients. Fresh fruits and vegetables are good food choices.

It's easier to make wise decisions if you have healthful choices in mind before you eat.

Healthful Food Choices	
Instead of . . .	**Choose . . .**
Potato Chips	Carrot Sticks
Ice Cream	Frozen Low-Fat Yogurt
Candy	Fresh Fruit
Soda	Unsweetened Juice or Water

Food Labels

Knowing how to read labels on food packages is important. It will help you make wise choices. The **food label** shows information that tells the buyer what is in the product and who made it. The law states that all packaged foods must have a label.

It takes time to read food labels, but your health is worth it. First you need to understand all the facts that are shown on food labels. Then you can judge whether or not a food is good for you. The food label shown on the next page is from a container of orange juice.

PRACTICE REFUSAL SKILLS

What Would You Do?

Your sister is trying to talk you into buying some sweets on the way home from school. How would you tell her that you plan to make a more healthful choice? What would you choose?

Food Labels

A food label contains nutrition facts about the food in the package. All the information on the label is for a serving size. The serving size is shown at the top of every label. One serving for this orange juice is 8 ounces, or 1 cup. Read labels carefully. Serving sizes are different from food to food. They even change for the same types of food.

This part tells you about each serving of this orange juice. You learn the number of servings. You also learn the number of calories in one serving. Calories are the amount of energy available in a food.

These parts show the percent (%) daily value of nutrients that the juice gives your body. One serving of this orange juice gives you all the vitamin C that you need for one day—100%.

An **ingredient** is a substance that is mixed together with others to make food. The law states that the ingredients printed on a label must be listed in order from the greatest amount to the least amount. Understanding the order of ingredients on a food label helps you determine how healthful a food is.

Nutrition Facts

Serving Size 8.5 oz. (240 ml)
Serving per container 8

Amount Per Serving

Calories 120

	% Daily Value*
Total Fat 0g	0%
Sodium 300mg	0%
Potassium 430 mg	12%
Total Carbohydrate 29g	10%
Sugars 27g	
Protein 1g	

Vitamin C	100%
Thiamin	10%

Not a significant source of calories from fat, saturated fat, cholesterol, dietary fiber, Vitamin A, calcium and iron.

*Percent Daily Values are based on a 2000 calorie diet.

INGREDIENTS: WATER, CONCENTRATED ORANGE JUICE.

SUNNY TIME ORANGE JUICE CO., INC.
3000 Main Street, Orangetown, FL 32880

Sometimes you may be unfamiliar with some ingredients listed on a label. Some of these ingredients are additives. An **additive** is something added to food. Additives may make food more healthful, last longer, look better, or taste better.

The manufacturer's name and address appears on the food label or somewhere else on the packaging.

Figure Out Food Labels

LIFE SKILL MAKE DECISIONS

You will need: food labels from a variety of foods

1 Work with a group. List the nutrients from each label. Note which nutrient each food has the most of and the least of. Note the serving size and number of servings for each package.

2 Compare the facts for all the food labels. Decide which foods you think are the most healthful. Which would make the best snacks? Which might be good to include in a balanced diet?

3 Decide which foods are not good for you. What facts on the label led you to make this decision?

LESSON WRAP UP

Show What You Know

1. Why is it important to include fresh foods in your diet?

2. Why is it important to know the serving size shown on a food label?

3. Why is the list of ingredients on a food label important to consider when selecting a food?

4. **THINK CRITICALLY** Fresh foods are often considered better choices than similar packaged foods. In what ways might additives make packaged foods more healthful?

Show What You Can Do

5. **PORTFOLIO APPLY HEALTH ACTIVITY Make Decisions** Compare the food labels of two brands of your favorite cereal. Write a brief report explaining which brand is more healthful and why.

6. **LIFE SKILL PRACTICE LIFE SKILLS Practice Refusal Skills** Work with a partner. Write a skit to show how you would say "no" if someone offers you a snack that is not good for you. Take turns acting out your skit.

In this lesson, you will learn:

▶ how the amounts and kinds of foods you eat affect your health.

▶ how stress and diet are related.

▶ about diseases caused by a lack of nutrients.

VOCABULARY

calorie (kal′ə rē) a unit for measuring the amount of energy contained in food

deficiency disease (di fish′ən sē di zēz′) a disease caused by the lack of a nutrient

anemia (ə nē′mē ə) a condition in which the blood has too few red blood cells

QUICK START You ate lunch only two hours ago. However, the smell of pizza makes your mouth water. You feel like eating again. What's going on? Does your body really need food now?

It's important to recognize the messages your body sends when you are hungry. If you eat whenever you are faced with food, you will eat more than your body needs. But if you regularly skip meals, you might develop health problems. With proper nutrition, there is a balance between food coming in and energy that you use up.

Eat three nutritious meals each day.

A Balanced Lunch	Calories
2 slices whole wheat bread	130
Tuna Fish (3 ounces)	127
Mayonnaise (1 teaspoon)	33
Lettuce (2 leaves)	5
Tomato (1/2, sliced)	13
Apple Juice (8 ounces)	120
Orange (small)	100

Calories Expended	
Activity	Calories per Minute
Basketball	5–6
Bicycling	4–6
Running	6–9
Sitting	1
Skating	3–5
Skiing	5–6
Sleeping	1
Soccer	4–5
Swimming	5–7
Volleyball	2–3
Walking	3–4

Calories

A calorie is a unit of measure, like an inch or a pound. **Calories** measure how much energy food gives your body.

Calories also measure how much energy you use up when you do something active. For example, suppose you eat a banana. The cells in your body can get about 100 calories worth of energy from the banana.

Suppose you then ride your bicycle for 20 minutes. Your body needs energy to ride a bicycle. Your body uses about 100 calories during a 20-minute bicycle ride. So you "burn" all the calories that were in the banana.

In Lesson 2, you learned about balanced diets. The easiest way to have a balanced diet is to eat a variety of foods at each meal. A balanced lunch, such as the one in the chart above, provides many different nutrients your body needs. How many calories would your body get from this lunch?

If you added up all the calories in this lunch, you would see that your body had taken in 528 calories. Your body would use some of those calories to breathe, digest food, and so on. Your body could use the other calories to be active.

Different kinds of activities use up different amounts of calories. The chart above shows how you might use these calories after lunch.

LIFE SKILL

MAKE DECISIONS

What Would You Do?

Suppose that before dinner you would like to work off at least 100 of the calories you took in at lunch. Which of the activities in the chart above would you choose to do? For how many minutes might you do each one?

Food and Your Weight

Your weight stays the same when the number of calories you take in from food equals the number of calories your body uses to maintain itself and be active.

Sometimes a person takes in too many calories or is not very physically active. Then he or she may not use all of the calories taken in. These unused calories are stored as fat. Over time, the person might become overweight. To be *overweight* means to weigh more than is normal for someone of the same height and build. Being overweight is not healthy.

Sometimes a person eats too few calories or is very active. Then the body may not have enough energy to fuel its cells. The person will lack energy and not be able to think clearly. Over time, he or she may become underweight. To be *underweight* is to weigh too little for someone of the same height and build. Like being overweight, being underweight is unhealthy.

The number of calories in the foods you eat is important. Where the calories come from is important, too. All food contains calories, but the calories in some foods are easier for your body cells to use. Experts recommend that you get about half of your calories from carbohydrates. Proteins should provide about one-fifth of your calories. Fats should provide no more than one-third of your calories.

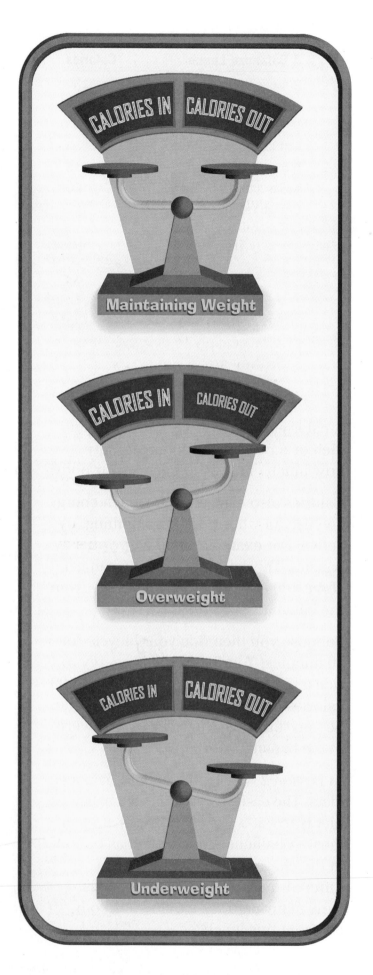

Managing Your Weight

There are many things you can do daily to stay at a healthy weight.

- Eat three balanced meals over the course of a day. A good breakfast will prepare your body and your mind for morning activities. A good lunch will give you energy for the afternoon. A healthful dinner will give your body the energy it needs to work and grow.

- Eat the right foods. Get the calories you need from foods that have a lot of nutrients. Stay away from junk foods. They may be easy to get and quick to eat, but they are not good for your body. Plan ahead for nutritious snacks.

- Get plenty of exercise. Stop extra calories from being stored as fat by burning up the calories you take in. Playing active games and sports are great ways to use up extra calories. Being physically active, even just by walking every day, will help you stay at a healthy weight.

Managing Stress

It's not always easy to follow a healthful diet. For example, sometimes stress can cause a person to want foods that aren't healthful. Also, if you have a poor diet or skip meals, you will be less able to handle stress.

If you are not eating well, you won't have enough energy. You may develop problems in your school, play, and social life. You may find yourself being cranky with people for no reason or having trouble paying attention. A healthy diet, on the other hand, strengthens your body systems. You will be better prepared to respond to stress.

Eating the right foods will help you feel good and manage stress.

HEALTH ACTIVITY
Good Diet Dramas

1 Work in groups. Talk about how you might maintain good health and reduce stress. Include ideas for eating properly and staying active. Write down everyone's ideas.

2 As a group, choose three favorite ideas. Discuss ways these ideas can be acted out in a skit.

3 Write the skit and perform it for the class. Have one student from the group narrate the skit. The rest of the group should enact the skit.

HEALTH FALLACY

❝ **Sugary snacks like candy give you a lot of energy.** ❞

This is not true. Over several hours, the kind of sugar found in these snacks actually decreases your energy. The sugar enters the blood quickly. The quick rise in blood sugar causes the body to react by lowering natural blood sugar. The blood sugar level ends up being below normal. The person's energy level drops as a result.

Nutrients and Illnesses

If you don't get enough of a needed nutrient, you may become ill. A disease caused by the lack of any nutrient is a **deficiency disease**. *Deficiency* means a lack of something necessary.

Anemia is a deficiency disease. **Anemia** is a condition in which the blood has too few red blood cells. A person with anemia may feel weak most of the time. Anemia is often caused by getting too little iron. Iron is a mineral that is an important part of red blood cells. Eating foods that are rich in the mineral iron can prevent or treat this form of anemia.

HealthWise Consumer

Vitamin D to the Rescue!

In Lesson 3 you learned about food labels. You saw that vitamins and minerals are added to many foods we buy. These additives have many health benefits.

One important food additive is vitamin D. This vitamin helps the body use minerals to build stronger bones and teeth. Most processed milk and some breads that you see in the grocery store have added vitamin D.

Vitamin D also prevents rickets, a childhood disease which results in soft, curved bones. Because of this additive, cases of rickets are now very rare in the United States.

LESSON WRAP UP

Show What You Know

1. How does the amount of food you eat affect your health?

2. How do the kinds of food you eat affect your health?

3. **THINK CRITICALLY** Suppose you have anemia. What kinds of food should you eat more of?

Show What You Can Do

4. **PORTFOLIO** **APPLY HEALTH ACTIVITY** **Manage Stress** Write a scene for two characters. Have one character tell how he or she eats junk food when feeling stress. Have the other give advice on managing stress and still eating well.

5. **LIFE SKILL** **PRACTICE LIFE SKILLS** **Set Goals** Set a goal with your family to eat healthful breakfasts. Plan your breakfasts for one week. Give your shopping list to the grocery shopper in your family.

In this lesson, you will learn:

▶ how to tell when a food is unsafe to eat.

▶ how to handle, prepare, and store food safely.

VOCABULARY

spoil (spoil) to become rotten and unhealthy

bacteria (bak tîr′ē ə) a type of one-celled organism, or living thing

mold (mōld) an organism that can spoil food; can appear as a fuzzy growth

QUICK START You buy milk after school. You notice that the date stamped on the package has already passed. What would you do?

Sometimes food "goes bad," or spoils. When food **spoils**, it becomes rotten and is no longer healthy to eat. Spoiled food not only tastes bad. Eating or drinking it can also make you sick.

There are many reasons foods spoil. The food may have been stored too long or in an incorrect way. The spoiled food might not have been handled, prepared, or packaged correctly. It may have been left out in the air too long.

YUMMY!

Bacteria and mold are two common causes of spoiled food. What can be done to prevent food from spoiling?

A Proper Place

LIFE SKILL

MAKE DECISIONS

1 Draw a chart with three columns. In the first column, make a list of ten foods.

2 In the second column, write where each food would best be stored before using.

3 Make a decision about where you think each food should be stored after its packaging has been opened. Write your decision in the third column.

4 Fold your paper so only your food list is showing. Exchange lists with a partner and provide your own answers. Discuss answers that differ in order to arrive at the best decision.

Food	Where to Store	Final Decision
Jar of tomato sauce	Cupboard	Refrigerator

Storing Food

You can store food in a way that stops it from spoiling quickly. Dairy products can be kept cold in a refrigerator. Some foods can be stored in a freezer. Cold temperatures can stop the growth of some bacteria that cause foods to spoil. **Bacteria** are a type of one-celled organism, or living thing.

Some food spoilage is hard to spot. Fruit that is bruised or an egg with a cracked shell may contain food-spoiling bacteria. Bacteria can cause a can of food to bulge. If you see such things, the food may be spoiled. Many spoiled foods smell bad. This warns you that the food is not safe to eat. A bad taste can also be a sign of spoiled food.

An organism known as **mold** can sometimes grow on food and spoil it. Mold is often fuzzy and might cause the food to change color. Eating moldy food can make you sick.

Storing food in plastic wrap or in closed containers can keep mold and bacteria in the air from getting on it. Some food packages say "Keep Frozen" or "Refrigerate After Opening." These instructions tell you the best way to store the food so it does not spoil quickly.

Preparing and Handling Food

Cleanliness is very important while food is being prepared. Make sure that any surface you work on is clean. Knives, forks, and spoons should be clean, too. Of course, you should always wash your hands with soap before handling food. Always rinse fruits and vegetables with water before preparing or eating them. Cleaning up with soap and hot water after preparing food also helps stop the spread of bacteria.

MAKE DECISIONS

What Would You Do?

You are about to use a fork that you find lying on the counter. Should you use it? What special care should you take?

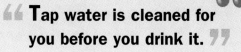

HEALTH FACT

" Tap water is cleaned for you before you drink it. "

One of the things you consume most is water. It is an important part of your diet. When you turn on the faucet at home, you expect to have clean, safe water. All public water supplies in the United States must be made safe to drink. The water is first cleaned. Then chemicals are added to kill bacteria.

Bottled water sold in stores is considered pure and does not need to be treated. But all public drinking water is made safe before it comes to your home.

LESSON WRAP UP

Show What You Know

1. What are three ways you can tell whether food is spoiled?

2. Where would you safely store and prepare each of the following foods—ice cream, fresh spinach, fresh chicken?

3. **THINK CRITICALLY** Many United States government workers inspect the foods we eat. They test for harmful chemicals and bacteria in food. How do these workers help consumers?

Show What You Can Do

4. **APPLY HEALTH ACTIVITY**
   Make Decisions Consider what foods might be safe to take on an overnight hiking trip. List the foods for one day's meals and two snacks. Describe ways that you would handle the foods and utensils while packing and during food preparation.

5. **PRACTICE LIFE SKILLS**
   Obtain Help Ask a parent to help you clean out the refrigerator. Decide whether any of the food is spoiled and needs to be thrown away.

YOU CAN MAKE A DIFFERENCE

Lunch for the Homeless

Donating food is an excellent way to help the homeless.

How long do you think it would take to make 400 sandwiches? Amber Coffman and her friends do it every Saturday morning. These kids have formed a group called Happy Helpers for the Homeless.

Amber and her friends convinced businesses in their town of Glen Burnie, Maryland, to donate food to their cause. With the donated supplies, the friends make lunch for homeless people in their town and in the nearby city of Baltimore.

Amber has been working with the homeless since she was eight years old. When she is older, her goal is to direct a shelter for the homeless. Already, her caring has helped many people.

Being a community volunteer like Amber is a great way to improve your own self-esteem. Imagine how good you would feel about yourself if you helped people on a regular basis. There are lots of possibilities right in your own neighborhood—your parents or teacher can help you find them.

LIFE SKILL

SET GOALS

PLAN A MENU

Imagine that you and a friend, like Amber, are going to make lunch for the homeless. Plan a nutritious and tasty lunch menu. Then, with your partner, look in the Yellow Pages of your phone book. Find and jot down the names of businesses that might donate food, such as a local bakery for bread, or an orchard or farm for fruit.

5 REVIEW

VOCABULARY

Write the word from the box that best completes each sentence. Use each word only once.

additive
anemia
balanced diet
calorie
ingredient
nutrient
spoil

1. Vitamin A is one kind of ___?___. (Lesson 1)

2. If you eat a variety of all the right kinds of food every day, you'll have a ___?___. (Lesson 2)

3. A unit for measuring the energy in food is ___?___. (Lesson 4)

4. A person with too few red blood cells may have ___?___. (Lesson 4)

5. Leaving milk out on the kitchen counter may make it ___?___. (Lesson 5)

REVIEW HEALTH IDEAS

Use your knowledge of nutrition from Chapter 5 to answer these questions.

1. Why is it important for the body to have food? (Lesson 1)

2. Which two nutrients does the body mainly use for energy? (Lesson 1)

3. Why should you eat foods from all five major food groups? (Lesson 2)

4. Why are fats, oils, and sweets not considered a major food group? (Lesson 2)

5. Why is it important to know how to read food labels? (Lesson 3)

6. Where can you find the number of servings in a package of food? (Lesson 3)

7. What are three things you can do daily to maintain a healthy weight? (Lesson 4)

8. What are two causes of being underweight? (Lesson 4)

9. A big bulge in a can of food may be a sign of what? (Lesson 5)

10. Why is it important to wash dishes and utensils with soap and hot water after use? (Lesson 5)

APPLY HEALTH IDEAS

1. If fiber isn't a nutrient, why is it important to eat foods that have fiber? (Lesson 1)

2. What does the size of each section in the Food Guide Pyramid tell you? (Lesson 2)

3. If sugar is the first ingredient listed on a food label, what does this tell you about the food? (Lesson 3)

4. **PORTFOLIO** **OBTAIN HELP** List all the snacks you ate last week. Ask a nurse or other trusted adult to help you judge how healthful your snacks were. (Lesson 3)

5. **LIFE SKILL** **PRACTICE REFUSAL SKILLS** A friend finishes his lunch and asks if he can have half of yours. How could you say "no" to him and explain the importance of you finishing your own lunch? (Lesson 4)

Which guideline from this chapter can you use at home every day?

Take a sheet of paper. Label it with the headings shown here. Make a list of guidelines that will be useful for everyone in your family.

Talk to your family about what you've learned and why it's important. Decide on a place at home to post your guidelines.

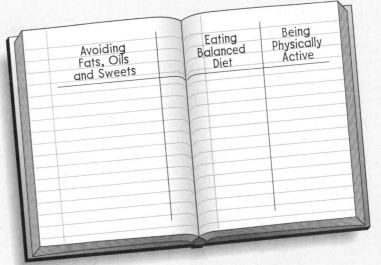

Avoiding Fats, Oils and Sweets		Eating Balanced Diet	Being Physically Active

Match the word or words in the box to the statements below. Use each letter only once.

a. calories
b. label
c. fats, oils, sweets
d. bacteria
e. minerals
f. additives
g. bad taste
h. fiber
i. refrigerate
j. serving size
k. carbohydrate

1. cannot be digested

2. can cause food to spoil

3. varies between foods, even for similar types of foods

4. the one part of the Food Guide Pyramid that is not a major food group

5. calcium and iron

6. lists ingredients found in a food

7. vitamins and minerals are sometimes put in foods as this

8. one way to store some foods to keep them from spoiling

9. an active person needs to take in more of these to maintain his or her weight

10. one sign that food is spoiled

Briefly answer each question.

11. Why does the body need food?

12. What is one benefit of eating fresh foods?

13–14. Name two ways to prepare and handle food safely.

15. Name a deficiency condition caused by the lack of a nutrient.

16–17. Name two signs that a food might be unsafe to eat.

18. Name one food group. What are the recommended daily servings for that group?

19. How can the amounts and kinds of foods you eat affect your health?

20. How does water help your body?

Performance Assessment

 The people in charge of your cafeteria have a number of important decisions to make each week. Suppose you have been put in charge. Create five lunch menus for one week. Consider nutrition and flavor.

PHYSICAL ACTIVITY AND FITNESS

THE BIG IDEA

Regular physical activity:

- keeps you fit.

- has a positive effect on your physical, emotional, intellectual, and social health.

In this lesson, you will learn:

▶ about the three parts of physical fitness.

▶ how diet and physical activity help you maintain a healthy weight.

▶ how physical fitness helps improve all parts of your health.

VOCABULARY

physical activities (fiz′i kəl ak tiv′i tēz) games, sports, exercises, and other actions that involve moving your body

physical fitness (fiz′i kəl fit′nəs) the condition in which your body works at its best

flexibility (flek sə bi′lə tē) the ability to bend and move your body easily

strength (strengkth) the ability to lift, push, and pull

endurance (en dùr′əns) the ability to be active for a while without getting too tired to continue

QUICK START You are watching a baseball game on TV. A friend calls. She asks you to play baseball with some friends. Should you continue to watch TV or join your friends? Which is the healthier choice?

Being fit means more than being able to run a race. It means more than being able to catch a ball. To be fit is to be as healthy in your body and mind as you can be.

Physical activity is fun!

What Is Physical Fitness?

Physical activities are games, sports, exercises, and other actions that involve moving your body. Physical activity makes your body strong. Physical activity helps you think clearly. It also helps you feel good about yourself and other people.

Physical fitness is a condition in which your body works at its best. When you are physically fit, you work, feel, and think well. There are three parts to physical fitness.

- **Flexibility** allows you to bend and move. Bending down to tie your shoes shows flexibility. Flexibility is important when you are dancing, swimming, and playing tennis, volleyball, or other sports.

- **Strength** is the ability to lift, push, and pull. It gives you the power to perform an activity successfully. When you kick a ball or carry a heavy box, you are using strength. Bicycling, handball, and cross-country skiing are activities that require strength.

- **Endurance** allows you to continue an activity, like hiking or running, for a long time before tiring. Another name for endurance is *stamina*. Dancing, swimmimg, and jumping rope all require endurance.

Flexibility, strength, and endurance can improve with regular physical activity. The more active you are, the more healthy and physically fit you will become.

Fitness and Body Weight

In Chapter 5, you learned that controlling the calories you take in can help you maintain a healthy body weight. Your diet is not the only thing that affects your weight. Your weight is also affected by how physically active you are.

Calories measure the amount of energy available to your body from the foods you eat. The more active you are, the more calories you use. A healthy diet and a regular physical activity program help you have a healthy body weight and a more healthy life.

Fitness and Your Physical Health

Physical fitness affects all the muscles of your body. The more you use your muscles, the stronger they become. The stronger muscles are, the better they can work.

Physical activity makes your heart strong so it can do its job. Your heart is a muscle in your chest. Your heart pumps blood through your body.

With each breath you take, your lungs take in air. The air you breathe has oxygen in it. This oxygen is picked up by the blood moving through your lungs. The oxygen is then carried to all parts of your body.

Your blood also takes waste gas back to your lungs. This waste gas is removed when you breathe out. When you have healthy lungs and a strong heart, you have good endurance.

" Physical activity helps you sleep better. "

It's true that people who don't exercise their muscles can't relax fully. They wake up more often during the night. Exercise and physical activity tire your body, helping you sleep better. Sleep helps refresh your body and mind. For children, it is also the time when bones grow. But be careful about when you do physical activities. Physical activity in the late afternoon helps you sleep at night. Close to bedtime, physical activity can keep you awake.

Fitness and Your Emotional and Intellectual Health

Being active does more than strengthen your body. Physical fitness affects your emotional and intellectual health, too. When your mind and body work well, you feel good about yourself. Your self-esteem, or self-confidence, improves. Being physically fit helps you:

- stay alert and think clearly.

- manage stress and deal with problems more effectively.

- feel good about your health and appearance.

Hiking does more than benefit your physical health. In what ways can hiking benefit your social, emotional, and intellectual health?

Fitness and Your Social Health

You can do physical activities alone or with family, friends, and classmates. Hiking, dancing, and team sports are healthy activities that are fun to do with others.

When you are active with others, you can meet new friends. Physical activities allow you to spend time with people you like. You have a chance to talk about what is going on in your life. Being active with others improves your social health along with your physical health!

LIFE SKILL

MAKE DECISIONS

What Would You Do?

Your best friend invites you to join the school hiking club on a nature walk. However, you're not sure you can keep up. What decisions can you make to prepare for the hike?

We Can Be Fit!

You will need: large paper, markers

1 Sketch yourself being active. Include at least one activity showing flexibility, one showing strength, and one showing endurance.

2 How much time do you spend doing each activity in a week? Write a short paragraph that describes how you feel before and after you are active. Which of these activities help you deal with stress?

3 Which activities are most popular among your classmates? Would any of them help you deal with stress?

flexibility

LESSON WRAP UP

Show What You Know

1. Describe the three parts of physical fitness.

2. Explain how physical activity and diet are both important to maintaining healthy body weight.

3. **THINK CRITICALLY** Explain how a team sport you like can improve your emotional, intellectual, social, and physical health.

Show What You Can Do

4. **PORTFOLIO** **APPLY HEALTH ACTIVITY**
   Manage Stress For one week, keep a log of all the physical activities you do. Tell how you feel before and after each activity. Then identify those activities that help you manage stress.

5. **LIFE SKILL** **PRACTICE LIFE SKILLS**
   Set Goals Set a goal to do more physical activities. Write a paragraph that describes what you would like to achieve. Tell how you would go about reaching your goal.

In this lesson, you will learn:

▶ how your fitness skills are used every day.

▶ the six basic fitness skills.

VOCABULARY

agility (ə jil′i tē) the ability to move easily

balance (bal′əns) the ability to keep your body in a steady position

coordination (kō ôr′də nā′shən) the ability to use more than one body part at a time to perform a task

speed (spēd) how quickly you move

reaction time (rē ak′shən tīm) the time it takes to notice and respond to something

power (pou′ər) the combination of strength and speed

QUICK START On your way home from school, you carry a heavy book bag and jump across a puddle. Then you step aside quickly when a dog runs toward you. What skills do you use to do these everyday activities?

A dancer leaps across the stage. A painter dips a brush into a paint can. A child chases a ball that rolls away. To be good at what they are doing, these people need good fitness skills. You use fitness skills every day— at school, at home, and on the playground. Your ability to do your best depends on how fit you are.

Being Fit
Helps You Every Day

Being fit plays an important part in your everyday life. To put on your socks while standing up, you use many different muscles. You use muscles in your back, legs, feet, and ankles to stand, raise your foot, and point your toes. You use muscles in your shoulders, arms, and hands to place the sock on your foot.

Can you name one or more fitness skills you would need to spin a basketball like this?

All these muscles are needed to do one simple thing—put on your socks while standing. Think about all the other things you do during the day. You need to be strong to carry your books home from school. Your whole body—not just your hands—needs to be ready to catch a baseball coming at you. No matter what activities you do during a typical day, the more fit you are, the easier your everyday physical activities will be.

HEALTH FALLACY

" Athletes are born, not made. "

This is not true. In fact, most athletes must work hard to improve the abilities they are born with. Many athletes have worked hard to turn their weaknesses into strengths. One example is athlete Wilma Rudolph. Wilma had polio when she was 4 years old. Because of the disease, she could not walk without a brace until she was 12. But with hard work and practice, 20-year-old Wilma went on to win three gold medals in sprinting at the 1960 Rome Olympics.

Wilma Rudolph, 1940–1994

Six Skills for Fitness

Do you play any sports? Do you like to roller skate with your friends? It may surprise you, but you use most of the six fitness skills every time you are active. The more you use these skills, the more you can improve them.

AGILITY **1**

Agility is the ability to move easily and smoothly. Agility—and all the other fitness skills—can be improved with practice. Sliding into third base takes agility.

Coordination **2**

Coordination involves different parts of your body working together to do a task. Playing the drum takes a lot of coordination!

Balance **3**

Balance is the ability to keep your body in a steady position. Balance stops you from falling down, even when you are jumping or bending your body. Keeping your balance is important for many activities.

Speed 4

Speed is how fast you move. Remember, people are different, and they move at the speed that's good for them. Just be the best you can be.

POWER 5

Power is the combination of strength and speed. Almost every sport or activity uses power at some point.

REACTION TIME 6

Reaction time is the time it takes you to respond to something. You can work on this skill by playing games and sports that involve catching, throwing, or hitting objects.

Activities That Build Physical Fitness

In this lesson, you learned about the six fitness skills. In Lesson 1, you learned about three parts of physical fitness—strength, endurance, and flexibility. Together, they make up physical fitness.

Look at the chart below. Find the activities that you enjoy. Use the key to compare how they help build the three parts of physical fitness as well as a healthy heart. What fitness skills do they use?

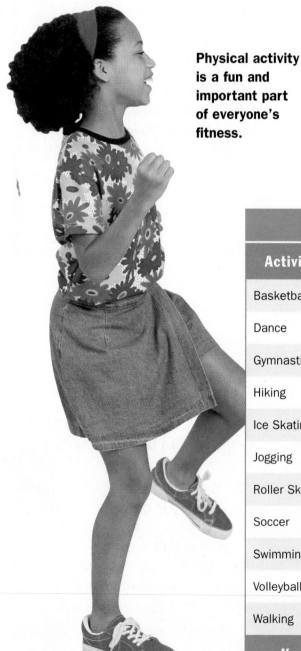

Physical activity is a fun and important part of everyone's fitness.

LIFE SKILL

SET GOALS

What Would You Do?

You want to build up your strength, endurance, and flexibility. Which activities would you do to reach your goals? Use the chart below.

Activities That Build Fitness				Healthy Heart
Activity	**Strength**	**Endurance**	**Flexibility**	
Basketball	★	★	★	★★★
Dance	★★	★★	★★★	★★
Gymnastics	★★★	★★★	★★★	★
Hiking	★	★★★		★★
Ice Skating	★★	★★	★	★★
Jogging		★★		★★★
Roller Skating		★		★
Soccer	★	★★		★★★
Swimming	★	★★★	★	★★★
Volleyball	★			★
Walking	★	★★		★★

Key: ★ = Fair ★★ = Good ★★★ = Excellent

HEALTH ACTIVITY
Skills Scope

OBTAIN HELP

1 Work in a group. Choose five activities that your group members like to do.

2 Find out more about each activity. Obtain help from a physical education teacher or coach to find books and magazines about the activities. You might also talk to a librarian or teacher. Decide which of the six fitness skills are most important in each activity.

3 Classify the activities according to the fitness skills needed to do them. Present your categories to the class. Which skill or skills show up most often? Why do you think this is so?

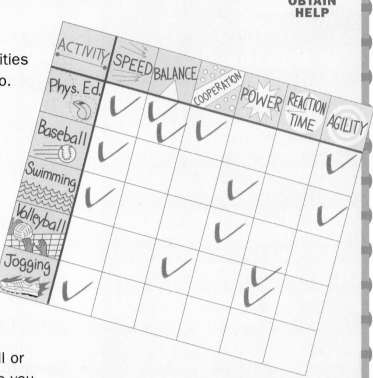

LESSON WRAP UP

Show What You Know

1. How does being physically fit help you every day? Give at least one example each from school, home, and the playground.

2. Name the six basic physical fitness skills. Explain the importance of one of them.

3. **THINK CRITICALLY** Which fitness skill do you think is most important when you walk? Why?

Show What You Can Do

4. **APPLY HEALTH ACTIVITY**
   Obtain Help Write a letter to a health or sports expert. Ask for information about a favorite activity. Decide what fitness skills are involved in the activity. Summarize your information for others.

5. **PRACTICE LIFE SKILLS**
   Practice Refusal Skills
   You are trying to become a good volleyball player. Act out how you would refuse a friend who is urging you to skip practice.

In this lesson, you will learn:

▶ about the importance of warming up and cooling down.

▶ how to create the best physical fitness program for you.

▶ how to be sensible about your physical fitness.

VOCABULARY

warm-up (wôrm′up) gentle movement that prepares the body for exercise

cool-down (kül′doun) gentle movement that relaxes the body after exercise

aerobic exercise (â rō′bik ek′sər sīz) physical activity that uses oxygen over a long time to provide energy for working muscles

QUICK START John enjoys running. He's fast in short races, but he wants to run in longer races. What can he do to prepare?

Staying fit helps more than your physical health. Fitness helps your emotional, intellectual, and social health, too. There may be parts of your fitness you want to improve. Perhaps you want to build up your endurance. There are many ways to reach your fitness goals. The first step is to think about what you would like to do, and what you are willing to do, to get there.

Running in a race can be a lot of fun— even if you don't cross the finish line first!

These activities can be used for warming up or for cooling down. See pages 294–297 of the Handbook for complete warm-up and cool-down activities and instructions.

Reach for Your Toes   **Ankle Pull**   **Wall Stretch**

Enjoy Your Road to Fitness

Every time you are active, you improve your physical fitness. Fitness should be fun. Choose physical activities that you enjoy. Playing your favorite sport or game is a good way to stay fit.

If you enjoy a popular sport such as basketball, play it regularly. There are many sports that can strengthen your heart. Swim—if it's fun for you. It will build your endurance. Hiking is also good for endurance. Do you like gymnastics or dancing? They're both great for improving flexibility.

Warming Up and Cooling Down

You should warm up before physical activity. **Warm-up** activities are gentle movements that prepare your body for exercise. These activities get your heart beating faster. They help blood flow to your muscles. *Muscles* are the tissues

that help your body move. Warming up also prevents injuries such as pulled muscles.

After physical exercise you should do a cool-down. **Cool-down** activities are gentle movements that relax your body after exercise. A good cool-down allows your heart rate to slow down. The cool-down also stretches your muscles. It helps prevent cramps. You can find examples of other warm-up and cool-down exercises on pages 295–297 of the Handbook.

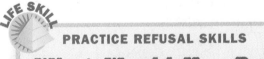

LIFE SKILL

PRACTICE REFUSAL SKILLS

What Would You Do?

After playing soccer, your friends want to leave before you have time to cool down. What would you say to them?

A Physical Fitness Program

Before you begin a fitness program, measure your fitness. One way is to try the five exercises that make up the President's Challenge, shown on pages 300–301 of the Handbook. Do these exercises only with a teacher's supervision.

A physical fitness program should help you reach the fitness goals you set. To improve your endurance, try aerobic exercise. **Aerobic exercise** uses oxygen over a long time to provide energy for muscles. It causes you to breathe deeply. It makes your heart beat quickly. Jumping rope, running, walking, and riding a bicycle are good aerobic exercises. Stretching exercises will improve your flexibility. Bicycling will strengthen your leg muscles.

If you have a physical fitness program that is just right for you, you are more likely to stick to it. You will also look and feel better.

Push-ups will build strength in your arms and upper body. See pages 298–299 of the Handbook for more exercises to build strength.

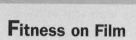
Be Sensible— Make the Right Moves

Whatever physical activities you do, be sensible. Always keep the following in mind.

- Gradually increase how long you perform an activity. As your fitness improves, you can increase your time.

- Set up a regular physical activity schedule. A regular schedule usually means three to five times a week, 30 minutes each time.

- Pay attention when your body tells you that it's tired. Take a rest or stop the activity.

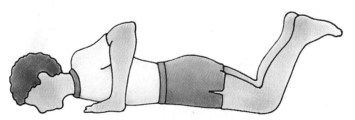

Push-up: Figure 1
Start on your hands and knees. Lower your chest to the floor.

Push-up: Figure 2
Push yourself off the floor while keeping your knees on the ground and your back straight. Lower yourself and repeat.

Get With the Program!

SET GOALS

Check with your physical education teacher before doing any fitness program.

1 Work in small groups. Plan a 30-minute physical fitness program to use 3 to 5 times a week.

2 Create a fitness program that sets clear goals for each member. Decide which part of physical fitness each group member would like to improve. Will it be endurance, strength, or flexibility?

3 Follow your program. After one week, report to the class. Tell about the effect of the program on group members. Did the fitness program help you reach the goals you set?

LESSON WRAP UP

Show What You Know

1. Why are warming up and cooling down important parts of any physical activity?

2. Explain why it is important for you to have a sensible physical fitness program.

3. **THINK CRITICALLY** Is it important for people to include activities that they enjoy in a fitness program? Or should they do only activities that "should" be included? Why or why not?

Show What You Can Do

4. **PORTFOLIO** **APPLY HEALTH ACTIVITY**
Set Goals Work with a partner. Interview each other about the goals you set to improve your endurance, strength, and flexibility. Record your interview on tape or in writing for others to share.

5. **PRACTICE LIFE SKILLS**
Obtain Help Identify two people who could help you create a personal fitness program.

In this lesson, you will learn:

▶ when to stop or slow down a physical activity.

▶ the importance of using safety equipment.

▶ fair play and good sportsmanship.

VOCABULARY

safety equipment
(sāf′tē i kwip′mənt)
materials designed to reduce the risk of injury

competition
(kōm′pi tish′ən) a contest between people or teams

QUICK START You want to go in-line skating. Your helmet and pads are upstairs. However, your friends are at the door. They want to start right away. What should you do?

Regular physical activity is the key to physical fitness. This is true only if you do it safely and correctly. You can hurt yourself if you are not careful. You can also injure yourself if you do not use the right safety equipment. Remember that an injury can stop you from enjoying any physical activity until you have had time to heal.

What is this girl doing to stay safe?

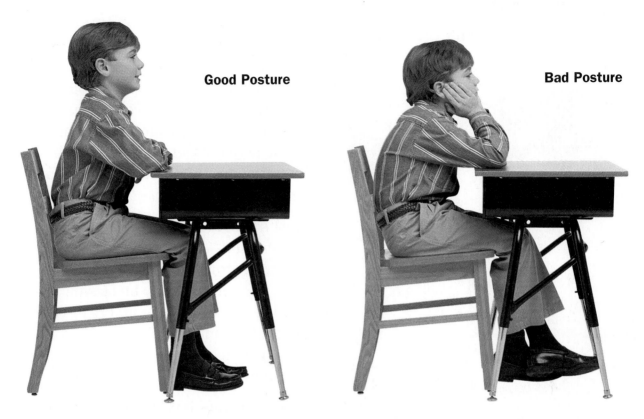

Good Posture

Bad Posture

Good posture while sitting involves three things—head and shoulders balanced over hips, back straight, and both feet flat on the floor.

Know Your Body

It is important to know your limits in anything you do. This is especially true with physical activity. If you try to do more than you are able to, you take the risk of injuring yourself.

Each person is different. Each person has different abilities. You may even find that your own abilities differ from day to day. It's best to go at your own pace. You will enjoy the activity and not get frustrated.

Some activities are so much fun that you don't want to stop. Or there may be other reasons you don't want to stop. For example, you may want to impress others. It's important to pay attention to your body. It will let you know when you do too much. If you feel tired or sore, take a rest or stop for the day.

Warm up before you start any physical activity. This prepares your body for the action to come. Also, cool down at the end of the physical activity. Give your body a chance to slowly recover. If you warm up and cool down, you're less likely to become injured or sore. Drink plenty of water to make up for water lost when you sweat.

Pay attention to what you are doing. Don't show off. Use good form whenever you are active. Good form involves good posture as well as proper body movement. As you learned in Chapter 1, posture is the way you hold your body. Good posture helps bones, joints, and muscles stay in place. Good posture also helps your lungs work well. Good posture and proper body movement lower the risk of injury.

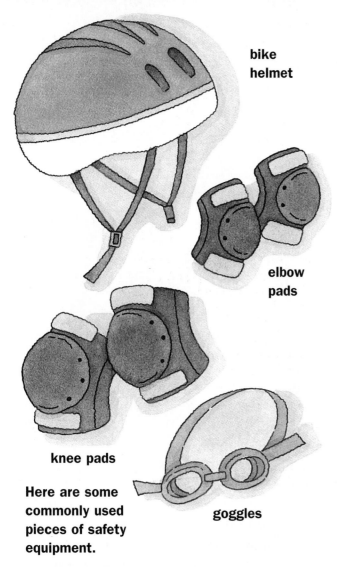

bike helmet

elbow pads

knee pads

goggles

Here are some commonly used pieces of safety equipment.

Use Safety Equipment

Skates are essential equipment for skating. You need ropes to jump rope. For some activities you need other equipment such as helmets and pads to keep you safe. **Safety equipment** protects you from injury. The right kind of equipment is important for your enjoyment and safety. Be sure all your equipment is in good condition. You can't enjoy an activity if you get hurt!

Don't start an activity until you know what equipment you need. Make sure you have all the equipment on hand before you begin. Always read directions before trying new equipment. Ask an adult for help when you use new safety equipment.

Be a Good Sport

Some activities can be done alone, like running. But many activities are enjoyed with other people. Group activities can improve your social health along with your physical health. These activities let you spend time with friends. They also help you make new friends.

Most social activities involve some *cooperation*—in other words, working or playing together to reach a common goal. Cooperation may be as simple as sharing chores with members of your family. Or it may involve working closely with others as a team over a long time.

All team sports involve **competition**, a contest between people or teams. Competition to win is not the same thing as conflict. Team sports have rules that must be learned before you can play. These rules make the game safer. They also make the game fair to all players.

HEALTHWISE CONSUMER

Bargains Abound, So Shop Around

It pays to shop around for safety equipment. Prices change all the time. One way to get the best price is to buy last year's model, not the new model. Retail shops usually lower prices on older models to get consumers to buy. Many times, a discount doesn't change the equipment, just what you pay for it.

HEALTH ACTIVITY
Good Sports

LIFE SKILL

MAKE DECISIONS

You will need: markers

1 Work in a group to create a "Good Sport Handbook." Start by discussing qualities that make someone a "good sport."

2 List each quality of good sportsmanship suggested. Together, make decisions about good examples of each quality.

3 Each group member should write and illustrate a page for one quality on the list. Sew the pages together to make a "Good Sport Handbook."

CULTURAL PERSPECTIVES

Soccer—The World's Most Popular Sport

Baseball, basketball, and football compete for the title of most popular sport in the United States. But throughout the world, the game of soccer is more popular than any other sport. Soccer is growing more popular in the United States. Fans from South America and Europe brought their love of the game with them when they moved to the United States. Pelé, a Brazilian soccer player, holds the record for the most number of career goals: 1281.

Team sports involve competition between teams. One goal is to see who can win. However, winning is not the only goal of team sports. Having fun, relaxing, and becoming physically fit are also goals.

You already saw that learning how to cooperate and playing by the rules are goals, too. So is showing respect to players on the other team. These last three goals are part of fair play and being a good sport. If you play with all these goals in mind, you will have fun, no matter if you win or lose.

Be a Team Player

In a team sport you must cooperate with other players. In basketball, you might pass the ball to a teammate to shoot. It might be best for the team if you played defense. That may not be as much fun as scoring, but it is still important for the team.

LIFE SKILL

RESOLVE CONFLICTS

What Would You Do?

Suppose you are playing a team sport and some of the other players keep breaking a rule. What would you do?

LESSON WRAP UP

Show What You Know

1. What might happen if you don't stop exercising when you get tired?

2. Name two activities for which it is important to wear a safety helmet.

3. **THINK CRITICALLY** What are your two favorite physical activities? Think about your abilities and limits. How can you enjoy these activities without risking injury?

Show What You Can Do

4. **PORTFOLIO** **APPLY HEALTH ACTIVITY** **Make Decisions** One of your teammates suggests a way to win by cheating. Write an explanation of your decision not to cheat and the importance of good sportsmanship.

5. **LIFE SKILL** **PRACTICE LIFE SKILLS** **Resolve Conflicts** You and a teammate are arguing about the need to use a safety helmet in a baseball game. Write a paragraph explaining how you would solve the problem.

YOU CAN MAKE A DIFFERENCE

Gymnastics Academy

Michelle Reohr, Gymnastics Trainer

Q: What sorts of activities do your students do?

Ms. Reohr: We start them out with simple floor exercises such as forward rolls and handstands. Later, they learn to use all the equipment that Olympic gymnasts use.

Q: What makes a child especially good at gymnastics?

Ms. Reohr: Good muscle development and balance are important. So is body control. Our students work on balancing and jumping. We use mirrors to help them see how their bodies work. Dance is also a big part of gymnastics. It helps the kids improve their coordination.

Q: How do you make sure your students don't get hurt?

Ms. Reohr: We focus on safety. The gymnasts learn the rules of using our equipment. We make certain they warm up. This gets their muscles ready for the work of gymnastics.

LIFE SKILL

MAKE DECISIONS

CHOOSE A PROGRAM

You and your friend want to study gymnastics. How would you decide what program to join? Work with a partner to make a checklist of things you would look for in a gymnastics program. Think about your schedule, your abilities, and safety issues.

VOCABULARY

Write the word from the box that best completes each sentence. Use each word only once.

aerobic exercise
balance
competition
cool-down
cooperation
coordination
endurance
flexibility

1. You need ___?___ to be active for a period of time. (Lesson 1)

2. It takes the ___?___ of many muscles to swim. (Lesson 2)

3. A(n) ___?___ makes you breathe deeply. (Lesson 3)

4. After jogging, do ___?___ exercises to relax your body. (Lesson 3)

5. To reach a common goal, ___?___ is needed. (Lesson 4)

REVIEW HEALTH IDEAS

Use your knowledge of physical activity and fitness from Chapter 6 to answer these questions.

1. What are the three parts of physical fitness? (Lesson 1)

2. How does physical activity affect your heart and other muscles? (Lesson 1)

3. What two factors are important in maintaining a healthy weight? (Lesson 1)

4. Name two fitness skills. Explain their importance. (Lesson 2)

5. What fitness skill do stretching exercises improve? (Lesson 2)

6. Which part of your physical fitness will aerobic exercise most likely improve? (Lesson 3)

7. Why should you warm up before physical activity? (Lesson 3)

8. Why are posture and proper form important during physical activity? (Lesson 4)

9. Why is it important to know your body's limits? (Lesson 4)

10. When playing team sports, what are three things to keep in mind? (Lesson 4)

APPLY HEALTH IDEAS

1. How can physical fitness improve your self-esteem? (Lesson 1)

2. Why is it a good idea to measure your physical fitness skills? (Lesson 3)

3. Why is it a good idea to use safety equipment such as helmets and pads? (Lesson 4)

4. **PORTFOLIO** **SET GOALS** Set a goal to create your own physical fitness program. Write down the steps you would take. (Lesson 3)

5. **LIFE SKILLS** **OBTAIN HELP** If you wanted to join an after-school sports club, where could you obtain help deciding which sport to play? (Lesson 2)

YOUR HEALTH AT HOME

Can you use what you've learned from Chapter 6 to choose a fitness program with your family?

Have your family determine what fitness skills they want to develop. Then make a list of activities that you will all enjoy. Include warm-ups and cool-downs. Make a schedule that shows the days and times for each activity.

Keep a diary of each day's activities and how you and your family felt after doing them.

Saturday

Warm-ups
• Stretched and then jogged to park

Activity
• Played baseball with three families on the block

• Had lots of fun. Mom hit the winning home run!

Cool-down
• Stretched and walked back home. Felt tired but had a great time!

Choose the correct word to complete each sentence.

1. More calories are used up when you are ___?___. (active, inactive)

2. Playing by the rules is an example of good ___?___. (fitness, sportsmanship)

3. Stretching exercises are good activities to improve your ___?___. (flexibility, endurance)

4. Exercises that strengthen your muscles are best to build up your ___?___. (reaction time, power)

5. It is a good idea to ___?___ an activity when your muscles feel sore. (stop, continue)

Write a sentence to answer each question.

6. Why is physical fitness important?

7. Define the term coordination as a fitness skill.

8. How can physical activities help maintain your body weight?

9. Why is it important to know your physical limits?

10. What is one important thing to know before you begin a sports activity?

11. Name an activity that improves each of the three parts of fitness.

12. What makes a person a good sport?

13–14. What are two important reasons to play by the rules?

15. Why is a cool-down exercise important after a physical activity?

16. Why is cooperation important in team sports?

17. What physical activities could improve your social health?

Write True or False for each of the following statements.

18. Your fitness skills remain the same throughout your life.

19. Stretching can be good for warm-up and cool-down exercises.

20. The more inactive you are, the more you should eat.

/ **Performance Assessment**

 Suppose you have been hired to write about health for your local paper. Make a list of all the reasons why people should include physical activities in their daily lives.

DISEASE PREVENTION AND CONTROL

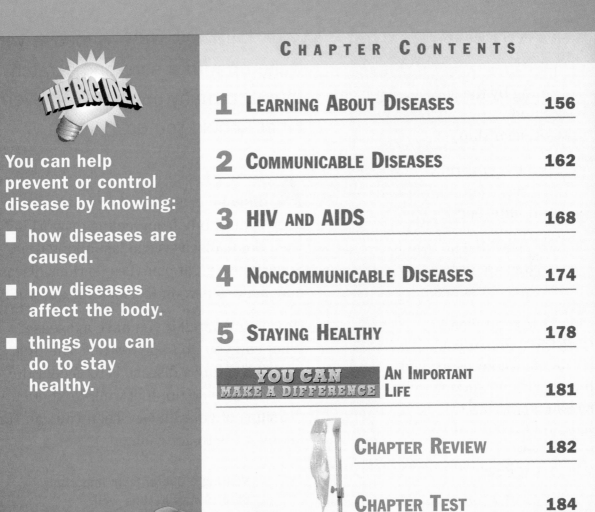

THE BIG IDEA

You can help prevent or control disease by knowing:

■ how diseases are caused.

■ how diseases affect the body.

■ things you can do to stay healthy.

In this lesson, you will learn:

▶ **how people feel when they are ill with certain diseases.**

▶ **what to do if you get sick.**

▶ **how some organisms can cause disease.**

VOCABULARY

disease (di zēz′) a condition that keeps the body from feeling or working well; an illness

symptom (simp′təm) a sign of a disease

microbe (mī′krōb) a tiny organism or particle, visible only with a microscope

virus (vī′rəs) a tiny particle that can only reproduce inside living cells

fungus (fung′gəs) an organism that feeds off other living or dead organisms

QUICK START Suppose you wake up with a sore and scratchy throat, a runny nose, and a fever. What should you do?

A **disease** is an illness or condition that keeps your body from feeling or working well. Some diseases can last a long time. Some cause great pain. Less serious diseases may make a person feel sick for a few days.

How can you tell if you have a disease? What can you do to get better? The first step in fighting a disease is to accept the fact that you do not feel well. Next, identify the signs of your illness. Then you can start taking steps to get well.

Visiting a doctor is an important step toward getting well.

Some Diseases and Their Symptoms		
Disease	**Length of Illness**	**Symptoms**
Common cold	About 1 week	Sore throat, cough, stuffy nose
Strep throat	About 1 week	Coating on tonsils, painful swallowing, often fever
Chicken pox	5–10 days	Rash, then blisters and dark itchy scabs, fever
Measles	7–10 days	Runny nose, cough, then fever and rash
Mumps	7–10 days	Fever, swollen glands at the sides of face and below chin

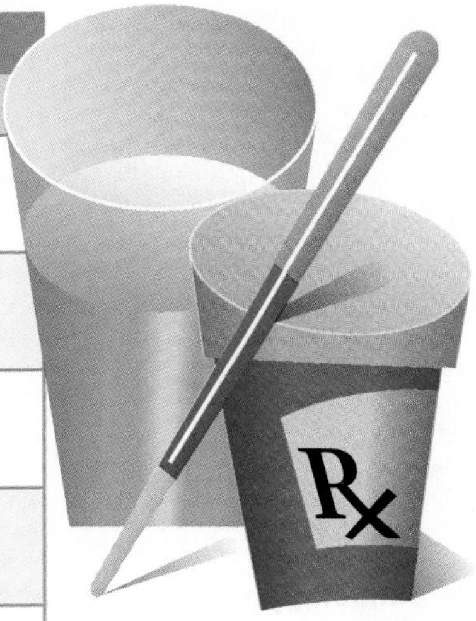

Symptoms of Disease

When you are healthy, you feel alert and strong. But when you are ill, you may not feel well at all. The signs of a disease are called **symptoms**. Here are some symptoms of common diseases.

- feeling tired, weak, or dizzy

- body aches

- sore throat

- sneezing or coughing

- headache

- earache

- rashes (spots) or sores

- an upset stomach

- *fever*, or high body temperature

Children get some diseases, such as strep throat and chicken pox, more often than adults. The chart above shows the symptoms of some common childhood diseases. Later you will learn about ways people prevent or treat some of these diseases today.

Treatment of Disease

Suppose you have symptoms such as fever, coughing, sore throat, or stomach pain. Symptoms such as these can be signs of a serious disease. You should tell a parent or another trusted adult, who can make health decisions for you. For example, a parent may give you medicine or take you to a doctor.

A doctor examines you carefully. After noting all the symptoms, the doctor will try to help you get well. You may need medicine and rest. You may also need to stay home from school, because many diseases can be spread to others.

You may or may not need medicine to get better. You can also help your body repair itself by following a few rules when you are sick.

- Follow your doctor's advice.

- Get enough rest and sleep.

- Drink plenty of juice and water.

- Eat healthful foods.

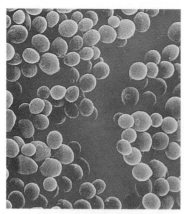

Magnification: 10,994×

Pneumonia is caused by round bacteria such as these. Strep throat and some kinds of meningitis are also caused by round bacteria.

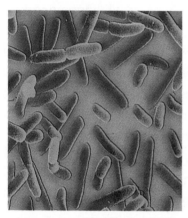

Magnification: 3,150×

When certain rod-shaped bacteria enter a person's body, they can cause serious stomach problems. Another type of rod-shaped bacteria causes tuberculosis. This disease affects the lungs.

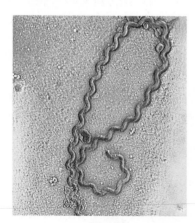

Magnification: 9,680×

Spiral bacteria such as these can also cause disease.

Some Causes of Disease

There are many causes of disease. Some are passed on from parent to child. Other diseases are caused when part of your body stops working well. But many diseases are caused when certain tiny *organisms*, or living things, enter your body. Bacteria, viruses, and fungi are three of these kinds of organisms.

Sometimes people call bacteria and viruses *germs*. Germs are microbes that can make you ill. A **microbe** is an organism or particle so tiny that it can only be seen with a microscope. Many microbes are harmless, and some are helpful. But as you will learn in this lesson, some microbes and fungi can cause disease.

Bacteria

Bacteria are tiny, one-celled microbes. There are many different kinds of bacteria. Some can be found living almost anywhere on Earth. Bacteria can even be found in and on our bodies. In fact, millions of bacteria are living on you right now!

Some bacteria are helpful. For example, helpful bacteria live in your intestines. They help break down the food you've eaten into smaller pieces.

Some bacteria can be harmful. If they grow and multiply in your body, they may cause disease. Different kinds of bacteria cause different diseases. Bacteria usually are one of three shapes: round, rod-shaped, and spiral.

Viruses

A **virus** is a tiny particle that can reproduce only inside living cells. Viruses can also cause diseases. They are much smaller than bacteria. They can be seen only with a very powerful microscope.

Viruses need to live inside a cell. A virus becomes attached to a living cell, passes into the cell, then takes it over. The cell acts like a factory, making "copies" of the virus. When the cell is full, it bursts.

New viruses spill out and attack other cells. Those cells make more copies of the virus. In this way, viruses spread through a person's body. You will learn more about how viruses and other microbes spread from person to person later in this lesson.

Viruses can cause colds, the flu, cold sores, and fever blisters. They can also cause many childhood diseases, such as chicken pox, mumps, and measles.

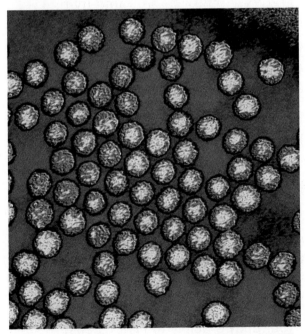

Magnification: 715,000×

This virus causes the common cold. Microscopes can magnify such viruses by more than one million times!

Fungi

A **fungus** is an organism that feeds off other living or dead organisms. Although many fungi look like plants, they are not plants. They have no true roots, stems, or leaves. They can't make their own food as plants do.

Some fungi are tiny microbes. Others, like mushrooms, are large and have many cells. Fungi can grow in warm, wet places or in cool, dry places. Many fungi grow on or in plants and animals—and even you!

About 30 human diseases are known to be caused by different kinds of fungi. For example, certain fungi cause athlete's foot and other types of ringworm. Some fungi also appear beneath toenails and fingernails.

Not all fungi are harmful or cause disease. In fact, some medicines—such as penicillin—are made from fungi.

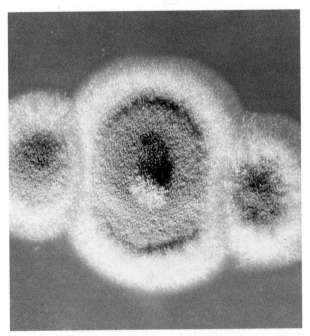

Magnification: 9.75×

Penicillin was first made from this type of fungus. Penicillin fights many diseases and has saved many lives.

How Microbes Get Into Your Body

Disease-causing microbes can get into your body in many ways. Some bacteria move through the air on dust and water drops. So do many viruses and tiny fungi. You may breathe them into your lungs. From there, your blood spreads them throughout your whole body.

Your skin is like a wall that prevents most microbes from entering. But bacteria, viruses, and microscopic fungi can get in through cuts and scratches. These microbes can then be carried throughout the body by your blood.

Microbes can also enter your body if you touch something and then put your fingers into your mouth or eyes. For example, a person may sneeze into their hands and then touch a doorknob. If you touch the doorknob right after that person, you may end up with their microbes on your hands.

Spoiled food or unclean water may contain bacteria and viruses. If you eat or drink them you can spread microbes through your digestive system.

Your body has many defenses against disease-causing microbes. You'll learn more about this in the next lesson.

When you help someone, be careful that the injury has been cleaned and that you do not come into contact with the person's blood.

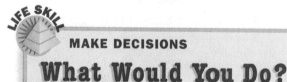

MAKE DECISIONS

What Would You Do?

Your sister has a bad cold but wants to go to school for a special concert. Should she go to school or stay home? How would you help her make a decision?

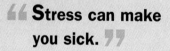

HEALTH FACT

" Stress can make you sick. "

This is true. Do you ever feel as if you can't relax? If so, you are feeling *stress*. Stress is emotional strain or tension. Stress can affect your health in a number of ways.

Stress can produce extreme tiredness, called fatigue. It can also cause headaches, stomach aches, and muscle soreness. Over a long period of time, stress can weaken your body's ability to fight disease. Harmful microbes can multiply in your body more easily.

HEALTH ACTIVITY
Health Help

LIFE SKILL

OBTAIN HELP

You will need: index cards

1 Work in a group. Create a list of some common illnesses, such as colds and chicken pox. Write each illness and its symptoms on the front of an index card.

2 Decide who or where you might go to for help if you had each illness. Write the name of that person or place on the back of the card. On the back of each index card, list the things a person with that illness might do to feel better.

3 Use the index cards to create a "Health Help" brochure. Share your group's brochure with the class.

LESSON WRAP UP

Show What You Know

1. What are some symptoms that might make you decide that you were sick?

2. Suppose you wake up one morning with a sore throat. What should you do?

3. What are three types of organisms that can cause disease?

4. **THINK CRITICALLY** Why is it helpful to learn about diseases?

Show What You Can Do

5. **PORTFOLIO** **APPLY HEALTH ACTIVITY**
Obtain Help Create a TV ad. Describe one illness and its symptoms. Tell who or where a person with the illness could go to for help.

6. **LIFE SKILL** **PRACTICE LIFE SKILLS**
Practice Refusal Skills You want to tell an adult that you feel ill. Your friend tries to convince you not to tell. He doesn't want you to have to stay home and miss a party. How would you respond?

In this lesson, you will learn:

▶ ways that some diseases can be spread.

▶ how the body defends itself against disease.

▶ ways you can try to prevent the spread of disease.

VOCABULARY

communicable disease
(kə mū′ni kə bəl di zēz′)
a disease that can be spread to a person from another person, an animal, or an object

immune system
(i mūn′ sis′təm) all of the parts and functions of your body that fight germs

antibody (an′ti bod′ē)
chemicals made by the body that help destroy or weaken bacteria, viruses, and other microbes

immunity (i mū′ni tē)
protection against or ability to fight a disease

QUICK START Your best friend is home from school with strep throat. He asks you to come over to explain what was covered in class. What would you do?

Think about the last time you had a cold or an illness like strep throat or the flu. Perhaps you felt tired or weak. Maybe your body ached, or you had a fever. Do you remember if a friend or family member had the same illness before you got sick?

Many diseases are communicable. **Communicable diseases** can be spread to a person from another person, an animal, or an object. If you know how they are spread and how to avoid catching them, you can help prevent communicable diseases.

The Spread of Disease

Microbes are everywhere. They're on doorknobs, coins, oranges, and pencils. They're even on your skin. Microbes are so common, it's no wonder people get colds and the flu so often. But if you understand how microbes enter your body, you can learn how to defend yourself against them.

There are four main ways that communicable diseases can be spread.

- through the air
- by contact with another person or with an object
- from animals, including insects, that have the disease
- through food and water

When you sneeze or cough, you release microbes into the air around you. Covering your face with a tissue is the best way to avoid the spread of such microbes.

Diseases Spread Between People

Some communicable diseases are easily spread from person to person through the air. A cold or the flu can be spread when a person sneezes or coughs. The microbes travel through the air on tiny water drops. Chicken pox can also be spread through the air.

Some diseases can also be spread by contact. Suppose someone with a cold sneezes into his or her hands. You might touch the person's hands. Or you might touch something that the sick person had touched, such as a doorknob. Then the microbes can get on your hands. They could enter your body through a cut, or when you touch your own mouth or eyes.

Some diseases are spread when you and a person with the disease use the same areas or things. For example, the fungi that cause athlete's foot can live on the warm, moist floor of a locker room. The fungi can infect the skin on your feet if you come in contact with them.

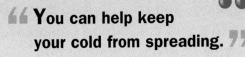

HEALTH FACT

" You can help keep your cold from spreading. "

This is true. If you have to cough or sneeze, you should use a tissue. If you don't have a tissue, at least cough or sneeze into the crook of your arm. Microbes are less likely to spread from there than from your hands. Always cough or sneeze away from people. Wash your hands often. In these ways, you can help make sure that others do not catch your cold.

This tiny deer tick can spread the microbes that cause Lyme disease.

Magnification: 16.8×

Other Ways Diseases Are Spread

Some diseases are spread by insects, ticks, and other animals. For example, malaria—a common tropical disease—is spread by mosquitoes. Lyme disease is spread by ticks. Rabies is most often spread by the bite of an infected animal, such as a dog or a raccoon.

Some diseases can be spread through food. Spoiled food may contain harmful bacteria that can cause food poisoning. Food that isn't cooked enough may contain tiny roundworms. These roundworms can cause a disease called trichinosis.

Untreated water may contain bacteria that cause diseases like cholera and typhoid. In some parts of the world, it is very difficult for people to find clean water to drink. Many people in these areas suffer from diseases spread by unclean water.

How Your Body Defends Itself

Your body has many ways to help guard against disease. On the outside, your skin acts like a protective suit. It stops most microbes from entering your body. Eyelashes and eyelids keep microbe-containing dust out of your eyes. Tears and sweat act to kill some harmful bacteria.

Your body also protects itself from the inside. Hairs inside your nose trap dirt and dust particles in the air you breathe. So do tiny hairs inside your windpipe. These keep microbes from entering your lungs.

Mucus is a thick fluid that protects the insides of your nose, mouth, and throat, as well as other parts of your body. The sticky mucus catches microbes. They are forced out when you sneeze, cough, or blow your nose.

Your Immune System

You've just read about your body's first line of defense against getting sick. Still, disease-causing microbes do get into your body sometimes. Then they are met by another powerful weapon—your immune system. Your **immune system** is all of the parts and functions of your body that fight germs.

Some illnesses bring on a *fever*—a body temperature higher than normal. That is a sign that your immune system is working. The high temperature helps stop the microbes from spreading.

Your immune system also protects you by making white blood cells. Your body makes different kinds of white blood cells that help fight microbes when they enter your body. When you have an illness, your body makes extra white blood cells. Some of them surround and destroy the harmful microbes.

At the same time, some white blood cells make antibodies. An **antibody** is a chemical that helps weaken or destroy microbes. The antibodies stick to the microbes, making them harmless. Other white blood cells get rid of the dead microbes.

Immunity

Have you ever had chicken pox? If so, you will probably never have it again. Your body has the ability to build up protection against some diseases, and chicken pox is one of them.

The first time you get sick from a virus or other microbe, your white blood cells start making antibodies. These antibodies help you fight off the invading microbes. Your body can produce millions of different antibodies. Each antibody protects you from only one kind of microbe.

Now, suppose the same kind of microbe enters your body at another time. The antibodies are probably gone. But white blood cells can make them "remember" the microbe. They can make the antibodies very quickly this time. Usually, the antibodies attack the microbe so fast that you don't become sick again.

This kind of protection against or ability to fight disease caused by microbes is called **immunity**. This is how your immune system protects you from getting some diseases more than once.

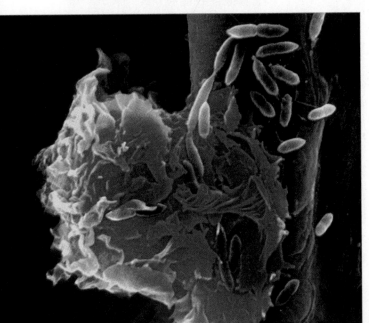

Disease-causing microbes enter the bloodstream. The large white blood cell (shown in purple) moves in to surround and destroy them. Antibodies attach themselves to the microbes and make them harmless. Other white blood cells remove the dead microbes.

HEALTH ACTIVITY
Antibodies to the Rescue!

You will need: art paper, scissors, colored pencils

1 Work with a group to make a comic book. First, identify and discuss the ways your body can fight off disease.

2 Think of characters that could show the body's actions. For example, you might include Annie Antibody or Willie the White Blood Cell.

3 Draw your comic book. Show how each character helps your body fight against disease. Share your comic book with the rest of the class.

Fighting Disease

The best way to defend yourself against disease is to avoid being exposed to it. You can also help by keeping your immune system in top condition. Protect yourself by eating properly, getting enough rest, and staying active.

Sometimes your immune system needs help defending your body against disease. You may be given medicines to fight some diseases. Medicines can help cure diseases caused by bacteria or fungi. They cannot cure diseases caused by viruses. However, some medicines can treat the symptoms of viruses. That can help you feel better.

Taking good care of yourself helps your immune system fight disease.

Preventing the Spread of Disease

Follow these simple rules to help prevent the spread of some of the more common communicable diseases.

- Wash your hands before eating and after using the restroom.

- Use tissues when you cough or sneeze. Then throw them away.

- Wash cuts with soap and water and cover them with bandages.

- Don't share toothbrushes, towels, eating utensils, cups, straws, or combs and brushes.

- Don't eat foods that haven't been cooked or stored properly. Be especially careful with pork and chicken. Don't eat food from a sick person's plate.

- Don't drink untreated water from lakes, streams, and rivers.

HEALTHWISE CONSUMER

Microbe Killers

Many first aid products act to kill microbes in and around a wound. The next time you are in a store, look for products that say they are antibacterial or antiseptic. *Anti-* is a prefix that means against. Also look for disinfectants. Check labels to find out the purposes of these products and how they are used.

LIFE SKILL

MAKE DECISIONS

What Would You Do?

During lunch, a friend with a cold reaches across the table to take a piece of food from your plate. What would you do?

LESSON WRAP UP

Show What You Know

1. What are four ways diseases can be spread?

2. How do white blood cells help protect you from disease?

3. **THINK CRITICALLY** Suppose you are in school. You start to sneeze and cough a lot. What can you do to help make sure your classmates do not get sick?

Show What You Can Do

4. **PORTFOLIO** **APPLY HEALTH ACTIVITY** **Science Connection** Write a pamphlet for children visiting a doctor's office. Describe the immune system. Include a flowchart showing how your body fights microbes.

5. **LIFE SKILL** **PRACTICE LIFE SKILLS** **Resolve Conflicts** You stop your younger sister from picking up the TV remote control, because she has just sneezed into her hands. She gets annoyed. What can you say and do to resolve the conflict?

In this lesson, you will learn:

▶ **how HIV affects the immune system.**

▶ **what happens when a person with HIV develops AIDS.**

▶ **about ways HIV can and cannot be spread from one person to another.**

VOCABULARY

AIDS (ādz) [Acquired Immune Deficiency Syndrome] a very serious disease in which the immune system is extremely weak; caused by infection with HIV

HIV (āch ī vē) [Human Immunodeficiency Virus] a virus that attacks the immune system and leads to AIDS

QUICK START A friend says that a person can get AIDS by shaking hands with someone. How can you find out if this is true?

Not long ago, few people had heard of AIDS. Today, sadly, it is a term most people hear a lot. There is much we still have to learn about AIDS and HIV, the virus that causes AIDS. The best protection against AIDS is being informed. Then you can act responsibly to avoid it.

Many people have false ideas about HIV and how it is spread. This lesson will help you learn the facts. In that way, you will be joining the global effort to defeat AIDS.

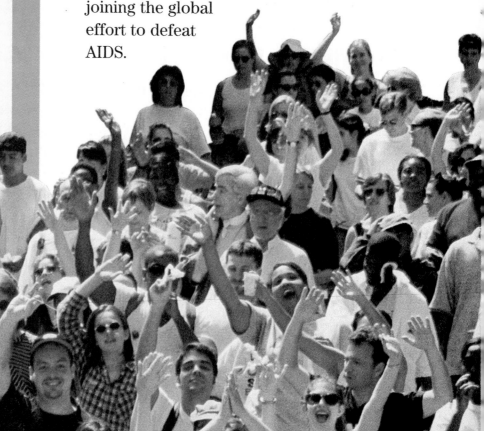

What Is AIDS?

AIDS is a very serious disease in which the immune system is extremely weak. AIDS stands for *Acquired Immune Deficiency Syndrome*. *Acquired* means that the disease is caught from other people. *Immune deficiency* means that a person's immune system lacks something necessary, or is *deficient*. A *syndrome* is a collection of symptoms associated with the same condition. AIDS is caused by infection with HIV.

What Is HIV?

HIV is the virus that attacks the body's immune system and leads to AIDS. The letters stand for *Human Immunodeficiency Virus*. HIV weakens people's immune systems. It kills certain white blood cells that a healthy immune system uses to fight diseases.

The goal of the people in this walk-a-thon is to make others aware of the need for research to treat AIDS patients.

Some people infected with HIV show no symptoms until after they develop AIDS. Or they may have fever, weight loss, exhaustion, swollen glands, and digestive problems. With or without symptoms, however, an HIV-infected person can still spread HIV to others. People can find out if they have HIV by taking a blood test.

AIDS—The Final Stage of HIV Infection

As time passes, HIV kills more and more white blood cells, which severely weakens the person's immune system. At this stage, the HIV infection becomes AIDS.

Because their immune systems are so weak, people with AIDS often get diseases that people with healthy immune systems do not get. Often, a person is diagnosed with AIDS when symptoms of these other diseases begin to appear. Some examples of AIDS-related diseases are certain rare skin cancers and certain kinds of pneumonia.

The amount of time that passes before an HIV-infected person develops AIDS can vary a great deal. But most HIV-infected people show symptoms of a disease related to AIDS after 5 to 10 years. Many people who develop AIDS will die within a few years.

People who have AIDS need the love and support of their family and friends. Their family and friends need support as well. The effects of this disease are painful to live with—and also painful to watch.

HOW HIV INFECTION LEADS TO AIDS

STEP 1

HIV enters a person's body. The virus is spread by blood or other body fluids from a person who already has the HIV virus.

STEP 2

Once HIV is in the bloodstream, it damages certain white blood cells called T-cells. T-cells are essential for a healthy immune system.

STEP 5

People who have AIDS eventually die. The cause of death is one or more of the diseases which their weakened immune systems could no longer fight.

STEP 3

HIV multiplies and kills more and more T-cells. As time passes, the immune system grows weaker and weaker.

STEP 4

The weakened immune system cannot fight against certain illnesses. At this point, the HIV-infected person has developed AIDS.

How HIV Is Spread

HIV is communicable, like some of the other diseases you've read about. But unlike a cold, it is not easily passed on. Scientists believe that HIV can only be spread from person to person in a few ways. Each of these ways requires very close contact with an infected person.

- HIV can be spread only through certain body fluids, such as blood.

- A person can get HIV by using needles that have touched infected blood. Many drug users get HIV by sharing needles with an infected person.

- A mother who is infected with HIV can pass the virus to her unborn baby. These babies can be born with HIV.

How HIV Is Not Spread

There are many false ideas and unnecessary fears about how HIV is spread. Some people think that they can get the virus from sharing clothing or from using the same toilet as an infected person. This is not true. HIV is not spread through air, water, or food. People cannot get HIV from insect or other animal bites, either.

Since HIV is not spread through the air, people cannot get it from simply being in the same room as an infected person. Scientists have found no cases in which HIV had been passed on by hugging, sneezing, coughing, or by other casual contact. Nor have they found any cases in which HIV had been passed on through tears, saliva, or sweat.

LIFE SKILL

OBTAIN HELP

What Would You Do?

One of your friends falls, gets cut, and bleeds while playing a game. Why should you ask an adult for assistance in helping your friend?

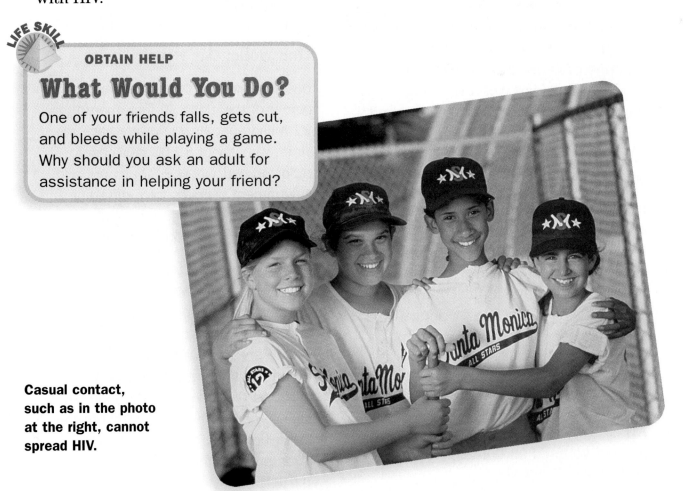

Casual contact, such as in the photo at the right, cannot spread HIV.

Counselors and health advisors can give you up-to-date facts about HIV and AIDS.

Treatment for AIDS

People infected with HIV can often help themselves by strengthening their immune systems. Eating nutritious foods, getting plenty of rest, being physically active, managing stress, and following a healthful lifestyle may help delay the onset of AIDS.

Today, AIDS is still *incurable*. That means scientists have not discovered a way to get rid of the virus entirely. However, scientists have developed some medicines that slow down the progress of the infection. Thousands of scientists around the world are searching for a cure to this deadly disease.

The healthiest action you can take is to educate yourself about HIV and AIDS. By being informed, you can help protect yourself and others against HIV and AIDS.

CULTURAL PERSPECTIVES

One World, One Hope

HIV has infected people in every corner of the globe. In fact, more than 22 million people worldwide have the virus, with about 8,500 new cases reported every day. Researchers and government officials from different cultures are working together to find solutions to this global problem.

Recently, representatives from 125 different countries attended a meeting. Its theme was "One World, One Hope." The goal of this meeting was to share new information about treatment and prevention of HIV and AIDS. As one person at the meeting said, "The challenge is to ensure that these hopes extend to *all* those threatened by the disease."

HEALTH ACTIVITY
Fact Finders

SET GOALS

1 Work with a group to create a TV ad. First, consider ways HIV can and cannot be spread from one person to another.

2 Set a goal for your ad to meet. For example, you may want your ad to reduce people's unnecessary fears by giving factual information on how HIV is spread.

3 Assign different jobs to group members. For example, two people might write the words while two others choose images.

4 Present your ad to the class. Discuss how it meets the goal you set for it.

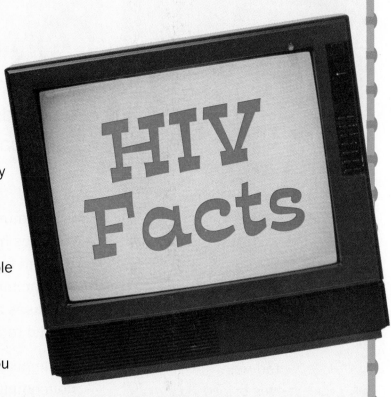

HIV Facts

LESSON WRAP UP

Show What You Know

1. How does HIV harm the immune system?

2. What is the difference between being infected with HIV and having AIDS?

3. **THINK CRITICALLY** Why is HIV called "communicable"?

Show What You Can Do

4. **PORTFOLIO** **APPLY HEALTH ACTIVITY**
Set Goals Set a goal for communicating information about AIDS to others in your school or community. Design a poster that reflects your goal.

5. **LIFE SKILL** **PRACTICE LIFE SKILLS**
Obtain Help Where can someone go to find out more about HIV and AIDS? Do some research to make a list of local resources. Include places on your list where people can go for support.

NONCOMMUNICABLE DISEASES

In this lesson, you will learn:

▶ **what a noncommunicable disease is.**

▶ **about risk factors that can lead to noncommunicable diseases.**

▶ **about some common noncommunicable diseases.**

VOCABULARY

noncommunicable disease
(non′kə mū′ni kə bəl di zēz′)
a disease that cannot be spread to a person from another living thing

risk factor (risk fak′tər)
something that increases the possibility that a person will get a certain disease

allergy (al′ər jē) a sensitivity to a certain substance

chronic (kron′ik)
lasting for a long time

QUICK START A friend tells you that she has an allergy. What is this disease? Do you think you could catch it?

You know that you can catch some diseases from a person, from an animal, or from food and water. These diseases are communicable. **Noncommunicable diseases** are diseases that cannot be spread to a person from a living thing.

Some people are born with a certain noncommunicable disease. For example, some babies are born with hearts that do not work properly. People can also develop noncommunicable diseases, such as allergies, during their lifetime.

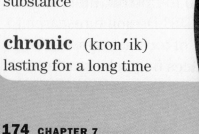

Some noncommunicable diseases can be passed from parent to child. But inheriting the risk for a disease does not necessarily mean that a person will get the disease.

Causes of Noncommunicable Diseases

A **risk factor** is something that increases the possibility that a person will get a certain disease. There are three main kinds of risk factors.

- Hereditary—the risk for some noncommunicable diseases can be passed on through heredity. For example, the risk of developing sickle cell anemia is passed down from parent to child.

- Environmental—some risk factors are in the environment. Air pollution is a risk factor that can cause lung disease, for example. Too much sun can lead to skin cancer.

- Lifestyle-related—your *lifestyle*, or pattern of behaviors, can put you at risk for some noncommunicable diseases. For example, people who do not get enough vitamin C in their diet can develop a disease called scurvy.

- Besides poor eating habits, other lifestyle behaviors can be risk factors, too. Too much stress or too little physical activity can lead to disease. So can abuse of tobacco, alcohol, and drugs. However, you can reduce these risk factors by making lifestyle choices that will help you stay healthy!

LIFE SKILL
MAKE DECISIONS
What Would You Do?

You love to lie on the beach in the sun. Your parents warn you that too much sun can be dangerous. What should you do?

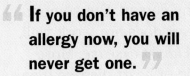

HEALTH FALLACY

" **If you don't have an allergy now, you will never get one.** "

This is not true. You can suddenly become allergic to something that has never bothered you before. Even if you have been exposed to something safely for years—for example, eaten peanuts or lived with your pet cat—you can develop an allergy to it. If you suspect that you have a new allergy, tell a trusted adult. They can take you to a doctor, who will test you to see whether you are allergic. If you are, the doctor can treat the allergy or help you manage it.

Allergies

Allergies are the most common noncommunicable diseases. When you have an **allergy**, your body has a sensitivity to a certain substance. You are *allergic* to it. Some people are allergic to a substance in the fur of cats and dogs. Many people are allergic to certain foods.

The most common symptoms of allergies are sneezing, a stuffy nose, and watery eyes. Sometimes, though, allergic reactions can be very dangerous. Allergies to bee stings and to shellfish can be fatal.

Most allergies are much less serious chronic diseases. A **chronic** disease is one that lasts for a long time. Its symptoms can come back again and again. Most allergies can be managed with good care.

Heart Disease

You know that you need a healthy heart to be a healthy person. But sometimes a person's heart does not work well. This is called *heart disease*. More Americans die of heart disease than from any other cause.

Heart disease can develop if something keeps the heart from pumping blood through the body properly. Sometimes, for example, fatty substances stick to the walls of blood vessels. This reduces the flow of blood and makes it harder for the heart to work. If a blood vessel becomes completely blocked, a person may have a *heart attack*.

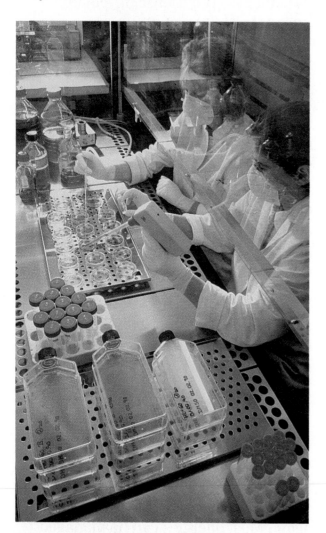

Researchers work every day to find new treatments for diseases.

When people develop heart disease, doctors can often help them. For example, complex operations can sometimes repair a damaged heart. But the best thing to do is try to keep your heart healthy. For a healthy heart, it helps to eat foods that are low in fat, get plenty of rest, be physically active, manage stress well, and avoid alcohol, tobacco, and drugs.

Cancer

After heart disease, *cancer* is the leading cause of death in the United States. Cancer is caused when body cells divide and multiply in ways that are not normal. The cells may form a growth called a *tumor*. Cancer cells invade and destroy healthy body tissue.

Different kinds of cancer have different symptoms and treatments. Sometimes cancerous tumors can be removed from the body with surgery. Sometimes cancer patients are treated with radiation or chemicals.

Scientists do not know what causes all cancers, but they do know the risk factors for some of them. For example, smoking tobacco is the greatest single risk factor for developing lung cancer.

Working to Cure Diseases

Each year millions of dollars are spent on medical research. Much of this money goes to scientists who are trying to find cures for noncommunicable diseases. New treatments and new cures for these diseases are developed every year. However, you can reduce your own risk factors for disease by limiting the risks in your environment and lifestyle.

Do It Right

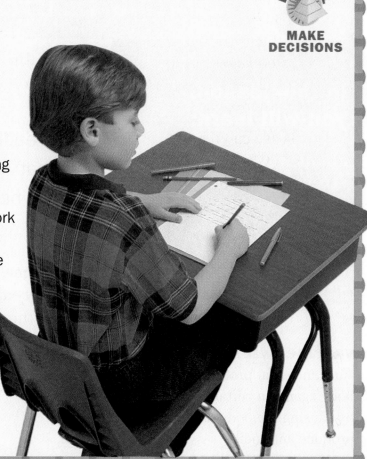

LIFE SKILL

MAKE DECISIONS

You will need: colored markers

1 Think about actions that you can take to reduce risk factors for noncommunicable diseases—eating healthful foods, for example.

2 Decide which areas you need to work on to reduce your risk factors. Decide on two actions you can take in each area, such as eating more vegetables or getting more sleep.

3 Make a list of your risk-reducing ideas. Check up on yourself once a week. Have you followed your own advice?

LESSON WRAP UP

Show What You Know

1. How are noncommunicable diseases different from communicable diseases?

2. What are the three main types of risk factors for noncommunicable diseases?

3. THINK CRITICALLY In what ways are allergies similar to heart disease and cancer? In what ways are they different?

Show What You Can Do

4. **PORTFOLIO** **APPLY HEALTH ACTIVITY**
Make Decisions Make a chart with the headings *environment* and *lifestyle*. For each of these risk factors, decide on two actions you can take to reduce your risk for noncommunicable diseases.

5. **LIFE SKILL** **PRACTICE LIFE SKILLS**
Obtain Help You have never had any allergies. However, one day after eating a bowl of strawberries you notice that a rash developed on your skin. What should you do?

In this lesson, you will learn:

▶ about ways to strengthen your immune system.

▶ the importance of early treatment of disease.

VOCABULARY

vaccine (vak sēn′) a substance that protects the body against a certain disease by causing the body to produce antibodies

QUICK START A flu virus is spreading throughout your school. What are two things you can do to stay healthy?

Some illnesses can't be prevented, but many can. As you've seen in this chapter and throughout this book, there are steps you can take to stay healthy. And if you do become ill, early treatment may prevent your disease from becoming more serious.

Receiving a flu shot is just one way to help yourself stay healthy.

Disease Detectives

You will need: reference books

1 Work in small groups. Select three of the following diseases to investigate: diphtheria, influenza, measles, mumps, polio, whooping cough, chicken pox, rubella, or tetanus. Each of these diseases can be prevented by vaccine.

2 Work together to find out more about each disease. Answer the following questions. How is the disease spread? What are the symptoms? For how long can the vaccine protect a person?

3 Make a chart showing your findings. Share your chart with your class.

Disease	Symptoms	Spread	How Long Vaccine Protects For
German measles	red spots, fever	by contact with virus	about 15 years

Taking Action to Stay Healthy

You've already studied many ways you can help prevent certain diseases. For example, you can avoid catching some colds by washing your hands. You can reduce your risk of getting certain diseases by eating well and avoiding stress. You can make sure that you get enough sleep. And you can stay away from people who are ill.

You have learned that your immune system plays an important role in your staying healthy. Choosing healthful behaviors helps strengthen your immune system. That way, it can respond more quickly when you do get sick.

Vaccines

Once you have had certain diseases, your body builds up immunities to them. This usually keeps you from getting those diseases again. Vaccines also work by strengthening the immune system.

Made from live, weakened, or inactive viruses, **vaccines** are substances that are either swallowed or injected. Vaccines produce antibodies that protect the body from disease-causing microbes. Some vaccines can protect you for your whole life. Other vaccines offer temporary protection and may require a booster shot later.

The Importance of Early Treatment

If you do become ill, get treatment as soon as you can. Some illnesses are serious and require immediate medical attention. Minor illnesses can often become more serious if left untreated. Here is a list of some symptoms that require immediate attention by a doctor. If you ever have any of them, be sure to tell an adult right away.

- a temperature over 101°F
- difficulty breathing
- bluish lips
- loud, raspy cough
- extreme drowsiness
- twitching or jerking muscles
- any severe pain
- repeated vomiting

OBTAIN HELP

What Would You Do?

You are playing during recess. A friend suddenly has trouble breathing. What would you do?

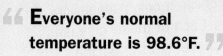

HEALTH FALLACY

" **Everyone's normal temperature is 98.6°F.** "

This is not true. Most people have a body temperature of 98.6°F most of the time. But some people may have a slightly different normal temperature. Also, your temperature can vary several degrees during the day. For example, your temperature is lowest early in the morning.

LESSON WRAP UP

Show What You Know

1. Describe two ways of strengthening the immune system.

2. Why is early treatment of diseases important?

3. **THINK CRITICALLY** Your best friend seems to get the flu several times each year. What advice can you give her?

Show What You Can Do

4. **PORTFOLIO** **APPLY HEALTH ACTIVITY**
   Science Connection
   Make your own vaccine checklist. Find out which vaccines you have received. If possible, list the date of each vaccine and which will need a booster shot.

5. **PRACTICE LIFE SKILLS**
   Set Goals Make a class goal for everyone to wash their hands often. Work with a partner to create classroom posters to remind classmates to wash their hands.

An Important Life

Cubby dePrince

Cubby dePrince was born August 11, 1981. He had a disease called *hemophilia*, which meant that his blood did not clot correctly. When Cubby was a toddler, he became infected with HIV through a clotting medicine made from infected blood.

By age six, Cubby knew he would not have the chance to become an adult. Cubby chose to teach people about living with AIDS. He spoke to reporters and appeared on television. He asked people to sponsor him in the Walk of Champions parade, which raised money to help people with AIDS.

Cubby died on June 9, 1993. He was eleven years old. Hundreds of people attended a celebration of his life. From his family to the governor of his state, Cubby had touched people with his courage and desire to help others. Today, people are carrying on in Cubby's memory. They continue to raise money to help people with AIDS and to teach AIDS awareness. Even now, Cubby's life is important.

LIFE SKILL

MAKE DECISIONS

LEAD AN IMPORTANT LIFE

Cubby found a way to make his life important and meaningful. Could you follow his example? Think of a way you could touch others and make a difference with your caring, your teaching, or your actions. Write a step-by-step plan showing how you might reach that goal.

VOCABULARY

Write the word from the box that best completes each sentence. Use each word only once.

communicable

HIV

microbe

noncommunicable

risk factor

symptom

vaccine

1. A tiny organism or particle that can cause disease is a(n) __?__. (Lesson 1)

2. A disease that can be spread from one person to another is __?__. (Lesson 2)

3. The virus that leads to AIDS is known as __?__. (Lesson 3)

4. Lifestyle can be a(n) __?__ for getting a noncommunicable disease. (Lesson 4)

5. A(n) __?__ is a substance that protects against disease. (Lesson 5)

REVIEW HEALTH IDEAS

Use your knowledge of disease prevention and control from Chapter 7 to answer these questions.

1. Describe a virus. (Lesson 1)

2. Why is it important to cover your mouth with a tissue when sneezing or coughing? (Lesson 2)

3. How is rabies spread? (Lesson 2)

4. How can your skin protect you from disease? (Lesson 2)

5. Which body system does HIV attack? (Lesson 3)

6. What causes AIDS? (Lesson 3)

7. Name one common symptom of an allergy. (Lesson 4)

8. Name two communicable diseases and two noncommunicable diseases. (Lesson 4)

9. How does a vaccine build immunity? (Lesson 5)

10. What might happen if a disease is not treated early? (Lesson 5)

APPLY HEALTH IDEAS

1. Why would it be unfair to your classmates if you went to school when you had a communicable illness? (Lesson 2)

2. Many communities have programs for giving vaccines. How might this help people where you live? (Lesson 5)

3. Your neighbor has AIDS and has difficulty leaving the house. What are some things you could do to try to help? (Lesson 3)

4.  **SET GOALS** Write a list of four goals that people can set to have a healthier lifestyle. (Lesson 4)

5. **LIFE SKILLS** **OBTAIN HELP** During lunch at school, a friend begins complaining that it is painful to swallow. What should you do? (Lesson 1)

YOUR HEALTH AT HOME

Which health behaviors from Chapter 7 can you use at home everyday?

Label a sheet in your diary or notebook with the headings shown above.

Make a list of suggestions for everyone in your family to follow and use. Make time to talk with your family about what you learned about disease prevention.

Preventing Disease | Building Your Immunity | Avoiding Risk Factors

Write True or False for each statement. If false, change the underlined word or phrase to make it true.

1. Disease-causing microbes can get into your body through <u>open cuts</u>.

2. Lyme disease is spread by <u>fleas</u>.

3. One common symptom of illness is <u>fever</u>.

4. Microbes can be destroyed by <u>white blood cells</u> in the body.

5. Common colds and the flu are caused by <u>fungi</u>.

6. HIV <u>cannot</u> be spread by hugging someone.

7. AIDS can develop <u>before</u> HIV.

8. Cancer is a <u>communicable</u> disease.

9. <u>Smoking</u> is a risk factor for some diseases.

10. Vaccines cause the body to make <u>microbes</u> that fight disease.

Write a sentence to answer each question.

11. Name three ways you can strengthen your immune system.

12. Describe two ways that microbes can enter your body.

13. Describe one way that HIV can be spread.

14. What is one symptom of heart disease?

15. What can you do to help keep a cold from spreading to other people?

16. What is the role of the immune system?

17. Describe how HIV can lead to AIDS.

18. What are some things you should do if you get sick?

19. What are two activities that might increase someone's risk for noncommunicable diseases?

20. What is one reason to get early treatment for an illness?

Performance Assessment

 Suppose you are asked to make a pamphlet about disease prevention for younger children. Fold over a sheet of paper so that it has four panels. In each panel, draw a picture and write a rule to help prevent the spread of some communicable diseases.

ALCOHOL, TOBACCO, AND DRUGS

THE BIG IDEA

Drugs can be:

■ used to treat or cure illnesses when taken correctly.

■ harmful to physical, emotional and intellectual, and social health when misused or abused.

DRUG-
FREE
SCHOOL
ZONE

In this lesson, you will learn:

▶ how medicines are different from other drugs.

▶ how prescription medicines are different from over-the-counter medicines.

▶ how to find information on a medicine label.

VOCABULARY

drug (drug) a substance, other than food, that causes changes in the body

medicine (med′ə sin) a drug used to prevent, treat, or cure disease or injury

prescription (pri skrip′shən) a written order from a doctor, usually for medicine

pharmacist (fär′mə sist) a person trained and licensed to prepare medicines and give them out to doctors' patients

QUICK START A friend is visiting at your home. What if she tells you she has a headache? What would you tell her to do?

What do you do when you don't feel well? Sometimes when you feel ill, getting some rest or eating a healthful meal can help you feel better. At other times, a trusted adult might choose to give you some kind of pill or liquid to help you feel better. Or that person may choose to take you to a doctor or other health care worker, who will then treat you.

In this lesson, you will learn how to make safe choices to help you get well.

Health care workers can help when you are ill.

Drugs Used to Treat Illness

A **drug** is a substance, other than food, that causes changes in your body. Drugs can change the way you feel, think, or behave. Some drugs are legal. For example, medicines are legal drugs. Other drugs are illegal—buying, selling, or using them is against the law.

A **medicine** is a drug used to treat, cure, or prevent disease or injury. Used properly, medicines can improve the way you feel or speed up your recovery when you are ill. They can also protect you from illness. However, never take any medicine without the guidance of a trusted adult.

Prescription Medicines

In order for you to get certain medicines, a doctor must examine you and write an order for them. The doctor's written order for medicine is called a **prescription**. The doctor considers your height, weight, age, and medical history before ordering a medicine. The medicine the doctor orders is for <u>you</u>. You should <u>never</u> share prescription medicines with another person.

To get a prescription medicine, you must have the prescription filled by a pharmacist. A **pharmacist** is a person trained and licensed to prepare medicines and give them out to doctors' patients. You can find a pharmacist in the pharmacy section of a store or in a drug store.

A pharmacist prepares prescription medicines.

When a pharmacist prepares medicine for a patient, he or she also makes labels with information meant only for the patient receiving the medicine. The label tells the *dosage*, or how much of the medicine to take. It also tells how often to take it.

LIFE SKILL

PRACTICE REFUSAL SKILLS

What Would You Do?

You have a sore throat like the one your brother has had for a few days. He tells you that you should try some medicine that was prescribed for him. What would you say to refuse your brother's offer?

Over-the-Counter Medicines

Not all medicines require a prescription. People can buy many medicines in stores, right off the shelves. These are known as *over-the-counter* medicines. You may have been given some of these medicines for colds or coughs. Or perhaps you've used lotions for rashes or insect bites.

Most over-the-counter medicines are for health problems that are not very serious. Even so, be sure to be careful when using them. Over-the-counter medicines can harm you if you don't use them correctly.

An over-the-counter medicine should have a label with information for anyone who might use it. The label tells about the product and has directions for its use.

The label may also include some warnings. For example, the warnings may tell a person not to use the product if he or she has a certain condition, such as asthma or heart disease. The label may tell the person to call a doctor if any problems develop, such as certain side effects or allergic reactions.

An *expiration date* should appear on the label of an over-the-counter medicine. The medicine should not be used after that date.

Over-the-counter medicines are sealed for safety reasons. They should never be bought if the seal has been broken.

Remember, never take any medicine without guidance from an adult. If a medicine doesn't seem to help you, you should tell a trusted adult. He or she can call your doctor for advice.

VITAMIN C

ASPIRIN-FREE
PAIN RELIEVER

OUGH YRUP

Adults and children 12 years of age and older: Take 2 tablets, 3 or 4 times a day. Do not exceed 8 tablets in any 24 hour period. **Children:** Do not give this product to children under 12 except under the advice and supervision of a doctor.

WARNINGS: Do not use for more than 10 days. If pain or fever persists or gets worse, consult a physician immediately. Keep this and all drugs out of the reach of children. In case of an accidental overdose, seek professional care or contact a poison control center immediately. As with any drug, if you are pregnant or nursing a baby, seek the advice of a health professional before using this product.

HEALTHWISE CONSUMER

Stop the Pain!

A pain reliever is a medicine that can help you feel better if you have a headache or other kind of body ache. There are many brands of over-the-counter pain relievers. Some contain aspirin. Aspirin can cause someone your age to become very ill. Pain relievers that don't contain aspirin can make you feel better, and they are also safer for someone your age.

Read the Label!

LIFE SKILL

OBTAIN HELP

You will need: an over-the-counter medicine label

1 Work with a partner. Read an over-the-counter medicine label.

2 Look for directions on the label. When might someone need to take this medicine? How much should a person take? How often? What warnings are on the label? After what date should the medicine no longer be used?

3 Think about what you've learned from the label. Discuss with your partner why it is important to obtain help from an adult whenever you take medicine. Share your thoughts with the class.

LESSON WRAP UP

Show What You Know

1. How are medicines different from other drugs?

2. What are some differences between prescription and over-the-counter medicines?

3. **THINK CRITICALLY** Why should an adult read the label before giving you any over-the-counter medicine?

Show What You Can Do

4. **PORTFOLIO** **APPLY HEALTH ACTIVITY** **Obtain Help** Ask an adult at home to help you read an over-the-counter medicine label. Describe the medicine. Include directions for use, any warnings, and the expiration date.

5. **LIFE SKILL** **PRACTICE LIFE SKILLS** **Make Decisions** Suppose you are a parent. Your daughter has a cold. You might decide to give her an over-the-counter medicine. Or you might take her to the doctor. How would you make a decision?

In this lesson, you will learn:

▶ the risks connected with taking medicine.

▶ the differences between misuse and abuse of drugs.

▶ rules for medicine safety.

VOCABULARY

side effect (sīd i fekt′) an unwanted result of using a medicine

dependence (di pen′dəns) a strong need or desire for a medicine or drug

misuse (mis ūz′) to use a legal drug improperly or in an unsafe way

abuse (ə būz′) to use an illegal drug; to use a legal drug in an unsafe way on purpose

QUICK START Suppose you are not feeling well. A friend offers you her cold medicine. What would you do?

When you become ill, it is important to make healthful decisions about seeking treatment. Often it is hard for people to know why they feel ill. They don't always know the best way to treat the illness. Some treatments may help a person feel better. Some may not help at all. Some treatments may even be harmful. Your family can protect you by seeking medical advice for you. You can help by following that advice.

It is important to know how serious an illness is before choosing a treatment.

Treating Illness

Sometimes people who feel ill try to find treatments on their own. This is called *self-medication*. People who buy over-the-counter medicines are practicing self-medication. Some people try *home remedies*, treatments for illness using natural substances. They are also practicing self-medication. Drinking hot lemonade and honey for a cough is one example of a home remedy.

People who practice self-medication take some risk. Their illness could get worse if the treatment is not right. The treatment itself could make the illness worse or cause new problems. A parent, guardian, or other trusted adult should talk with a doctor if he or she isn't sure what to do about treating you for an illness. Never choose a treatment on your own. Check with your family first.

The Risks of Taking Medicines

Almost all treatments for illness carry some risk. And some medicines affect different people differently. Some risks of taking medicines are described below.

Sometimes a medicine can cause unwanted changes in your body, such as sleepiness or dizziness. These unwanted results of using a medicine are called **side effects**.

You can have an allergic reaction to a medicine. Some people are sensitive to certain substances. This sensitivity is known as an *allergy*. An allergy can cause a person to have a rash, run a fever, or have trouble breathing. People should not take medicines to which they are allergic. They should stop taking a medicine if it causes an allergic reaction.

People sometimes become so used to taking a medicine or other drug that they feel they can't do without it. They develop a strong need or desire for it, or **dependence**. When people are dependent on a drug, it is very difficult for them to stop using it.

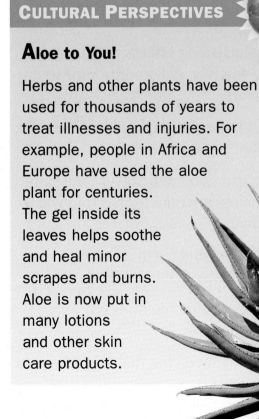

Aloe to You!

Herbs and other plants have been used for thousands of years to treat illnesses and injuries. For example, people in Africa and Europe have used the aloe plant for centuries. The gel inside its leaves helps soothe and heal minor scrapes and burns. Aloe is now put in many lotions and other skin care products.

Adults: Take one tablet every four to six hours.

Children: Do not give this product to children under 12 except under the advice and supervision of a doctor.

Adults and children over 12: Apply ointment to affected area not more than 3 or 4 times daily.

Children under 12 years of age: Do not use this product. Consult a physician.

 Adults and children 12 years and older: 2 teaspoons (tsp) every 4 hours

 Children 6 years to under 12 years: 1 teaspoon (tsp) every 4 hours

 Children under 6: Do not use this product. Consult a physician.

Children often take a different dosage of medicine than adults.

Misuse and Abuse

Another risk in using medicines involves how well a person taking the medicine can follow directions. Medicines can harm you if they are misused.

To **misuse** a legal drug means to use it improperly or in an unsafe way. For example, taking too much or too little of a medicine is misuse. Also, taking someone else's prescription medicine is misuse. All these kinds of misuse can cause harm.

When people use illegal drugs, or when they use legal drugs in an unsafe way on purpose, they **abuse** drugs. Using medicines for any reason other than to prevent or treat illness is abuse. Drug abuse can be very harmful to a person's health.

Rules for Medicine Safety

Drug companies test each medicine they make for safety. From these tests, they set safe dosages and provide warnings for consumers. Doctors also study a person's illness. They choose the best and safest medicine for treatment. You can also help reduce your risk of harm.

- Take medicines only under the supervision of a trusted adult.

- Follow the directions on the label. Take the correct dosage for your size and age.

- If you have side effects, tell a trusted adult, who can call your doctor if necessary.

- Take a prescription medicine only if it is meant for you.

- Never use two medicines at the same time unless your doctor has told you to take them.

- Store all medicines in a locked cabinet, away from children's reach.

- Never use medicine after its expiration date.

- Never buy medicine that has a broken safety seal.

LIFE SKILL

PRACTICE REFUSAL SKILLS

What Would You Do?

After your doctor gives you ear drops, your ears continue to hurt. Your friend tells you to try doubling the dosage. How would you say "no" to your friend?

On the Safe Side

MAKE DECISIONS

1 Work with a partner. Act out being a parent and a sick child. Begin by having the child describe his or her illness. Write down the description.

2 Make a list of the decisions the parent and child can make to treat the illness safely. How will they use medicines safely? Who can they ask for help?

3 Compare your decisions with those made by other pairs.

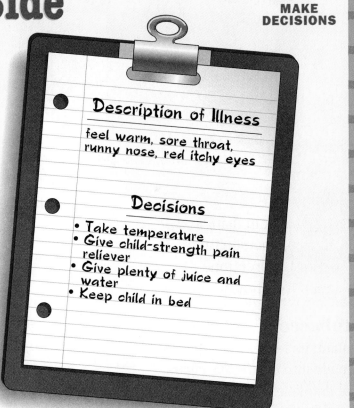

Description of Illness

feel warm, sore throat, runny nose, red itchy eyes

Decisions

- Take temperature
- Give child-strength pain reliever
- Give plenty of juice and water
- Keep child in bed

LESSON WRAP UP

Show What You Know

1. What are the risks connected with taking a medicine?

2. How is drug misuse different from drug abuse?

3. **THINK CRITICALLY** Why is it important for you to take medicine only with the help of a trusted adult?

Show What You Can Do

4. **PORTFOLIO** **APPLY HEALTH ACTIVITY**
   Make Decisions Make a small pamphlet about medicine safety. Choose the three medicine safety rules you think are the most important. Explain why you chose these rules.

5. **LIFE SKILL** **PRACTICE LIFE SKILLS**
   Obtain Help Suppose you are taking a medicine that your doctor has prescribed for you. After a few days, you develop a rash. What should you do?

3 TOBACCO AND HEALTH

In this lesson, you will learn:

▶ about the effects of tobacco products on the body.

▶ why it is hard to stop using tobacco products.

VOCABULARY

tobacco (tə bak′ō) a plant; its leaves are dried and made into cigarettes, cigars, or smokeless tobacco

nicotine (nik′ə tēn′) a drug; a poisonous, oily substance found in tobacco

carbon monoxide (kär′bən mon ok′sīd) a poisonous gas produced when tobacco burns (as well as when a motor vehicle gives off exhaust)

tar (tär) a sticky, brown substance found in tobacco

QUICK START A friend offers you a puff on a cigarette. "C'mon! One puff won't hurt you." How can you refuse your friend's suggestion?

When you are out with your family and friends, you may see people smoking. Most likely, you know at least one person who smokes. You might wonder why people smoke. Some try smoking because they are curious. Some try it to go along with friends. Others may not realize it is harmful. The fact is, people who smoke are breathing in a dangerous drug.

Tobacco products are harmful to your health.

TOBACCO AND THE BODY

Tobacco is a plant. Its leaves are dried and used to make cigarettes, cigars, pipe tobacco, smokeless tobacco, and other products.

All things made with tobacco have a drug called nicotine. **Nicotine** is a poisonous, oily substance found in tobacco. As a smoker puffs on a cigarette, most of the nicotine in the cigarette is taken into the body.

Nicotine can cause certain changes in the body.

It affects the way the brain sends and receives messages.

It raises blood pressure.

It speeds up heart rate.

It raises the amount of fat in blood.

Tar is a sticky, brown substance found in tobacco.

It can cause bad breath, stained teeth, and deadened taste buds.

More importantly, it can damage lungs.

Carbon monoxide is a poisonous gas produced when tobacco burns.

When a smoker inhales cigarette smoke, carbon monoxide takes the place of some of the oxygen that is normally taken into the lungs. As a result, the smoker can become short of breath.

Short-Term Effects of Smoking

It doesn't take long before smoking will affect the health of a smoker. Bad breath results from the first puff. A reduced sense of smell and taste quickly follows.

Other body changes can occur within a few weeks of smoking.

- rapid heart rate

- higher blood pressure

- shortness of breath

- nagging cough

- red, itchy eyes

- stuffy nose

- tiring easily during physical activity

Long-Term Effects of Smoking

You have read about some of the short-term effects that smoking has on the body. These include a rapid heart rate, higher blood pressure, bad breath, and deadened taste buds. As awful as these sound, the long-term effects of smoking are even more drastic!

The effect of nicotine on the heart, blood, and blood vessels raises a person's risk of heart disease. Each year, heart attacks kill many people who smoke.

Lung cancer also causes many deaths each year. Tar in smoke can cause lung cancer. Lung cancer destroys the lungs, making it impossible for a person to breathe on his or her own without the help of machinery.

It is easier to enjoy your favorite activities if you do not smoke.

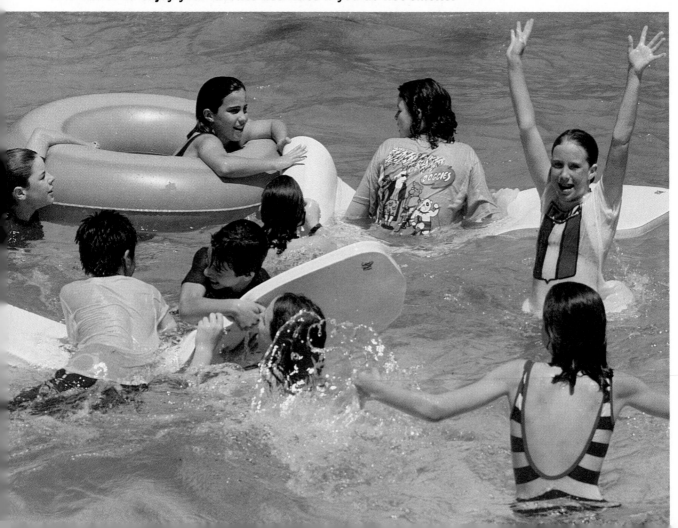

The Effects of Smoking on the Lungs

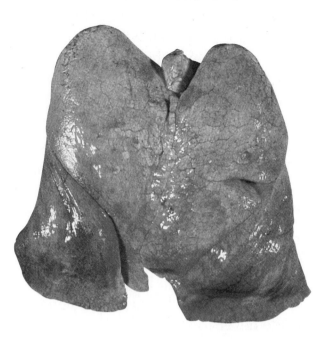

The lungs of a nonsmoker are healthy and pink.

Some lung damage from smoking can never be repaired.

Smoking causes other lung diseases, too. Some of these diseases damage the lungs so badly that doing even simple tasks becomes impossible. A person with serious, permanent lung damage may have a hard time climbing stairs or even blowing out a candle.

HEALTH FACT

" Even cigarettes that are low in tar and nicotine are not safe to smoke. "

This is true. It doesn't matter what kind of cigarette or what brand of cigarette a person smokes. All people who smoke damage their lungs. Smoking any kind of cigarette has been shown to cause life-threatening heart and lung diseases.

Smokeless Tobacco

People who use *smokeless tobacco*—also called chewing tobacco or snuff—hold it in their mouths between their cheeks and gums. The nicotine from smokeless tobacco enters the bloodstream through the gums.

Using smokeless tobacco has the same effects on the heart as smoking cigarettes. Some other effects of smokeless tobacco are listed below.

- reduced sense of smell and taste

- stained teeth and bad breath

- cracked or stinging gums and lips

- gum damage and worn-away teeth

- sores and white spots

- cancers of the lip, tongue, mouth, and throat

Why Is Tobacco Hard to Give Up?

Young people often start smoking because their friends smoke. Peer pressure leads them to start something that is very dangerous to their health and also very hard to stop. It is hard to stop smoking because the nicotine in tobacco is *addictive*. When a drug is addictive, it causes dependence.

A person addicted to nicotine craves its effect. Some people feel the need to smoke as often as every hour, or even more than that. And the more they smoke, the more their health is affected.

The physical act of smoking or chewing becomes a habit. The desire to smoke or chew can last for months after quitting. In addition, giving up nicotine can cause nervousness, dizziness, sleeplessness, and sadness. These symptoms do not last long, however. And once a person stops using tobacco, his or her risk of developing a serious tobacco-related illness decreases.

Quitting Tobacco Use

People quit using tobacco in different ways. Some people slowly reduce the amount they use. Others quit all at once. Some join a group of people who help them make it through the difficult parts of quitting. Others visit their doctors to receive nicotine substitutes. It may take a person several tries to really quit, but it is important that the person keep trying.

The easiest way to "quit" using tobacco is to never start using it at all. If you think about how smoking can affect your health, it will be easier for you to decide never to start.

LIFE SKILL

RESOLVE CONFLICTS

What Would You Do?

Your best friend's sister has started smoking. You worry that your friend might start smoking too. What should you do?

Organizations such as the American Cancer Society offer smokers encouragement and help them to stop smoking.

No Smoking

Great American SMOKEOUT®

AMERICAN CANCER SOCIETY®

No Smoking, Please!

LIFE SKILL

PRACTICE REFUSAL SKILLS

You will need: a piece of chalk, a jar lid

1 Work with a partner. Imagine that the chalk is a cigarette and that the lid is a tin of smokeless tobacco.

2 Offer the "cigarette" to your partner and give a reason for smoking it. Your partner should turn it down. Then he or she should explain why smoking is harmful to the body and hard to stop.

3 Have your partner offer you some of the "smokeless tobacco." Turn it down and tell your partner why it is harmful to use and difficult to stop using.

LESSON WRAP UP

Show What You Know

1. In what way does the tar in tobacco products affect the body?

2. Why is it hard for a person to quit using a tobacco product once he or she has started using it regularly?

3. **THINK CRITICALLY** Why should a person who enjoys running refuse tobacco products?

Show What You Can Do

4. **PORTFOLIO** **APPLY HEALTH ACTIVITY**
   Practice Refusal Skills
   Write a short skit in which the human body talks to its hands. Have the body give reasons for refusing to smoke the cigarette one of the hands is holding.

5. **LIFE SKILL** **PRACTICE LIFE SKILLS**
   Obtain Help Use a local phone book. Find out where in your community tobacco users can get help if they want to quit. Make a list of the phone numbers and addresses.

4   TOBACCO USE IN THE COMMUNITY

In this lesson, you will learn:

▶ about the risks of smoking to the health of nonsmokers.

▶ about some laws that regulate smoking and tobacco advertising.

▶ to analyze tobacco advertising.

VOCABULARY

passive smoke
(pas′iv smōk) tobacco smoke that is inhaled by someone other than the smoker

nonsmoking section
(non smōk′ing sek′shən) a part of a public place set aside for people who do not smoke

QUICK START In your favorite restaurant, you are sitting in a section where smoking is not allowed. Someone nearby lights a cigarette. What could you do?

You might think that if you don't smoke, you are safe from the harm that tobacco smoke causes. But did you know that even if you don't smoke, other people's smoke can harm you?

When you sit in a room where others are smoking, the smoke in the air you breathe in can cause health problems. Many communities have passed laws to protect people from other people's smoke.

How can smoke from cigarettes harm people who do not smoke?

These warnings on cigarette packages help educate the public about the dangers of smoking.

Dangers of Smoke to Nonsmokers

Smoke from someone else's burning cigarette can get into your lungs. So can the smoke that someone else breathes out. When you breathe in other people's cigarette smoke, you are breathing in **passive smoke**. That smoke can cause harm, just as if you had smoked.

In Lesson 3, you learned how carbon monoxide harms the body of anyone who smokes. When you breathe in passive smoke, the amount of carbon monoxide in your blood becomes greater, too. Being around someone who smokes can cause these symptoms.

- Your eyes might burn and get watery.

- Your throat might become scratchy, and you might develop a cough.

- You might have an allergic reaction.

People who don't smoke, but who live with people who do, have a higher risk of becoming ill. They are more likely to develop heart and lung diseases, just like people who smoke. Children of parents who smoke are more likely to have asthma, pneumonia, sinus problems, and ear infections than the children of people who don't smoke.

Smoking and the Law

Many laws and regulations protect both people who smoke and people who don't smoke. Cigarette packages have to carry warnings about smoking. These warnings alert people to the dangers of smoking. In most states, businesses are not allowed to sell cigarettes to people who are under a certain age. This helps protect children.

Many communities ban or limit smoking in public places. In most public plazas and public transportation, people are not allowed to smoke at all. In some places, such as restaurants, people may smoke, but only in certain areas. These buildings usually have a **nonsmoking section—** an area for people who do not smoke.

You won't see tobacco products advertised on TV. Congress banned these ads on TV to protect children from being tempted to smoke.

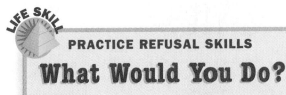

LIFE SKILL

PRACTICE REFUSAL SKILLS

What Would You Do?

A friend asks you to get your older brother to buy cigarettes for him. What would you say to refuse him?

Tobacco Advertisements

Advertising is important for the sale of many products, including tobacco. You may have seen ads on billboards or in magazines. Tobacco ads are designed to get people to use tobacco. But what you see is <u>not</u> what you get.

Look at the chart. It shows ways advertisers try to persuade people to buy their products. Each approach has a hidden message. For example, the picture of a smoker in an expensive car sends you an unspoken message. It implies that smokers are rich people who can afford fancy cars. No matter what approaches are used, you should know how smoking really affects a person. Don't be fooled!

Smoking and Advertising

Many ads show people having fun and looking good while they smoke. But these ads don't show the harmful effects of smoking. They don't tell how the smell of smoke is on a smoker's breath and clothing. You would never guess from ads that smoking bothers other people, either.

The next time you see an ad for cigarettes, think about the approach the ad is using. Try to imagine a more realistic picture instead.

ADVERTISING APPROACHES AND THEIR HIDDEN MESSAGES		
Type of Approach	**Example**	**Hidden Message**
BANDWAGON	Group of People	I should use this product because everyone else does.
Beautiful People	Models and Actors	I will look as good as these models and actors if I use this product.
FUN AND GAMES	Physical Activity	I will have fun if I use this product.
STATUS	Expensive Car	I will look successful if I use this product.
Symbols	A Well-Known Character	I will be popular like this character if I use this product.

What's the Message?

LIFE SKILL
MAKE DECISIONS

You will need: magazines, scissors, tape

1 Work with a group. Cut out at least three cigarette ads from magazines. Tape each ad to a sheet of paper.

2 Use the chart on page 202. Decide which approaches each ad uses to persuade people to buy the product. Identify the hidden messages. Write the approaches and the messages under each ad.

3 Think about each ad. Decide what information the advertiser has left out of the ad. Write the missing information under the ad.

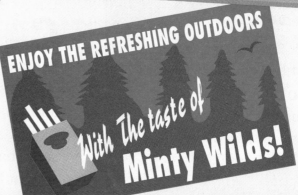

LESSON WRAP UP

Show What You Know

1. What makes passive smoke a health risk to nonsmokers?

2. Describe a law that helps prevent young people from starting to smoke.

3. **THINK CRITICALLY** Do you think fewer people would smoke if there were no cigarette ads? Why or why not?

Show What You Can Do

4. **PORTFOLIO** **APPLY HEALTH ACTIVITY**
Make Decisions Make a "real" tobacco ad. Decide on ways to show how smoking really affects people. Use some of the same techniques used in the ads you cut out.

5. **LIFE SKILL** **PRACTICE LIFE SKILLS**
Resolve Conflicts Prepare a short skit with a classmate. Show how you would deal with a best friend who tries to smoke when you are together.

ALCOHOL AND HEALTH

In this lesson, you will learn:

▶ about the effects of alcohol on a person's health and safety.

▶ about alcohol advertising.

VOCABULARY

alcohol (al′kə hôl′) a drug found in beer, wine, and liquor and in some medicines

QUICK START You are at a friend's house. Your friend's older brother tries to get you to drink a can of beer. How would you refuse the offer?

Certain beverages and medicines contain a drug called **alcohol**. Alcohol changes the way a person feels, thinks, and acts. It also changes the way the body works. All beverages with alcohol have the same basic effects on a person. The body cannot tell which beverage the drug came from. Alcohol from one source is just as harmful to your health as the same amount of alcohol from another source.

Alcohol can affect the drinker and anyone around the drinker.

Each of these drinks includes about the same amount of alcohol:

mixed drink		can of beer		glass of wine
1 ounce of liquor	=	8 ounces of beer	=	4 ounces of wine

Amount of Alcohol Consumed in 2 Hours			Effect of Alcohol on a 100-Pound Person
1 drink	or 1–2 drinks	or 1–2 drinks	Slower reaction time, clumsiness, some confusion
2–4 drinks	or 3–5 drinks	or 3–5 drinks	Unable to think clearly, loss of control of muscles, problems seeing
5–6 drinks	or 6–8 drinks	or 6–8 drinks	Unable to move, loss of control of emotions, and problems seeing, hearing, and judging distances
7 drinks	or 9 drinks	or 9 drinks	Passing out, brain unable to control breathing, possible coma or death

Alcohol in the Body

You may already know that alcohol is found in wine, beer, and liquor. Alcohol is also in some medicines, like cough syrup. It is important to know what alcohol does to the body, because it is in some products that people often use.

When a person drinks alcohol, it gets into the body's organ systems very quickly. First, the drug moves from the stomach and small intestine into the bloodstream. The blood then carries some of the alcohol to the brain. It takes only a few minutes for this to happen.

When a person drinks too much, the liver can't break down the alcohol fast enough. More of the alcohol will be in the person's blood. This affects the brain even more. The way a body reacts to alcohol depends on many factors, including the person's body weight and the amount of food eaten recently. A person who drinks a lot of alcohol in a short time may pass out, or even die, from alcohol poisoning.

Physical Health and Alcohol

Too much alcohol in the blood affects a person's physical health. Alcohol can affect almost every part of the body. The more alcohol there is in a person's blood, the more health problems the person is likely to have.

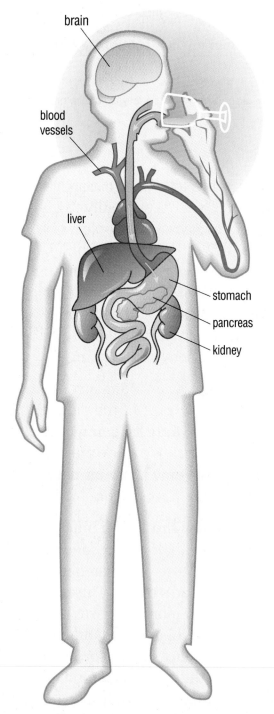

Alcohol can cause harm throughout the body.

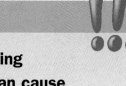

HEALTH FACT

" **Drinking during pregnancy can cause serious damage to the unborn child.** "

This is true. The alcohol the mother drinks passes from her bloodstream to the fetus. In some cases, the child may be born with Fetal Alcohol Syndrome. This syndrome can cause a child to be born with both physical and mental handicaps.

Alcohol slows down messages between the brain and the rest of the body. This can result in dizziness, loss of balance, unclear speech, slower reaction time, and loss of muscle control.

When alcohol reaches the brain, it slows down the senses of sight, smell, hearing, taste, and touch. For example, a drinker might not be able to feel pain, not even from a burning match or from freezing temperatures. Alcohol can also cause memory loss.

In addition to affecting the way the brain works, alcohol causes other physical problems. Alcohol use can cause damage to nerves. For example, heavy alcohol users might feel burning pain in their feet and legs.

Drinking alcohol also makes the liver work overtime. This can lead to liver disease, which can kill heavy alcohol drinkers. Drinking alcohol can cause high blood pressure and can damage heart muscle, which can lead to heart disease. Alcohol use has also been linked to mouth and esophagus cancers.

A driver who has not been drinking would easily see a person walking across this street.

A driver who has been drinking would have vision problems, which might cause a serious injury.

Emotional and Intellectual Health and Alcohol

A person drinking alcohol may act very differently than when he or she is not drinking. The alcohol can cause a person to engage in risky behaviors. A person who consumes alcoholic beverages may find it hard to remember events.

Anything that affects the brain also affects the way a person feels. Drinking alcohol can have serious effects on a person's emotional health. Many people who drink alcohol feel sad, or "down." Sometimes alcohol users also feel a lot of anger. It can be hard for them to control their emotions.

A person's intellectual health is affected by alcohol, too. The person could become confused more easily. Drinking alcohol can make it hard for a person to make decisions. Also, the person may have trouble judging distances. These problems combine to make a very dangerous situation, especially if the person tries to drive a car or operate other equipment.

Social Health and Alcohol

Drinking alcohol can also lead a pleasant person to act badly toward others. It makes some people more likely to become loud or to get into fights. It can cause people to treat friends and family with disrespect. Some people become very quiet and withdrawn. Some people are more likely to commit crimes when they are drinking.

You can see how drinking alcohol can be harmful. Because of the dangers of drinking alcohol, some communities have laws that don't allow the sale of alcoholic beverages. In most states, laws prevent a person from buying alcoholic drinks until he or she is of a certain age—for example, 21.

LIFE SKILL

OBTAIN HELP

What Would You Do?

Your friend tells you his older brother drinks a lot on weekends. He comes to you for help because he is worried. What would you tell him to do?

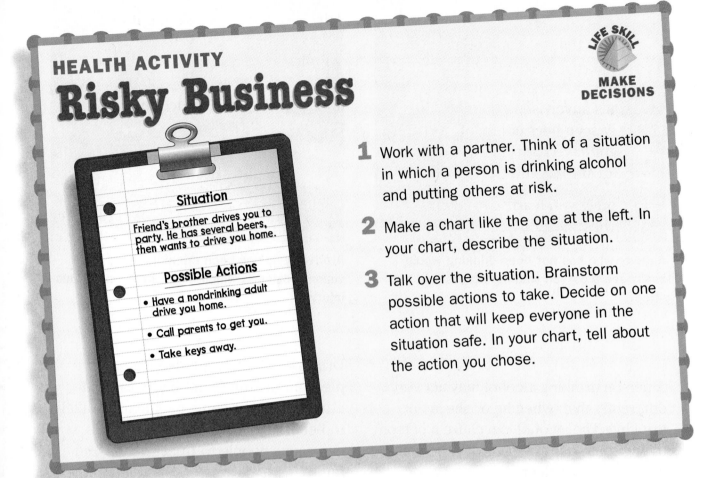

Risky Business

LIFE SKILL

MAKE DECISIONS

Situation

Friend's brother drives you to party. He has several beers, then wants to drive you home.

Possible Actions

• Have a nondrinking adult drive you home.

• Call parents to get you.

• Take keys away.

1 Work with a partner. Think of a situation in which a person is drinking alcohol and putting others at risk.

2 Make a chart like the one at the left. In your chart, describe the situation.

3 Talk over the situation. Brainstorm possible actions to take. Decide on one action that will keep everyone in the situation safe. In your chart, tell about the action you chose.

Safety and Alcohol

Because alcohol affects a person's ability to think clearly, people who drink too much alcohol are more likely to take risks. If you are around someone who is drinking, you may be at risk too—even if you never drink yourself.

People who drink and drive cause more deaths on roads than those who don't. Every year, drivers who have been drinking kill thousands of people—and often themselves. They leave thousands more people seriously injured.

Most states have laws against driving while intoxicated. These laws usually suspend, or take away, the license of any driver who is caught driving under the influence of alcohol.

Not all people of legal age abuse alcohol. Many legal drinkers use it safely. But alcohol is easy to abuse. Because alcohol affects a drinker's judgment, the person can drink too much and too often. Over time, the person can become dependent on alcohol.

Staying away from alcohol will help you stay healthy and safe from its effects. Remember, it is illegal for anyone your age to drink. You should always say "no" to alcohol. And if you find yourself around someone who has been drinking, use good judgment. Take steps to get away from the situation safely. Remember, you should <u>never</u> ride in a car with a driver who has been drinking.

Alcohol Advertisements

Companies that make alcoholic beverages advertise their products. Bars and stores that sell alcoholic beverages advertise, too. You have probably seen beer commercials on TV. You might have seen ads for wine, especially during holiday seasons.

In Lesson 4, you learned about some approaches tobacco advertisers use to try to persuade people. Advertisers of alcoholic beverages use the same approaches. The people in the ads look like they are successful adults. They seem to have many friends. And they appear to be having a lot of fun.

The ads do not show any of the terrible effects that alcohol can have. And they make it look like you need alcohol in order to have fun. This is not true. You can have more fun and be a healthier person without alcohol. And the effects of too much alcohol are <u>not</u> fun at all!

Advertisers do not talk about how alcohol affects health. However, laws in the United States require that labels on alcoholic beverages include warnings about the dangers of alcohol.

There are many healthful ways to have fun without drinking alcohol.

LESSON WRAP UP

Show What You Know

1. Describe how alcohol can affect a person's physical health.

2. How do ads for beer or for other alcoholic beverages try to persuade people to drink?

3. **THINK CRITICALLY** How does alcohol affect all parts of a person's health?

Show What You Can Do

4. **PORTFOLIO** **APPLY HEALTH ACTIVITY**
   Make Decisions Your friend's older brother offers to drive you home from a party. He has been drinking. Make a chart like the one on page 208. Decide on one action that will keep you all safe.

5. **LIFE SKILL** **PRACTICE LIFE SKILLS**
   Obtain Help Use a local phone book. Find phone numbers for programs or groups that help people or families with alcohol problems.

In this lesson, you will learn:

▶ **about the effects of marijuana on the body.**

▶ **about the effects of inhalants, stimulants, and depressants on the body.**

VOCABULARY

marijuana (mar′ə wä′nə) a drug made from the crushed leaves, flowers, and seeds of the cannabis plant

inhalant (in hā′lənt) a legal substance that gives off gas at room temperature; may be abused by inhaling

stimulant (stim′yə lənt) a drug that speeds up the activity of the body

cocaine (kō kān′) a stimulant made from the coca plant

depressant (di pres′ənt) a drug that slows down the activity of the body

QUICK START Suppose you walk to school. Your route takes you past some people selling illegal drugs. How could you stay safe?

What would you do if someone asked you to try an illegal drug? The person might say things about the drug to get you to try it. He or she might say that it would make you feel good. He or she might tell you that the drug couldn't possibly harm you. How do you know whether or not the person is telling the truth? The information in this lesson will help you understand that no illegal drug is safe.

Illegal drugs cannot solve problems. Talking things over with a trusted friend is a better choice.

You do not need to use illegal drugs to have fun.

Marijuana

Pot, grass, weed—these are all names for an illegal drug called marijuana. **Marijuana** is made from the leaves, flowers, and seeds of the cannabis plant. Most often, these parts are dried, crushed, and rolled in paper to make marijuana cigarettes. Marijuana is also smoked in pipes.

Like other drugs, marijuana changes the way the body works. Marijuana has many short-term effects. Here are some physical effects of smoking marijuana.

- bloodshot eyes
- dry mouth and throat
- increased heart rate
- increased appetite

Marijuana also affects the brain. Often, people who smoke marijuana have trouble remembering things. They can become confused easily and have trouble doing simple tasks. They may become nervous. Often, people using marijuana think that they are acting in a normal way, but they may not be. This makes them a danger to themselves and to others.

Marijuana can also affect a person's ability to judge distance and time. This makes it very dangerous for that person to drive.

Some long-term effects of smoking marijuana are like those of smoking tobacco. Marijuana can damage the lungs. It destroys lung tissue and might cause lung cancer.

Marijuana is an illegal drug. It's against the law to sell it, to smoke it, or even to have it in your possession. Just being around this drug can get a person into serious trouble with the law.

Inhalants

Inhalants are legal substances that some people abuse. An **inhalant** is a substance that gives off a gas at room temperature. Some common household items, such as paint thinner and spray paint, can be abused as inhalants. Inhaling the gas can cause nausea, headaches, and even brain damage and death.

HEALTH ACTIVITY
Not for Me!

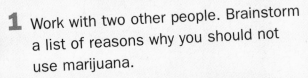

1 Work with two other people. Brainstorm a list of reasons why you should not use marijuana.

2 Act out a scene in which two people try to get a third person to try marijuana. That person should use the reasons in Step 1 to say "no" to using marijuana.

3 Change roles until each of you has played each role. Talk about the ways you thought of to say "no" to marijuana. Which ways worked best? Which made the most sense to you?

Stimulants

Drugs are grouped by their effect on the body. Drugs that cause similar effects are of the same type. Stimulants are one type of drug. **Stimulants** are drugs that speed up the activity of the body. They make the heart beat faster. Someone who takes a stimulant may feel nervous and jumpy. Stimulants can also decrease a person's appetite and cause sleeplessness.

Some stimulants are legal. Caffeine is a legal stimulant found in coffee, tea, and many soft drinks. In small amounts, it is harmless to most people. Consumed in large amounts, caffeine can cause people to have trouble sleeping. They may feel anxious and restless. Caffeine can also cause dependence.

The nicotine in tobacco is another legal stimulant. As you learned in Lesson 3, nicotine can harm the body. There are laws that control its use and help protect possible users.

Illegal Stimulants

Most dangerous stimulants are illegal. One of them is **cocaine**, a stimulant made from the coca plant. Usually, cocaine is used in powder form and breathed in through the nose. Cocaine puts a lot of strain on the heart. Many young people have suffered heart attacks when using cocaine. *Crack* is an especially harmful form of cocaine. It comes in the form of a pellet and is smoked in a glass pipe.

Milk and fruit juices are good choices for caffeine-free beverages.

Perhaps the most dangerous thing about stimulants is how addictive they are. Using cocaine—especially crack—can cause dependence very quickly. Dependence can lead to many long term health problems. These can include depression, seizures, heart failure, and even death.

Depressants

Depressants are another type of drug. **Depressants** are drugs that slow down the activity of the body. Depressants slow down heart rate. They also slow down nerve messages in the nervous system. They can make a person feel tired and forgetful.

Alcohol is a legal depressant. Like tobacco use, alcohol use is controlled by laws because of its harmful effects.

Sleeping pills and tranquilizers are medicines that are depressants. They are sometimes prescribed by doctors to treat nervousness or to help a person relax. Some low-dosage sleeping pills are sold over the counter. Because they are medicines, these drugs are legal. But they are often misused.

It's very easy to become dependent on depressants. Like stimulants, they can cause long-term health problems. It is hard to stop using them without a doctor's help.

Abusing depressants or any other kind of drug is not good for your health. Fortunately, you know many ways to live a healthful life. You know how to be healthy physically, emotionally and intellectually, and socially. And you know how to do it without alcohol, tobacco, or other drugs.

PRACTICE REFUSAL SKILLS
What Would You Do?

Suppose a friend offers you a diet pill, a stimulant that reduces hunger. You'd like to have less of an appetite so that you could lose some weight. What would you do? What would you say?

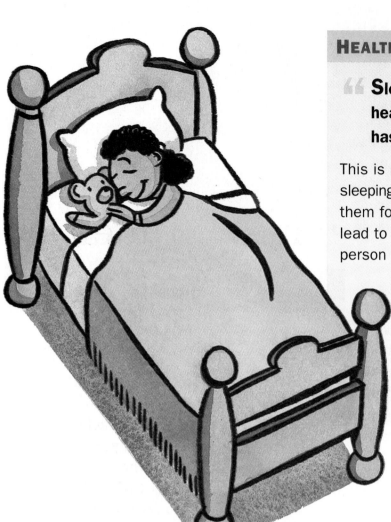

"Sleeping pills are a healthful choice when a person has trouble sleeping."

This is not true! It is not okay to take sleeping pills, unless a doctor prescribes them for you. Taking sleeping pills can lead to a dependence. Over time, a person needs more and more pills to become sleepy. Some people do have trouble sleeping. But they can make better choices than taking pills. They could try exercising during the day or relaxing and reading just before bedtime.

LESSON WRAP UP

Show What You Know

1. What are some of the harmful effects of marijuana on a person's body?

2. Give an example of a stimulant and explain its effects on a person's body.

3. **THINK CRITICALLY** How is crack cocaine different from alcohol?

Show What You Can Do

4. **APPLY HEALTH ACTIVITY**
   Practice Refusal Skills
   Write a dialogue between two people. Show how one person says "no" to trying the illegal drug offered by the other person.

5.  **PRACTICE LIFE SKILLS**
   Make Decisions
   Brainstorm some things people can do to have energy or to relax instead of taking drugs. Make a poster titled "Decisions Other Than Drugs."

YOU CAN MAKE A DIFFERENCE

Students Teaching Students

Members of SADD

Every 26 minutes, someone in the United States dies in a car accident involving alcohol. Students Against Driving Drunk, or SADD, are teenagers across the country who teach others about the dangers of drunk driving, alcohol, and illegal drugs.

SADD was started in 1981 by Robert Anastas, a health teacher in Wayland, Massachusetts. Today there are more than 25,000 chapters of SADD in schools throughout the United States. The seven million student members of SADD organize programs to deal with the problems caused by alcohol and drugs.

In middle schools, SADD provides students and parents with a special contract. This contract commits students to living a life free of alcohol and illegal drugs. SADD students also work to make their schools free of alcohol and drugs. In high schools, SADD teaches students about the dangers of driving while under the influence of alcohol or drugs. SADD also creates social events that are alcohol and drug-free.

LIFE SKILL — **PRACTICE REFUSAL SKILLS**

GOOD JUDGMENT

Imagine that you are a judge. In your courtroom, a drunk driver had just been found guilty. Write two paragraphs, showing what you would say to the driver. Tell the driver why he or she should never drive drunk again. Suggest some sensible ways to say "no" to alcohol.

8 REVIEW

VOCABULARY

Write the word from the box that best completes each sentence.

alcohol

cocaine

dependence

marijuana

nicotine

nonsmoking
  section

pharmacist

side effects

1. A person who prepares prescription medicines is a(n) __?__. (Lesson 1)

2. Unwanted changes in the body caused by a drug are __?__. (Lesson 2)

3. A drug found in tobacco is __?__. (Lesson 3)

4. A drug found in beer and wine is __?__. (Lesson 5)

5. A dangerous illegal stimulant is __?__. (Lesson 6)

REVIEW HEALTH IDEAS

Use your knowledge of alcohol, tobacco, and drugs from Chapter 8 to answer these questions.

1. If a doctor gives you a prescription, where do you get it filled? (Lesson 1)

2. Which drugs are medicines? (Lesson 1)

3. Why can self-medication be risky? (Lesson 2)

4. What is the difference between drug misuse and drug abuse? (Lesson 2)

5. What are some dangers of using smokeless tobacco? (Lesson 3)

6. What are the possible short-term effects of smoking? (Lesson 3)

7. How can cigarette smoke harm a nonsmoker? (Lesson 4)

8. How can alcohol affect a person's social health? (Lesson 5)

9. What effect can large amounts of caffeine have on the body? (Lesson 6)

10. What effects do depressants have on the body? (Lesson 6)

APPLY HEALTH IDEAS

1. Describe a situation in which it might be important to take a prescription drug. (Lesson 1)

2. Why should you always ask to be seated in a nonsmoking section in a restaurant? (Lesson 4)

3. Why might a person who regularly smokes marijuana have trouble doing well in school? (Lesson 6)

4. **PORTFOLIO** **MAKE DECISIONS** Write a letter to the president of a TV network. Explain why you think alcohol should not be advertised on TV. Decide what arguments you would present in your letter. (Lesson 5)

5. **LIFE SKILL** **PRACTICE REFUSAL SKILLS** Suppose your older sister's friends want to smoke marijuana and drink beer. They ask you to join them. Write three ways to refuse and try to convince them not to do it either. (Lesson 6)

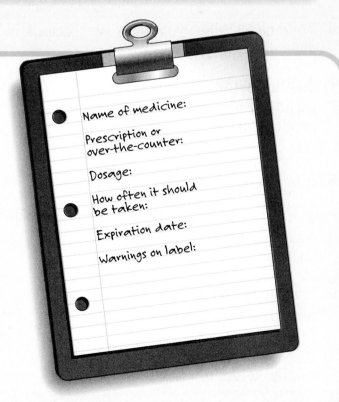

Can you use what you've learned from Chapter 8 to interpret the labels on medicines that you have at home?

Ask an adult to select at least three medicines in your home. Inspect the label on each medicine. For each medicine, prepare a sheet of paper like the one shown at the right. Fill in the information for each medicine. Talk about what you've learned.

Name of medicine:

Prescription or over-the-counter:

Dosage:

How often it should be taken:

Expiration date:

Warnings on label:

Choose the correct word to complete each sentence.

1. Cocaine (increases, decreases) heart rate.

2. A strong need for a substance is described as a (dependence, side effect).

3. Medicines that can only be purchased with an order from a doctor are (over-the-counter, prescription) medicines.

4. Cigarettes produce (carbon dioxide, carbon monoxide).

5. Unintentionally taking twice the dosage of a medicine is an example of (misuse, abuse).

6. Smokeless tobacco is likely to cause (brain, mouth) cancer.

7. A drug that makes it hard for people to stop using tobacco products is (carbon monoxide, nicotine).

8. It is against the law to show (beer, cigarette) ads on TV.

9. Alcohol can make people behave in a (concerned, risk-taking) manner.

10. Passive smoke (can, cannot) cause heart disease in a nonsmoker.

Write a sentence to answer each question.

11. How do alcohol ads try to influence people to drink?

12. Why is it so dangerous to drink alcohol and then drive?

13. How does tar in tobacco affect the mouth?

14. How does smoking marijuana affect the lungs?

15. How can a label on an over-the-counter medicine help you use the medicine safely?

16. How would you say "no" to someone who offers you marijuana?

17. How does a doctor help you use medicines safely?

18–20. Describe three approaches used in tobacco advertising.

✎ **Performance Assessment**

 Choose one drug mentioned in Chapter 8. Create a booklet describing its effects on the body and mind. Also tell why misuse or abuse of this drug can be dangerous.

SAFETY, INJURY, AND VIOLENCE PREVENTION

CHAPTER 9

THE BIG IDEA

You can prevent most injuries by:

- following safety rules.

- avoiding hazards.

- asking for help when needed.

CHAPTER CONTENTS

INJURY PREVENTION

In this lesson, you will learn:

▶ the difference between intentional and unintentional injuries.

▶ how to identify and remove hazards.

VOCABULARY

injury (in′jə rē) any kind of physical damage or harm to a person

hazard (haz′ərd) a thing or an action that creates a dangerous situation or risk of harm

first aid (fûrst ād) immediate treatment for a minor injury or illness; in an emergency, treatment given until medical help arrives

emergency (i mûr′jən sē) a serious situation that requires immediate help, usually from the police, the fire department, or medical personnel

QUICK START You need to put away an iron that is on the counter. You don't know if the iron is hot. What can you do to keep yourself safe from injury?

Any kind of physical damage to you is an **injury**. Injuries can be *intentional.* If someone hurts you by pushing, hitting, or throwing something at you on purpose, that's an intentional injury. More often, an injury is *unintentional*—the result of an unexpected event.

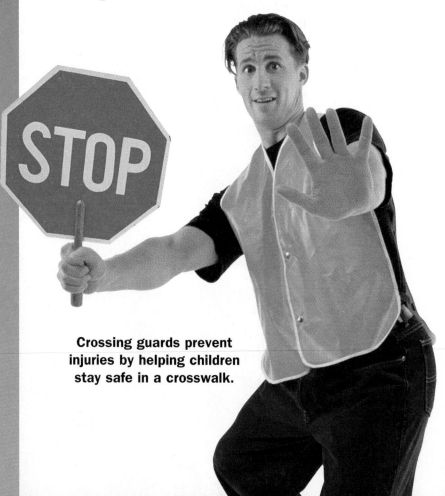

Crossing guards prevent injuries by helping children stay safe in a crosswalk.

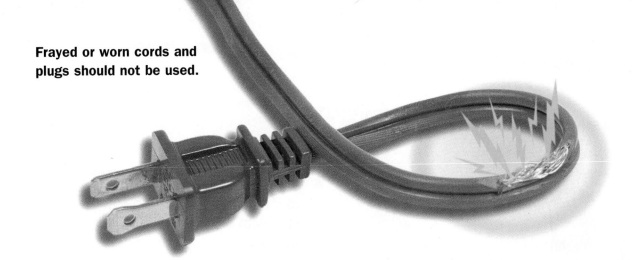

Frayed or worn cords and plugs should not be used.

Unexpected Events Will Happen

You can't always predict when or where unexpected events will occur. Nevertheless, many unintentional injuries are *preventable*—you can do things to keep them from happening.

The three keys to preventing unintentional injuries are:

- follow safety rules,
- avoid hazards, and
- ask for help when you need it.

Safety Rules

Sometimes you may feel that there are too many rules in your life. Family rules may have you locking the door at night. School rules may direct you not to run in the halls. Community rules may say that you must wear a safety helmet when bicycling. But when you think about it, aren't most of those rules intended to keep you safe from danger?

The best way to avoid injuries is to stay away from hazards. A **hazard** is something that creates a dangerous situation or risk of harm. Following are some common hazards and ways to stay away from them.

Electrical Hazards

Carelessness with electricity can lead to fire or to electric shock. These rules can help prevent burns and shocks.

- Don't overload electrical outlets.
- Don't use frayed or worn cords and plugs.
- Never go near water with an electrical appliance. Don't play a plugged-in radio near the tub. Don't use a hair dryer while you are standing over a filled sink.

HEALTH FACT

" Never touch a person who is receiving an electric shock. "

This is true. As long as the person is still touching the source of the shock, the shock can pass to you. Find the source of the shock. Then turn off the power. If you can't, then knock the source away from the person with a wooden stick or pull the person away with a dry rope or cloth. Do not use anything made of metal. Get emergency help right away.

Danger Detectives

1 Work in groups. Find hazards in your classroom, such as overloaded electrical outlets or clutter you could trip over.

2 With your group, create a plan to "safety-proof" the classroom. Present your plan to the class while a volunteer writes each new idea on the chalkboard.

3 Decide which ideas your group will carry out. For example, your group might be in charge of "clutter clean-up." Go to work to rid your classroom of hazards.

Heat Hazards

Burns don't always come from open flames. You can burn yourself on any hot surface or with any hot liquid. The following ideas can help keep you from getting burned.

- Immediately after use, turn off or unplug appliances that produce heat.

- Think before you touch any appliance that produces heat.

- Always use a heat-resistant glove when handling pots.

- Turn handles of pots and pans toward the back of the stove while cooking.

Falls

Falling down is the most common cause of indoor injury. You can prevent many falls by getting rid of hazards. These ideas can help you prevent falls.

- Clean up clutter, especially on or near staircases. Tuck away things like electrical cords that might make you trip and fall.

- Keep areas where people walk well lit. If a room is dark when you come in, turn on a light or use a flashlight.

- Use nonslip mats in tubs and showers.

- Don't use any chair as a ladder.

Road Hazards

Following are guidelines for road safety while in a car, in a bus, or walking.

- All passengers in a car should wear safety belts at all times. Keep car doors locked. Never sit in the back of a moving pickup truck.

- Avoid Danger Zones around a bus. Keep straps and clothing away from doors. Do not stick your head or arms out the bus window.

- Always look left, right, and left again before crossing the street. Do not ride your bike or walk behind any vehicle that is in operation.

Dealing With Injuries

If an injury happens and a trusted adult is present, ask for help. If you know first aid and there is no adult present, you could provide help. **First aid** is immediate treatment for a minor injury or illness. First aid may also be given in an emergency until medical help arrives.

An **emergency** is a serious situation that requires immediate help—usually from the police, the fire department, or medical personnel. In an emergency, calling 911 on the telephone may get you the help you need.

LIFE SKILL

OBTAIN HELP

What Would You Do?

You find your younger cousin lying on the floor. He does not respond to his name. What would you do?

LESSON WRAP UP

Show What You Know

1. What is an unintentional injury?

2. Name three hazards that could cause injuries. Explain how to remove each hazard.

3. **THINK CRITICALLY** Your friend jokes about how often he falls down in his house. What advice would you give him?

Show What You Can Do

4. **PORTFOLIO** **APPLY HEALTH ACTIVITY Make Decisions** Think about your kitchen at home. Are there any hazards there? What decisions could you make that would help remove them? Write a step-by-step plan. List four things you would do to remove the hazards.

5. **LIFE SKILL** **PRACTICE LIFE SKILLS Obtain Help** Find out where in your community you can take first aid courses.

In this lesson, you will learn:

▶ **what kinds of situations can lead to violence.**

▶ **how to avoid violence in and out of school.**

VOCABULARY

violence (vī′ə ləns) physical force intended to cause bodily injury or harm; behavior intended to cause emotional harm

weapon (wep′ən) a knife, gun, or other object used in an attack

QUICK START A bully in your school keeps trying to get you to fight. What can you do to stay safe?

If you are careful, you can avoid many unintentional injuries. But how do you avoid intentional injuries? If someone wants to hurt you, what can you do to stay safe?

Even good friends have disagreements sometimes, but violence never solves a problem.

The Road to Violence

Physical force intended to cause bodily injury or harm is **violence**. When people act violently, they use physical force instead of communication skills to show how they feel. Certain feelings can lead people to want to behave in a violent way.

You might think of violence as being physical—hitting, pushing, and so on. People can also be emotionally violent. Using mean words and making fun of other people are acts of *emotional violence*. They can hurt as much as slapping or kicking. Besides, angry words can lead to angry actions.

Resolving Conflicts Without Violence

A *conflict* is a strong disagreement between two or more people. Anger is often a part of conflict. Following are steps you can take to help keep a disagreement from ending in violence.

- Remain calm. Take a deep breath. Count to ten. This slows down your heart and gives you time to think.

- Talk about what the conflict is. Putting it into words helps keep a conflict under control. Use the word "I" and tell how you feel. Saying "When you make fun of me, I feel insulted" is less hostile than saying "You're so rude!"

- Listen carefully. The other person has a point of view, too. Take turns talking.

- Talk about solutions. Be willing to *compromise*—settle the argument by give and take. Agree on a solution that works for both of you. Then make sure you live up to your agreement.

CULTURAL PERSPECTIVES

Exporting Nonviolence

"I wanted to avoid violence. Nonviolence is the first article of my faith." These are the words of Mohandas K. Gandhi (1869–1948), a leader of modern India. Gandhi worked as a lawyer in South Africa for many years. He fought against South African laws that hurt Asians and Africans. Instead of acting violently, Gandhi used nonviolent methods. He held peaceful protest rallies. He quietly resisted certain laws. When Gandhi returned to his homeland, he used nonviolent methods to help end British rule in India.

Weapons and Violence

Acts of violence may involve the use of a **weapon**—a knife, stick, gun, or any other object used in an attack. One weapon that is especially dangerous is a handgun.

Guns should never be kept where children can find them. If you see a gun, leave it alone and tell an adult where it is. Never pick it up to show a friend, not even if you believe that it is unloaded. Never point a gun at anyone—not even a toy gun. More than one person has been shot by someone who thought that a real gun was a toy gun.

Movies, TV, and Violence

You make many choices that directly influence your health. Even the movies and TV shows you watch may make a difference in your health. Some people think that violent TV shows and movies may make children act in disrespectful and even violent ways.

When you see a show or a movie in which people end a disagreement with violence, does that change the way you solve problems? How do you and your family choose the movies and TV shows you watch?

When Words Don't Work

Words are powerful, but sometimes they are not enough. You may need to let people know that you do not want to take part in violence. You can choose not to fight. You can choose to walk away. You can choose to find help. At times, leaving the scene may be the only sensible and safe choice you can make.

MAKE DECISIONS

What Would You Do?

Your little cousin just destroyed something you worked for weeks to make. What decisions could you make to stop yourself from reacting angrily?

Walking away is often the best solution to a conflict.

Preventing Violence

LIFE SKILL

RESOLVE CONFLICTS

1 Work with a partner. Think of two situations that could lead to violence. Write them down.

2 Think of ways to keep each situation from getting violent. Talk them over. Write down the best idea for each situation.

3 Choose the situation for which you think you have the best solution. Act it out for the class. Talk about the idea you had for keeping the situation from becoming violent. Would it work in real life? What do your classmates think?

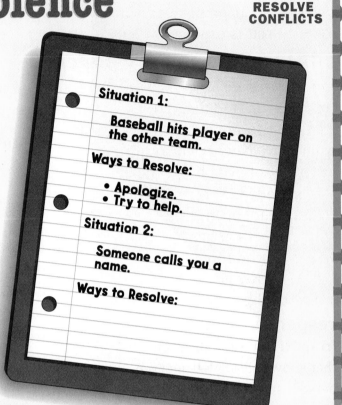

Situation 1:

Baseball hits player on the other team.

Ways to Resolve:

• Apologize.
• Try to help.

Situation 2:

Someone calls you a name.

Ways to Resolve:

LESSON WRAP UP

Show What You Know

1. Describe a feeling that can lead people to act violently.

2. Why is counting to ten a good way to keep from acting violently?

3. **THINK CRITICALLY** Suppose you saw a movie in which a younger brother is always being hit by his older brother. How could the two brothers end their conflict safely? What suggestions would you make to the brothers?

Show What You Can Do

4. **PORTFOLIO** **APPLY HEALTH ACTIVITY** **Resolve Conflicts** Think of a time when you saw TV characters acting violently. Write a scene that shows how they could resolve the conflict without violence.

5. **LIFE SKILL** **PRACTICE LIFE SKILLS** **Practice Refusal Skills** Work with a partner. Write a scene about an older bully and someone your age arguing. Show how the younger person refuses to fight. Act out the scene for the class.

INDOOR SAFETY

In this lesson, you will learn:

▶ safety rules to follow when you're home alone.

▶ the difference between respectful and disrespectful touches.

VOCABULARY

respectful touch
(ri spekt′fəl tuch) a touch that shows caring for another person, such as a handshake or a pat on the back

disrespectful touch
(dis′ri spekt′fəl tuch) a touch that shows a lack of caring for another person, such as hitting or kicking

QUICK START Suppose your family is out and you are home alone. A stranger knocks on the door. What should you do?

Maybe you think safety is something to think about only when you're away from home. But no home is completely free from safety problems. In this lesson, you'll learn ways you and your family can stay safe at home.

When you're home alone, keep your door locked.

Never tell a stranger on the phone that you are home alone.

Home-Alone Safety Rules

Work with your parents to plan what to do when you need to be home alone. Remember, when you're alone, you are in charge of your own safety.

- Don't play with dangerous objects. Stay away from matches, lighters, stoves, household chemicals, poisons, medicines, knives, and—of course— guns.

- Keep your door locked. Never let strangers in.

- Keep away from windows on upper floors, especially those with screens and no safety rails.

- If you answer the telephone, never admit to a stranger that there are no adults with you. Instead be polite and say, for example, "My mother can't come to the phone. May I take a message?"

- Keep a list of emergency numbers by the phone. In addition to 911, include numbers for your parents or other adults, the fire department, the doctor, the poison control center, and any other numbers you think might be useful.

HEALTHWISE CONSUMER

Crank Prank

Have you ever received a rude, or crank, phone call at home? Some people think it's funny to breathe heavily into the phone or to call and hang up over and over again. Your family could buy expensive equipment to trace such calls. But most experts agree that the best response is to simply hang up. If these calls continue, phone the police.

HEALTH ACTIVITY
Emergency Numbers List

LIFE SKILL

OBTAIN HELP

Emergency
Telephone Numbers

911   for any serious
          emergency

555-0123 Dr. Talbut's office

555-1023 Poison Control

555-2103 Police Station

You will need: local telephone book

1 Work with a partner. Brainstorm a list of emergency numbers you can keep by the phone in case you need help. Think of any numbers you might like to have on your list.

2 Use a local telephone book to find the numbers you need.

3 Design your emergency numbers list to be organized and easy to use. Should it be in A-B-C order? Which numbers are most important? You decide.

4 Share your finished list with your family. Post it by the telephone.

Finding Emergency Numbers

You can find many emergency numbers in your local telephone book. However, not all telephone books list emergency numbers in the same way.

- Some telephone books have a separate emergency numbers page.

- Some telephone books list emergency numbers on the inside cover.

- Some telephone books have the numbers listed in a community services section.

It's important to know where your local telephone book lists emergency numbers

before an actual emergency happens. No one has time to look for a phone number when there's a real emergency. Get to know how your telephone directory works. Mark the pages with emergency numbers or prepare your own list of emergency numbers.

LIFE SKILL

SET GOALS

What Would You Do?

You've moved to a new home in a new neighborhood. What are two things you could do to make your new home safe?

Respectful and Disrespectful Touches

A **respectful touch** is a touch that shows caring for another person. It says, "I like you and care about you as a person. I am touching you in a way you or I would choose to be touched." A handshake can show respect. A gentle pat or a hug from a friend can show respect.

A gentle pat on the back can show you care.

A **disrespectful touch** is a touch that shows a lack of caring for another person. It says, "I don't care what you think. I'm going to touch you any way I like." Any kind of hitting shows disrespect. So does any other touch you don't want.

You should never allow strangers to touch you. A stranger could be someone you have never seen before. A stranger could also be someone you have seen before—even every day—but don't know very well. Sometimes, a person you do know very well can touch you in a way you do not like.

Remember, you have a right to say "no" to anyone who tries to touch you in a disrespectful way. Always tell a trusted adult if someone touches you in this way. Don't worry that you might hurt the person's feelings—your feelings matter, too!

LESSON WRAP UP

Show What You Know

1. Name two important safety rules that you should follow if you are home alone.

2. Give one example of a respectful touch and one example of a disrespectful touch.

3. **THINK CRITICALLY** Suppose you are home alone. A person comes to your door to deliver a package. Should you let that person into your home? Why or why not? What might be the best way of handling the situation?

Show What You Can Do

4. **APPLY HEALTH ACTIVITY**
   Obtain Help Write a letter to a friend in another class. Explain how your friend can obtain help finding emergency numbers from a local telephone book.

5. **PRACTICE LIFE SKILLS**
   Practice Refusal Skills A neighbor touches you in a way that upsets you. Explain what you would you say to the neighbor.

In this lesson, you will learn:

▶ about fire safety equipment and how it can protect you.

▶ safety rules to follow in case of fire.

▶ how to make a fire escape plan.

VOCABULARY

smoke detector
(smōk di tek′tər) a machine that sounds an alarm when it senses smoke

fire extinguisher
(fīr ek sting′gwi shər) a machine that sprays chemicals onto a fire to put it out

QUICK START You're studying in the kitchen when you smell smoke. What should you do?

Firefighters see firsthand how dangerous fires can be. They know that fire safety equipment in homes can save lives. Can you name a fire safety device?

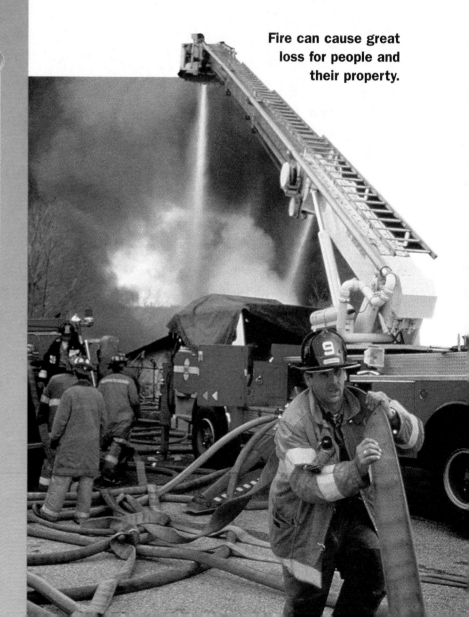

Fire can cause great loss for people and their property.

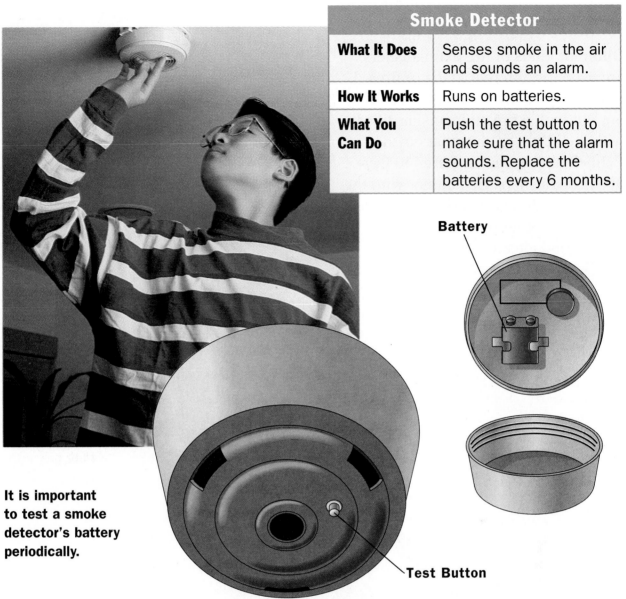

Smoke Detector	
What It Does	Senses smoke in the air and sounds an alarm.
How It Works	Runs on batteries.
What You Can Do	Push the test button to make sure that the alarm sounds. Replace the batteries every 6 months.

Battery

Test Button

It is important to test a smoke detector's battery periodically.

Fire Safety Equipment

Smoke detectors and fire extinguishers are devices that help protect you from fire. When a **smoke detector** detects smoke, it sounds an alarm. There should be a smoke detector outside each sleeping area and at least one on each floor of a house, according to the National Fire Prevention Association. A **fire extinguisher** sprays chemicals onto a fire to put it out. You will learn more about fire extinguishers on the next page.

HEALTHWISE CONSUMER

Battery Up!

About nine out of ten homes in the United States have at least one smoke detector. But smoke detectors can't keep you safe unless they work. In recent years, in about one third of the homes that have had fires, the smoke detectors were broken or didn't have batteries. Check every month to be sure your smoke detectors are in working order!

Fire Extinguishers

Different kinds of fire extinguishers are used for different kinds of fires. For example, electrical fires should be put out with a fire extinguisher filled with liquid gas or chemical powder. Public buildings are required to have fire extinguishers. Be familiar with the location of fire extinguishers in your school and other public buildings. It's also a good idea to have a fire extinguisher in your home.

Fire Extinguisher	
What It Does	Smothers fires with chemicals.
How It Works	Often, twisting the handle and pushing a button releases the chemicals. Instructions should be printed on the fire extinguisher.
What You Can Do	Check the expiration date to make sure that the chemicals will still work.

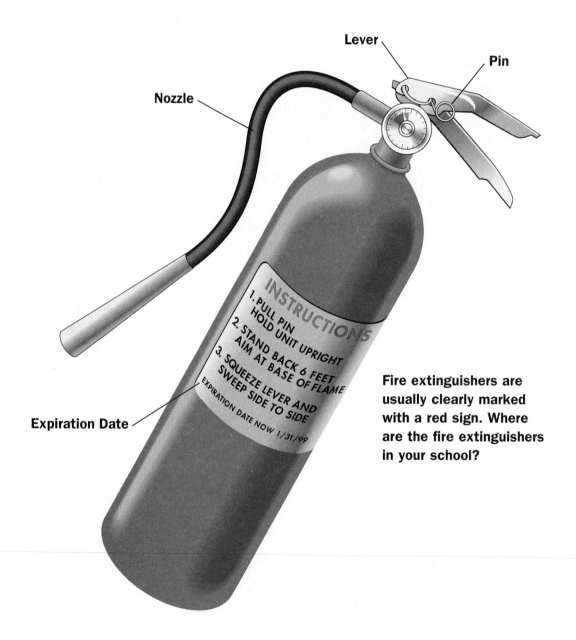

Lever

Pin

Nozzle

INSTRUCTIONS
1. PULL PIN HOLD UNIT UPRIGHT
2. STAND BACK 6 FEET AIM AT BASE OF FLAME
3. SQUEEZE LEVER AND SWEEP SIDE TO SIDE
EXPIRATION DATE NOW 1/31/99

Expiration Date

Fire extinguishers are usually clearly marked with a red sign. Where are the fire extinguishers in your school?

Follow cooking safety rules indoors and outdoors.

Cooking Safety

Fire extinguishers are often kept in the kitchen to put out small cooking fires. Knowing a few safety rules for cooking can help prevent fires.

You should cook only under adult supervision. Before you start cooking, make sure that the stove surface and areas around the stove are clear. Roll up your sleeves and tie back your hair to prevent them from catching on fire. Stay in the kitchen while the food is cooking. As soon as you have finished cooking, turn off the stove.

Be sure to clean stove burners and ovens regularly. Built-up grease can catch fire easily. Never put water on a grease fire. It only makes the fire worse. A fire extinguisher is the right tool for putting out grease fires. If you don't have one handy, pour flour or baking soda on the fire.

You also have to be careful to prevent fires when cooking outdoors. If you are using a grill, be sure that it is placed away from trees and buildings. If you cook over an open campfire, remember to pour water on and stir the smoldering ashes after you are done. Make sure the ashes are completely cooled before leaving the area.

LIFE SKILL

MAKE DECISIONS

What Would You Do?

Your neighbor has a smoke detector in her kitchen. Every time she cooks, it goes off. She decides to remove the batteries. What would you tell her? Is there a better solution to her problem?

Make a Fire Escape Plan

LIFE SKILL
MAKE DECISIONS

1 Your goal is to draw an escape route to use in case a fire starts in your school.

2 Walk through your school. Sketch two ways to leave your classroom and exit the building. Label windows and doors.

3 Test your fire escape plan. Does it show the best way to exit your classroom and leave the building? Does it explain how to behave while exiting? Could you improve the plan? Share your final plan with your classmates.

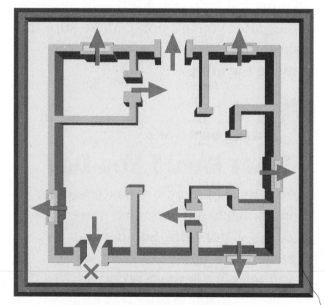

This escape plan shows possible exits and a meeting place in case of fire.

Planning Your Escape

Once a fire starts indoors, there is very little time to think about how to get out safely. It's a good idea to plan your fire escape ahead of time.

To be able to get out of a burning building safely, you need to know at least two ways out of every room. A floor plan, like the one pictured, shows all window and door exits. Your escape plan should include a meeting place outside the building. That way, you can be sure that everyone is safe.

Staying Safe During a Fire

If you are indoors when a fire starts, these rules can help you stay safe.

- Get out immediately, if possible. Never go back inside for any reason.

- Smoke rises. Crawl low under smoke. Cover your mouth and nose with a wet cloth to prevent choking.

- If a door feels warm to the back of your hand, the fire is very close. Don't open the door. Leave by another exit.

- If you can't leave by another exit, line doors with blankets or towels to keep smoke out.

- Open a window slightly. This will help you to breathe. Then you can shout for help.

- If your clothes are on fire, follow the "stop, drop, and roll" technique shown in these pictures. Stop everything, lie down, and roll on the ground.

STOP

DROP

ROLL

LESSON WRAP UP

Show What You Know

1. Name two pieces of safety equipment that can help prevent injuries from fire.

2. What safety rules should you follow during a fire?

3. **THINK CRITICALLY** Why is it always a good idea to have two fire escape routes planned?

Show What You Can Do

4. **PORTFOLIO** **APPLY HEALTH ACTIVITY Make Decisions** Make a map of the floor plan of your own home. Decide where smoke detectors and fire extinguishers are, or should be, placed. Draw two escape routes from your home.

5. **LIFE SKILL** **PRACTICE LIFE SKILLS Obtain Help** Find out which fire department number you should call in case of a fire. Add the number to your emergency phone list.

In this lesson, you will learn:

▶ safety rules to use in different places.

▶ how to protect yourself in heat, cold, and sunlight.

VOCABULARY

life preserver
(līf pri zûr′vər) a belt, vest, or ring made from a material that keeps a person afloat in water

sunscreen (sun′skrēn) a cream or lotion that blocks the sun's dangerous rays and prevents or minimizes sunburn

QUICK START You are swimming at a lake. Suddenly, there's a flash of lightning. What should you do?

What could be better on a hot day than a bike ride followed by a swim? The sun and water feel wonderful. However, they both can involve some dangers. Learning simple safety rules will allow you to stay safe as you enjoy many kinds of outdoor activities.

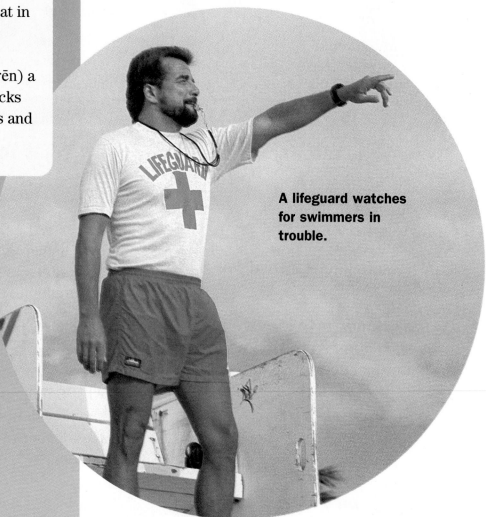

A lifeguard watches for swimmers in trouble.

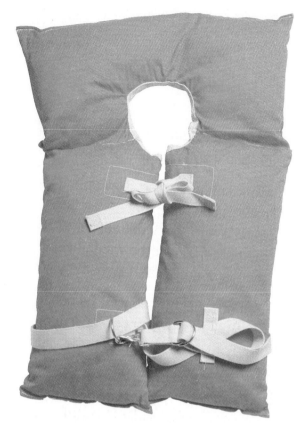

Life preservers save lives.

Safety Rules for Swimming

How many of these rules do you already know? Learn them all to stay safe while having fun in the water.

- Swim only where there is a lifeguard or an adult watching you.

- Learn to swim properly. If possible, take swimming lessons. Also, learn how to float.

- Read and follow all posted signs that explain swimming rules.

- Choose a swimming buddy and stay together. If one of you has a problem in the water, the buddy can help or get help.

- Do not swim too far or for too long. If you get tired or get leg cramps while swimming, leave the water. If you can't swim to shore, call loudly for help.

- If you hear thunder or see lightning, get out of the water immediately. Lightning can travel through water and injure swimmers.

- You should dive only in areas where a sign says it is safe to dive. Before you dive, check the conditions under the water. Make sure the water is deep enough. Look for rocks or other dangers.

- If you don't know how to swim, always wear a life preserver, or personal flotation device, when you are playing in or near the water. A **life preserver** is a belt, vest, or ring made from a material that can keep a person floating in water. It's always best to use a life preserver that is approved by the United States Coast Guard. In a boat, you should always wear a life preserver.

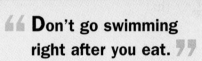

HEALTH FACT

❝ **Don't go swimming right after you eat.** ❞

This is true. You should wait at least an hour after you eat before going into the water. During that time, your stomach is busy digesting the food you ate. The blood that is usually in your arms and legs has moved to the stomach area. So your other muscles don't get enough blood. This makes it more likely that you will get cramps in your arms and legs. You may become tired more easily. You may also get an upset stomach.

HEALTH ACTIVITY
Sink or Float?

You will need: dishpan half-filled with water, equal-sized pieces of clay, balloon

1 Work with a partner. Blow up a balloon and tie it. Place it on the water's surface. What happens? Push the balloon under the water, hold it, then let it go. What happens? Why?

2 Roll one piece of clay into a ball. Press another as flat as possible. Put both pieces of clay on the water. What happens? Why?

3 Explain what these activities show about floating. How are your lungs like the balloon? How could you use your arms and legs to change your shape?

Helping Someone in the Water

Suppose your swimming buddy gets a leg cramp and can't swim to land. How can you help?

- Stay calm and call for help. Tell your buddy to be calm and to float. If your buddy can float on his or her back, it may be possible for you to gently rub the cramped area.

- Don't try to grab or hold onto your buddy, and don't try to swim while dragging your buddy. You could easily lose control and end up in an even more dangerous situation.

- If someone is in trouble in the water and you are on land, don't go into the water. You are only putting yourself in danger, too. And if you're in trouble yourself, you can't help someone else.

- If a life preserver or a flotation ring on a rope is nearby, throw it to the person. Hold on to something attached to the ground as you pull the person ashore. If there are no life preservers, use anything nearby that is long enough to reach the person, such as a pole, a tree branch, a shovel, or a towel.

Safety Rules for Bicycling

Bike riding is a favorite outdoor activity. Every year, however, more than 500,000 people are injured while bicycling. You can stay safe by following these rules.

- Make sure your bike is safe to ride. Both feet should touch the ground when you sit on the bike. Also, can you reach the brakes and handlebars easily? Do the brakes stop quickly and smoothly? Are the tires properly inflated, and have you tightened all loose screws? Does the bike have reflectors and a bell or horn?

- Always wear a helmet when riding a bicycle, even if it is not required where you live. A bicycle helmet could save your life!

- Always wear shoes, so that your feet won't slip off the pedals.

- It is always best to ride during the day. If you must ride at night, then wear brightly colored clothing with reflective stickers or patches. Also use rear reflectors and a headlight.

- Follow all traffic signs, especially stop signs. Signal all turns using the signals shown in the pictures below.

- Keep both hands on handlebars, except when signaling a turn.

- Never let anyone ride on your handlebars or ride behind you on your bike.

- Walk your bike across busy intersections.

- Ride on bike paths or sidewalks when possible. If you can't, ride near the curb on the right side of the road. Move in the same direction as traffic. Ride single file, not side by side.

- Watch for cars pulling out of parking spaces or driveways. Watch for car doors opening and for people crossing the street.

- Watch for weather conditions that can make the roads slippery.

LIFE SKILL

MAKE DECISIONS

What Would You Do?

You're riding your bike to the park. A friend runs up and asks you for a ride. What decision could you make so that both of you would stay safe?

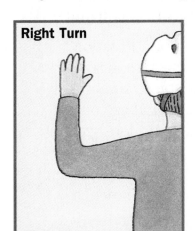

Right Turn

Left Turn

Stop

PLAYING IT SAFE
IN HOT AND COLD WEATHER

Hot Weather Safety

In the summer, high temperatures can be a problem. Following are some tips for keeping cool in hot weather.

- ✺ Wear light colors. Dark colors absorb heat from the sun. The cloth will heat up, and so will you!

- ✺ Wear loose clothes. Loose clothing allows your skin to stay cool.

- ✺ Wear a hat to help protect your face, scalp, and hair from sun damage and to keep your head from becoming too hot.

- ✺ Drink plenty of fluids to make up for water lost through sweating.

- ✺ Remember to use the proper sunscreen. A **sunscreen** is a skin cream or lotion that blocks the sun's dangerous rays. It prevents or minimizes burning.

Cold Weather Safety

Winter's low temperatures can be a problem, too. These tips will help protect you when the weather turns cold.

- ❄ Cover up before going into the cold. Your body loses heat through your skin.

- ❄ Dress in layers to trap body heat. If outer layers get wet from the rain or snow, take them off and put on new layers.

- ❄ Wear hats, gloves, and warm shoes or boots to hold in body heat.

- ❄ Wear dark, loose-fitting clothes. Heat absorbed by dark colors will build up in the layer of air between your skin and your clothes.

Rural Safety

People in rural areas—the countryside— might face hazards that other people don't. Following are a few rules for staying safe in rural areas.

- Only adults should operate farm equipment. Tractors and other machines can cause injuries if they are not used properly.

- Never allow extra riders on farm tractors or on other farm vehicles.

- Remember, never sit in the back of a moving pickup truck.

- Look carefully for oncoming traffic at road crossings. Even quiet road crossings can be dangerous.

- Never go near livestock, silos, or ponds unless there is adult supervision.

- Hazardous chemicals should be kept in secure, locked storage.

Playground Safety

Each year, nearly 200,000 children on playgrounds are injured seriously enough to need medical attention. Over three-fourths of all playground injuries are the result of falls or running into things. Here are some rules for playground safety.

- Play only within fenced areas of the playground.

- Play only in areas that are clear of stones, vines, bumpy tree roots, and other things that can cause injury.

- Do not play on broken playground equipment.

- Never play near a construction site or in an abandoned building.

Wherever you are—on a playground, in the water, or anywhere else outdoors— following simple safety rules will help you stay safe.

LESSON WRAP UP

Show What You Know

1. Name one safety rule that you should follow while swimming and one that you should follow while on a playground.

2. How can a hat protect you on a sunny day and on a cold day?

3. **THINK CRITICALLY** Suppose your family lives in a large city. Often, you go to visit friends on their farm in the country. Name three safety rules you would have to follow in both places.

Show What You Can Do

4. **APPLY HEALTH ACTIVITY**
   PORTFOLIO
   Science Connection Write an activity for your school's science club. Describe an experiment using toy blocks to find out why objects float or sink.

5. **PRACTICE LIFE SKILLS**
   Obtain Help Find out where in your community you can take swimming lessons.

In this lesson, you will learn:

▶ the difference between an emergency and a nonemergency.

▶ steps to follow during an emergency.

▶ first aid rules to treat minor injuries.

VOCABULARY

sprain (sprān) an injury caused by twisting muscles near a joint, such as the ankle or wrist

blister (blis′tər) a swelling of the skin filled with a watery fluid

QUICK START A friend collapses while playing and does not wake up. What should you do?

An *emergency* is any serious situation that requires immediate help. Minor injuries are not emergencies. When you have a small cut, nosebleed, or headache, you and your family can usually take care of the problem. But if the injury is an emergency, you would probably need outside help from a medical professional. Even minor injuries, however, should be handled under adult supervision.

A sprained ankle can be serious.

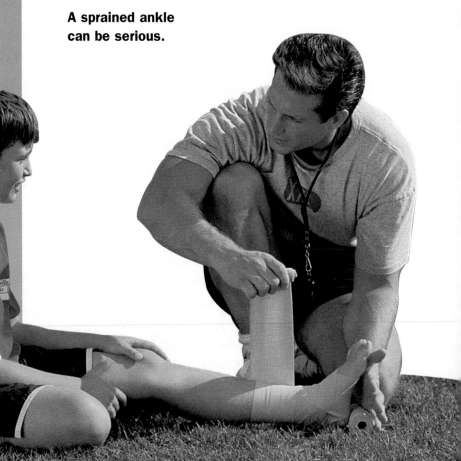

MINOR INJURIES
Slight headache
Scratches, scrapes, and small cuts
Small burns that turn red
Hurting your ankle a little
Coughing when you have a cold
Insect sting

SERIOUS INJURIES
Fainting or not being able to wake up after a fall
Cuts that are very deep or that don't stop bleeding
Deep burns that blister
Twisting your ankle so hard that you cannot move it
Having serious difficulty breathing
Allergic reaction including rash, swelling, and serious breathing problems

Minor and Serious Injuries

In the chart above you can see some of the differences between serious injuries and minor injuries. Serious injuries are emergencies. Minor injuries are nonemergencies.

What to Do in an Emergency

If there is an emergency, you need to contact emergency help. Tell a trusted adult what happened. If you are alone, call 911 or your local emergency number. Tell what happened, who is injured, and where you are. Mention street names and landmarks to help people find you. Stay on the phone until the operator tells you to hang up.

Until help arrives, follow these rules.

- Do not move an injured person. Moving an injured person can cause more harm.

- Cover the person with a blanket to keep him or her warm.

- Stay with the person. Talking can help the person stay calm. Say that help is coming.

Preparing for an Emergency

You never know when an emergency will happen, but you can still be prepared.

- Prepare an emergency supply kit. It should include a flashlight, extra batteries, and bottled water.

- Carry a card with your name, home address, and phone number.

- Watch for situations that can cause injuries.

- Always have a basic first aid kit on hand. Suggest to your parents that they keep one kit at home and another one in the car.

HEALTH FALLACY

" You don't need a doctor for a minor injury. "

This is not always true. Sometimes minor injuries become more serious. A minor cut might get infected and need a doctor's care. Headaches after a fall may seem minor but can mean more serious problems. Watch minor injuries carefully. If they don't get better quickly, see a doctor.

First Aid Kits

First aid kits are one good way to be prepared for an emergency. First aid kits contain a variety of items that help you treat minor injuries and handle other unexpected events.

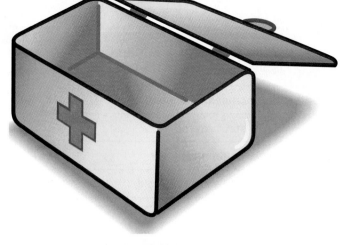

- **Soap** Use soap to clean cuts, scratches, and insect bites. Soap can also be used to wash sap from poisonous plants, such as poison ivy, off your skin.

- **Antibiotic Ointment** This ointment should be used on cuts and scrapes after they have been properly washed. This ointment helps keep wounds from becoming infected.

- **Instant Cold Pack** These packs contain chemicals that become cold when you squeeze them. Cold packs are perfect for treating sprains.

- **Sterile Bandage** Bandages come in many shapes and sizes. Sterile bandages are free of harmful germs and dirt. They should be placed over a cut, scrape, or burn after it has been properly cleaned.

- **Tweezers** Tweezers are useful for removing splinters, or small pieces of wood, that get stuck in your skin.

- **Latex Gloves** If you give first aid to another person, be sure not to touch their blood or wound with your bare hands. Some diseases are passed through blood from person to person. Keep a barrier, such as latex gloves, between yourself and the other person's blood.

Classroom Clinic

LIFE SKILL

MAKE DECISIONS

1 Work with a group in a "Classroom Clinic." Choose a role from this list—doctor, nurse, EMS worker, hiker, biker, runner.

2 Students who choose hiker, biker, or runner decide on their injuries. Each "patient" describes his or her symptoms to the "medical workers."

3 Students who choose doctor, nurse, or EMS worker decide what's wrong with each patient. They talk over the steps to follow in "treating" each patient.

4 If you like, change roles and try again. Talk about what you've learned.

EMERGENCIES ACT I

First Aid for Minor Injuries

Even with minor injuries, it is always important to let a trusted adult know what has happened. But if there is no adult nearby, keep these ideas in mind.

- Clean cut or scraped skin before putting on a bandage. This will help prevent an infection.

- Most insect stings are minor injuries. With a bee sting, it is important to remove the stinger as quickly as possible.

- A **sprain** happens when you twist a muscle near a joint. The area near the joint often swells and turns black and blue. If you think you have a sprain, don't get up. Call for help and put something cold on the sprain. Raise the injury above your heart to reduce the swelling. As soon as possible, wrap the area with an elastic bandage.

- If you burn your skin on a hot surface, gently apply cool water to the burned area and cover it with a loose bandage or cloth. Sometimes a burn can cause a **blister**—a swelling of the skin that looks like a bubble and is filled with watery fluid. Do not burst a blister. But if the blister breaks by itself you should wash it, pat it dry, and then apply a sterile bandage.

IF SOMEONE ELSE IS CHOKING	IF YOU ARE ALONE AND CHOKING

Wrap your arms around the person from the back. Make a fist with one hand and grasp it with the other.

Pull your fist into the person's stomach. Use quick, hard, upward pushes. Be sure not to press so hard that you break or injure a rib.

Lean with your stomach against the back of a steady chair.

Press against the chair with a quick, hard push. This will help force the food out of your throat. Be sure not to press so hard that you break or injure a rib.

First Aid for Choking

If food gets caught in your throat, it can block your airway. If someone cannot cough or speak, they may be choking. The steps in the chart above can help clear a person's airway. Do not practice them unless your teacher supervises you.

LIFE SKILL

OBTAIN HELP

What Would You Do?

You are eating a sandwich at home alone. A piece of food gets stuck in your throat and won't come out when you cough. What should you do?

LESSON WRAP UP

Show What You Know

1. Name one injury that is an emergency and one that is a nonemergency. What is the difference in how you would respond to these two injuries?

2. What three things should you tell a 911 operator in an emergency?

3. **THINK CRITICALLY** If you were the only other person around when someone was choking, which would you do first—call 911 or try to help the person? Explain your answer.

Show What You Can Do

4. **PORTFOLIO** **APPLY HEALTH ACTIVITY**
   Make Decisions Make a picture book for younger children. Teach them how to decide whether an injury is minor or an emergency.

5. **LIFE SKILL** **PRACTICE LIFE SKILLS**
   Set Goals Identify a career that involves responding to emergencies and giving first aid. What education would you need to get a job in this field?

TECHNOLOGY

Safe, Safer, Safest

Air bags inflate upon impact, protecting the passenger from injury.

Have you ridden in a car with an air bag? An air bag is a safety device that protects people in the front seat from injury in a front-end crash. It inflates like a big balloon upon impact.

In their first ten years of use, air bags probably saved over 1,000 lives. However, they had their dangers, too. A child or small adult could be badly hurt by the force of the inflating bag.

Car manufacturers put out the word—children age 12 and under should always ride in the back seat! The best place for an infant is in the rear-facing child safety seat buckled into the middle of the back seat. Other children should wear seat belts in the back seat.

Manufacturers also went to work to design a "smart air bag." One smart bag detects whether a child safety seat is being used in the front seat. If it is, the air bag shuts off automatically. Other smart bags adjust the force of inflation depending on the size of the passenger.

SCIENCE CONNECTION
THE SAFEST CAR YET

What else could be done to improve automobile safety? Design your own version of the safest car yet. Draw it or model it in clay and label its special safety features. Then display your car for the class and explain how it could help save lives.

9 REVIEW

VOCABULARY

Write the word or words from the box that best completes each sentence. Use each word only once.

conflict

first aid

hazard

respectful touch

sprain

sunscreen

violence

weapon

1. An overloaded electrical outlet is a(n) __?__. (Lesson 1)

2. A(n) __?__ can be resolved in a nonviolent way. (Lesson 2)

3. A handshake is an example of a(n) __?__. (Lesson 3)

4. Wearing __?__ can help keep your skin from burning. (Lesson 5)

5. Twisting a muscle near a joint can cause a(n) __?__. (Lesson 6)

REVIEW HEALTH IDEAS

Use your knowledge of safety, injury, and violence prevention from Chapter 9 to answer these questions.

1. Why is it important to keep staircases free of clutter? (Lesson 1)

2. What are some safety rules about riding in a car? (Lesson 1)

3. What can you do to try to prevent falls? (Lesson 1)

4. Why should you never pick up a gun or point it at anyone? (Lesson 2)

5. What should you say to a caller who asks if you're home alone? (Lesson 3)

6. What should you do if your clothing catches fire? (Lesson 4)

7. How can you protect yourself from the sun if you're invited to swim outdoors? (Lesson 5)

8. What is one thing you can do to help a friend who has fallen into the water? (Lesson 5)

9. What should you do if a friend is choking? (Lesson 6)

10. Why is it important to know what to do when someone is hurt? (Lesson 6)

APPLY HEALTH IDEAS

1. Why should you never leave the kitchen while you are cooking? (Lesson 4)

2. Why should both beginning and experienced bicycle riders wear safety helmets? (Lesson 5)

3. What are some differences between a minor injury and an emergency? (Lessons 1 and 6)

4. **PORTFOLIO** **PRACTICE REFUSAL SKILLS** Suppose you are home alone. Someone you have seen once or twice asks to come in. Write a skit about what you would do. (Lesson 3)

5. **LIFE SKILL** **RESOLVE CONFLICTS** Write a letter to your school's principal. Suggest rules to follow if a conflict occurs at school. Explain the reasons for these rules. (Lesson 2)

YOUR HEALTH AT HOME

Which rules from Chapter 9 can you use at home every day?

Take a sheet of paper and label it with the headings shown at the right.

Make a list of rules for everyone in your family to follow and use. Make time to talk to your family about what you've learned and why it's important. Decide on a place to post your rules.

Resolving Conflicts | Preventing Fire | Preventing Injuries

Write <u>True</u> or <u>False</u> for each statement. If false, change the underlined word or phrase to make it true.

1. Most rules in your life are meant to <u>keep you from having fun.</u>

2. <u>Fighting</u> is one way to help people reach solutions without violence.

3. If a stranger calls the house, <u>do not let him or her know you are alone.</u>

4. You should <u>not say anything</u> if someone touches you in a way that makes you feel uncomfortable.

5. A smoke detector can <u>put out a fire.</u>

6. If there is a fire in your house, <u>crawl beneath the smoke.</u>

7. It's a good idea to ride <u>side by side</u> when bicycling with a friend.

8. If you see a man struggling in the water, <u>jump in to help him.</u>

9. In an <u>emergency</u>, you should call 911 or your local emergency number.

10. <u>Tweezers, rubbing alcohol, and bandages</u> are important things to include in a first aid kit.

Write a sentence or two to answer each question.

11. How can you help a person who is receiving an electric shock?

12. What can you do to stay safe if you find a gun?

13. What is one example of a respectful touch?

14. How would you go about making a fire escape plan?

15. What should you do if you hear thunder while you are swimming?

16. When the temperature is very cold, how should you dress to avoid harm?

17–19. Name three situations that would be considered emergencies.

20. When you make a 911 call, what should you tell the operator?

/ **Performance Assessment**

Pretend that you are chosen to prepare your club for a camping trip. Make a checklist for club members. The list should include what clothes to bring and what first aid equipment is needed.

COMMUNITY AND ENVIRONMENTAL HEALTH

CHAPTER 10

THE BIG IDEA

The health of the community and the environment depends on:

- individual people.
- families.
- groups of people working together.

In this lesson, you will learn:

▶ how health care workers and health care facilities meet community needs.

▶ how health departments help maintain healthy communities.

VOCABULARY

outpatient
(out′pā′shənt) a patient admitted to a hospital or other health care facility for treatment and release the same day

health department
(helth di pärt′mənt) a local or state government agency that promotes community health

immunizations
(im′yə ni zā′shənz) vaccines to prevent certain diseases

outbreak (out′brāk) a sudden increase in the number of people with a disease or illness

QUICK START Suppose you injure your eye. Your mother calls your family doctor. Who else in your community could she call for help?

In some ways, you are responsible for your own health. You choose what to eat or how to be physically active. It is up to you to tell a parent or other trusted adult when you feel sick.

Adults in your family and community also play a part in keeping you healthy. They may cook healthful meals for you. They may take you to the doctor for checkups. They may work at health care jobs or at jobs that protect the environment. They all have one thing in common—they help to keep you and others in your community safe and healthy.

Your parents influence your health in many ways.

Health Care Workers

Many people in your community work to help you stay healthy. You might visit a doctor when you feel ill. Sometimes you might need the help of a *specialist* to treat a certain illness. A specialist is a doctor who has a lot of training and experience with certain illnesses or health problems. For example, an ear, nose, and throat specialist has a lot of experience with such illnesses as ear infections, sore throats, and colds.

Often, your regular doctor can provide the name of a specialist to see. Friends who have had a similar illness might be able to suggest a specialist. Health care organizations, local hospitals, or medical schools can usually help you to find a specialist. Specialists can also be found in the phone book.

A doctor is only one of many health care workers who can help you. The table below tells about other health care workers and what they do.

Health Care Workers and Their Jobs	
Title	**Role**
doctor	knows about health; treats illnesses; advises about health
medical specialist	treats only particular kinds of diseases or illnesses
pediatrician	treats babies and children
counselor, therapist	helps people by discussing their health problems with them
dentist	treats and takes care of teeth
dietitian	manages food preparation
physician assistant	performs routine medical procedures under a doctor's supervision
nurse, nurse practitioner	takes care of sick or injured people; assists doctors
pharmacist	prepares and distributes medicines according to a doctor's orders
emergency medical service worker, paramedic	assists people in a medical emergency

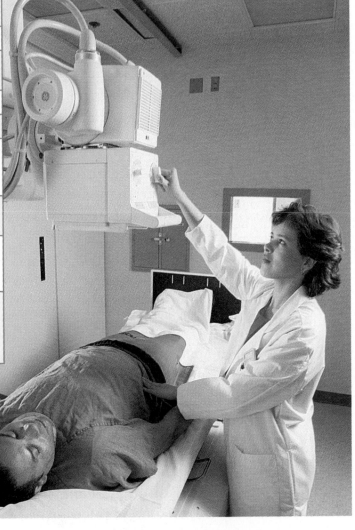

Doctors, physician assistants, and nurses are some of the health care workers who can help you stay healthy.

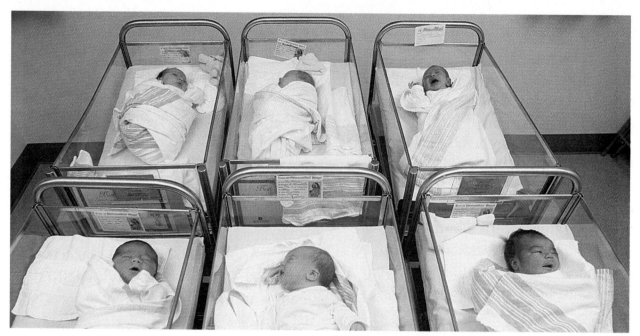

Many babies are born in hospitals, where special care
can be given immediately if needed.

Hospitals

Sometimes a person needs treatment
that cannot be given at home or in a
doctor's office. The person may need
emergency medical care, special tests,
or an operation. A person who needs
special treatment may have to stay in
a hospital.

As you know, there are regular
doctors and doctors who specialize in
certain illnesses. Similarly, there are
regular hospitals and hospitals that
specialize—in certain kinds of patients,
or in certain diseases. For example,
there are hospitals that treat only
children and hospitals that treat
only cancer patients.

In a hospital, the patient is cared for
daily by doctors, nurses, and other health
care workers. Usually, the patient stays
for several days or longer.

Sometimes, a person is treated as an
outpatient. An **outpatient** is a patient
admitted to a hospital or other health
care facility for treatment and released

the same day. Often, an outpatient must
make a return visit to the facility to
make sure he or she is getting better.

HEALTHWISE CONSUMER

Saving on Health Care

People make many choices about their
health care. Sometimes their choices
can save them money. For example,
your library might have free health
care information. Your doctor or a
local health care facility might have
free brochures.

Even when people are ill or hurt, they
can often make choices about their
care. Outpatient treatment usually
costs less than inpatient treatment.
Less-expensive generic versions of
over-the-counter medicines are often
available. With your doctor's permission,
a pharmacist might be able to fill your
prescription with a generic version of
the medicine you need.

Other Health Care Facilities

Everyone needs health care. A person may be ill or hurt—or may just need protection from the spread of a disease. There are probably many facilities in your community that provide for most people's health care needs. Some kinds of health care facilities are shown on the chart below.

OBTAIN HELP

What Would You Do?

As you ride your bicycle home one evening, you hit a bump and fall. You try to get up, but you can't stand on your left leg. Where might an adult take you to obtain help at this time of day?

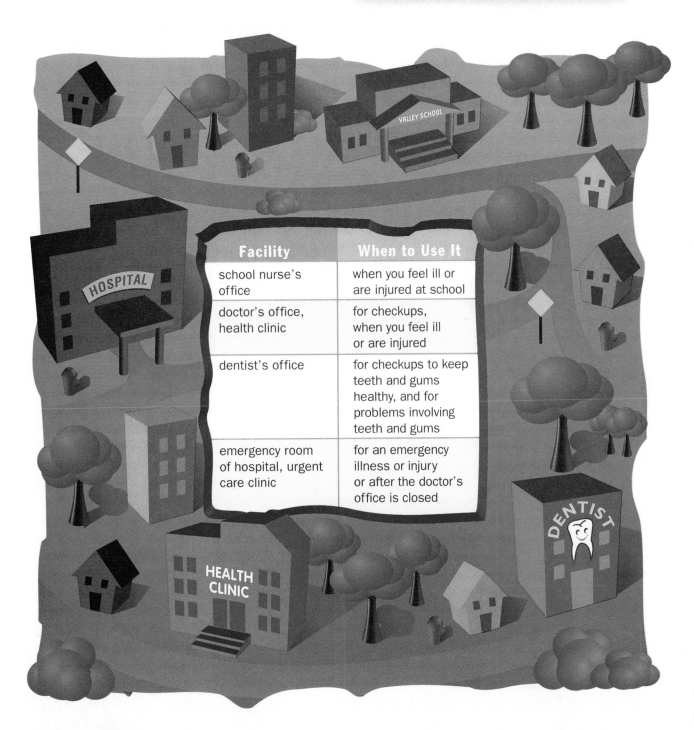

Facility	When to Use It
school nurse's office	when you feel ill or are injured at school
doctor's office, health clinic	for checkups, when you feel ill or are injured
dentist's office	for checkups to keep teeth and gums healthy, and for problems involving teeth and gums
emergency room of hospital, urgent care clinic	for an emergency illness or injury or after the doctor's office is closed

Health Departments

Health departments are local or state government agencies that promote community health. Preventing the spread of disease is an important goal of health departments. To reach this goal, health departments prepare health guidelines for the community. These sometimes become laws. For example, there are laws stating that all children must get some immunizations before they start school. **Immunizations** are vaccines to prevent certain diseases. When your parents took you to get your immunizations, they were obeying these laws.

Health departments also watch for any **outbreak** of disease—a sudden increase in the number of people with a disease or illness. Suppose a restaurant served some spoiled fish, and everyone who ate it got sick. Health workers would talk to the people who reported the same symptoms, to discover what they did that was the same. The source of the outbreak could then be traced to the restaurant and the fish it served.

Educating the public about staying healthy is another important job health departments do. Your doctor may have some free health department booklets that tell about diseases and how to stay healthy.

Health departments serve their communities in many other ways, too. They might offer free emergency medical care, supply special services, or have programs for people with financial needs. They may also offer treatment and support for drug-addicted people and their families. Health departments can do a lot to help create a healthy community!

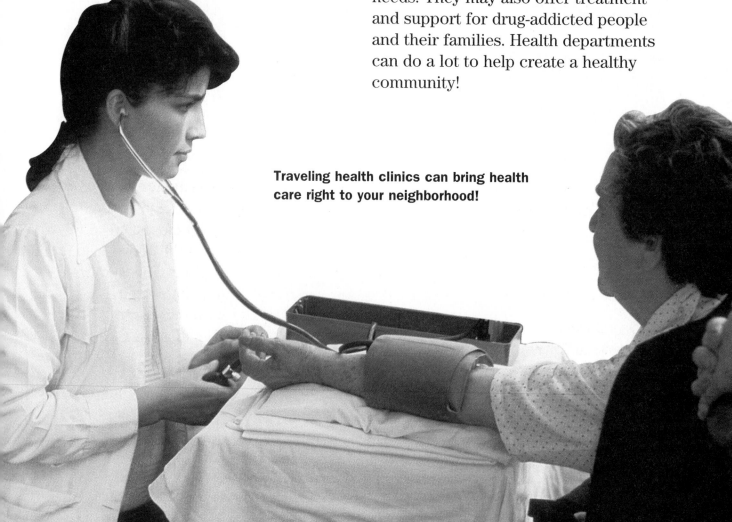

Traveling health clinics can bring health care right to your neighborhood!

Help in a Pinch

OBTAIN HELP

You will need: colored stick pins, local map, local phone book

1 Work in a group. Look in your local phone book for places that provide emergency medical services at or near your school.

2 List all the places you find. Choose a certain color stick pin for the hospitals. Choose another color for clinics and other services.

3 Place a stick pin on the map at each location. Figure out which emergency care service would be used if someone needed to obtain help quickly.

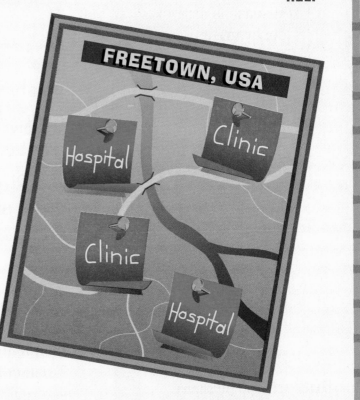

FREETOWN, USA

Hospital

Clinic

Clinic

Hospital

LESSON WRAP UP

Show What You Know

1. Name one type of community health care worker. Describe the role or job of this worker.

2. Name one type of health care facility and describe its role.

3. **THINK CRITICALLY** Why would it be important for a health department to find out the source of an outbreak?

Show What You Can Do

4. **PORTFOLIO** **APPLY HEALTH ACTIVITY**
   Obtain Help Find the health care facility closest to your home. Write down the address and phone number. Then write a short paragraph explaining why it is important to know where to get help in case of an emergency.

5. **PRACTICE LIFE SKILLS**
   Make Decisions Choose one of the health careers mentioned in this lesson. Make a list of reasons why you might like that job.

2 PUBLIC HEALTH LAWS AND SERVICES

In this lesson, you will learn:

▶ about guidelines and laws in your community that help protect your health.

▶ how community members and facilities help keep the environment safe and clean.

VOCABULARY

pollution (pə lü′shən) unhealthful substances that make the air, water, or soil dirty or impure

reduce (ri düs′) to decrease the number of things you throw out

reuse (rē ūz′) to find a new use for something that might otherwise be thrown out

recycle (rē sī′kəl) to set certain types of trash aside to be made into other products

QUICK START You are just finishing lunch with a friend at a park. You have a couple of cans, plastic wrap, and the paper bags you brought your lunch in. You don't see a trash can nearby. What would you do?

Communities pass public health laws and provide services designed to keep people in the community safe and healthy. Trash collection is one service that you may see regularly. But you may not know about the many other ways the health of your community is protected.

Trash collectors help protect your health.

A clean environment contributes to everyone's health—and enjoyment!

Keeping the Community Clean

People do things that add pollution to the environment. Fumes from cars pollute the air. Sewage may pollute water and land. **Pollution** includes unhealthful substances that do not naturally occur in the air, in water, or on land. Plants, animals, and people exposed to pollution may get sick.

Many communities have laws to help prevent pollution. For example, there are laws that prevent businesses from polluting. Most communities do not allow people to litter. Pet owners are required to clean up after their pets in most neighborhoods. These laws help eliminate the bacteria and poisons that arise from trash and other waste.

As you learned in Chapter 8, passive smoke can harm people who do not smoke. Some communities have laws that prohibit smoking in public buildings. Such laws help protect people from being exposed to harmful substances that can be released into the air from cigarette smoke.

MAKE DECISIONS

What Would You Do?

Suppose you and a friend are playing in a park. You see someone else litter. What would you do?

Water and Sewage Facilities

If you live in a rural area, you might get your water from a well on your own land. This water is pumped from underground. Then it is piped into a water storage tank, usually located in your basement. It stays there until you turn on the tap.

Since well water is usually clean, there is no need to filter it, or clean it. But it is important to test your well water from time to time, to make sure it has not become polluted.

If you live in a small or large city, you probably get your water from city pipes. City water usually comes from nearby rivers, lakes, or streams. Because these sources of water are often polluted, the water must be cleaned before you use it.

City water is cleaned in a water treatment plant. Water is pumped from local sources into large tanks. Wastes are removed, and chemicals are added to kill disease-causing microbes.

Once the water has been cleaned, air is often pushed through it to help get rid of unpleasant smells or tastes. The clean water is stored in large tanks for use by the people living in the city.

Many communities pipe *sewage*—liquid waste, either from households or from public facilities—to a waste treatment plant. There, the dirty water is treated to remove harmful substances. When the water is clean, it is piped back into local lakes or rivers. Unlike sewage, this clean water does not pollute the environment.

This water treatment plant cleans water for the people of Chicago and some of its suburbs. Located on Lake Michigan, the plant can clean almost 2 billion gallons of water a day.

Solid Waste Disposal

Have you ever thrown out a peach pit, a plastic bag, or some old rags? If so, you have created *solid waste*. Solid waste is any solid material, including garbage and trash, that is thrown out. Businesses, farms, and governments—as well as individuals—create a lot of solid wastes.

Solid wastes are usually taken to a dump. If you live in a rural area, someone in your family probably takes the garbage to a local dump. If you live in a city, your garbage is most likely collected by sanitation workers, put in a truck, and then hauled to a dump.

Disposing of solid wastes in open dumps can create problems for the community. Rotting garbage causes foul smells, attracts harmful insects and rodents, and is very unpleasant to look at. Many communities have outlawed open dumps. Instead, they might take solid waste to a *landfill*.

In a landfill, land is built up by dumping solid wastes and covering them with dirt. Each day, solid wastes are dumped, then tractors pack the material tightly and cover it with soil. When the landfill site is full, the community covers the area with even more soil. Eventually, the landfill can be used to make a park or to build homes on.

Another way to dispose of solid wastes is to burn them. Some communities have built *incinerators*, facilities that burn trash. But if products containing harmful chemicals are burned, the ash and smoke produced may contain poisons. If these poisons are released into the air, they may be harmful to breathe and might cause health problems.

There are no easy solutions to solid waste problems. The best answer is to create as little trash as you can. Try to reuse and recycle as much as you can.

HEALTH FALLACY

" Using batteries is safe for the environment. "

This is not always the case. Dead batteries that aren't rechargeable are thrown out and become solid waste. Most of these batteries contain mercury, a dangerous metal. At some point, the discarded batteries will leak the mercury into the soil. It can then travel to water supplies used by people.

If possible, use rechargeable batteries. Ask your local recycling center or sanitation department how to get rid of batteries that cannot be recharged.

READY 4U

SUPERCHARGE

Reduce, Reuse, Recycle

There are three important things everyone can do to help solve solid waste problems: reduce, reuse, and recycle as much as possible. Here are some tips.

REDUCE

You can *reduce*, or decrease, the number of things you throw out.

🌿 Buy products in large quantities, to reduce the amount of packaging you have to get rid of.

🌿 Buy products that are not harmful to the environment. Check the packaging for information about the product's impact on the environment.

REUSE

You can *reuse*, or find a new use, for something that might otherwise be thrown out.

🌿 Reuse paper bags when you go shopping. Or carry your own cloth bag to the supermarket and fill it with your purchases.

🌿 Reuse empty food bottles and cans to store household items.

🌿 Reuse old or torn sheets and towels as cleaning rags.

RECYCLE

Some types of trash can be *recycled*, or made into other products. Most communities have recycling facilities.

🌿 Buy products that are packaged in materials that can be reused, refilled, or recycled. Packages made from glass, paper or cardboard, and aluminum are good choices. Packages made from plastic are not.

🌿 Buy products that have the recycling symbol on the package. These products are made with recycled materials. If you use them, you will help reduce the amount of solid waste in the environment.

🌿 Find out about your community's recycling rules. Recycle everything you can.

HEALTH ACTIVITY
Waste No Time

1 Work in groups of three. Look for ways to reduce solid waste at your school. Consider things in your classroom that could be used less, reused, or recycled.

2 List things that all students could do to reduce waste. Set these as goals in your classroom.

3 Present these goals to younger students. Be sure to explain why reducing solid waste is important for a clean, healthful environment.

LESSON WRAP UP

Show What You Know

1. Name two laws that many communities have to protect the health of their citizens.

2. How does a water treatment plant help make water safe for people to use? What can you do to help keep water safe?

3. **THINK CRITICALLY** Most people talk about throwing used things "away." Is there really such a place as "away," where garbage can be sent? Explain your answer.

Show What You Can Do

4. **APPLY HEALTH ACTIVITY**
   Set Goals Design a poster to promote the goals of reducing, reusing, and recycling. Explain why these goals are important.

5. **PRACTICE LIFE SKILLS**
   Resolve Conflicts Your brother has a big box of things to throw away. You think he could find uses for some of them. He says, "I don't want to be bothered." How can you resolve the conflict?

In this lesson, you will learn:

▶ the effects of pollution on people's health.

▶ why Earth needs to be protected, and some ways to protect it.

VOCABULARY

emission (i mish′ən) a substance that is released into the air, such as smoke from a factory smokestack or exhaust from a bus or car

acid rain (as′id rān) rain that contains high levels of dangerous chemicals that can harm the environment

ozone layer (ō′zōn lā′ər) a naturally occurring layer of a special kind of oxygen in Earth's atmosphere; keeps some of the sun's harmful rays from reaching Earth

natural resource (nach′ər əl rē′sôrs) a substance or organism found in nature that is useful or necessary for life, such as water

QUICK START You're walking along a street. You notice a lot of gray smoke with a bad smell coming from the tailpipe of a bus. What can you do to protect your health?

Everyone shares the same environment. Everyone has the responsibility of taking care of it. Pollution causes stress, breathing problems, some forms of cancer, and other health risks. Protecting the "health" of the land, air, and water helps protect the health of the people living there.

Smog—smoke combined with fog—is a common sign of air pollution.

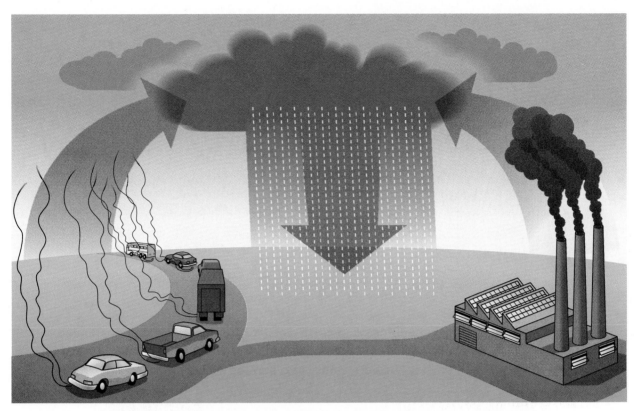

Acid rain can destroy crops and kill trees. How could this affect you?

Air Pollution

Automobiles burn gasoline. This causes emissions. An **emission** is a substance released into the air, such as smoke from a factory chimney or exhaust from a bus or car. Gasoline contains substances that—when burned—make car exhaust unhealthful.

Carbon monoxide is a poisonous gas that is produced when a motor vehicle burns fuel. Some factory emissions also contain a lot of carbon monoxide. Cigarette smoke has carbon monoxide in it. You can't smell, taste, or see this gas. If you breathe it in, however, it reduces the amount of oxygen your red blood cells can carry. This is very bad for your health.

Smog is a combination of smoke and fog. It's the thick, gray air that results when a lot of emissions are chemically changed by sunlight. Smog contains substances that hurt your lungs if you breathe them in. People who constantly breathe in smog have a higher risk of developing lung diseases.

The emissions produced by cars and coal-burning factories cause acid rain. **Acid rain** is rain that contains high levels of chemicals that can harm the environment. The emissions pollute the air, and the air pollutes the rain.

LIFE SKILL

PRACTICE REFUSAL SKILLS

What Would You Do?

Your community is under a smog alert. A friend calls and asks you to go out to play. What would you say to refuse?

Water from rain and other sources can carry weed-killing chemicals and pesticides into surface water, such as rivers. Chemicals and other wastes poured down a drain will travel into sewers. Sewers empty into surface water, too.

A Layer of Protection

Older refrigerators, air conditioners, and products in spray cans used chemicals called chlorofluorocarbons, or CFCs. Scientists have learned that CFCs are destroying the ozone layer. The **ozone layer** is a naturally occurring layer of a special type of oxygen in the atmosphere.

The ozone layer keeps some of the sun's harmful rays from reaching Earth. CFCs react with the ozone high in the air and destroy it. When ozone is destroyed, the harmful rays from the sun can come through to Earth's surface.

The atmosphere over some parts of Earth now has holes where ozone used to be. The sun's harmful rays make some people who live in these regions sick from diseases such as skin cancer. Laws have been passed to stop the use of CFCs. Many companies have obeyed these laws. Scientists are hoping that the ozone layer will get better.

Effects of Surface Water Pollution

Water pollution can affect people in different ways. Suppose you want to go to the beach, but it is closed because sewage is in the water and on the sand. Any contact with this pollution could make you sick.

Water pollution can affect what you eat. You might not find your favorite kind of fish at the market, because they were poisoned by river pollution. If you eat the fish, you could be poisoned too. Many people who fish for a living have no work, because there are fewer healthy fish to be caught.

Today there is less surface water pollution than there used to be. There are more laws against polluting water. People are also more aware of how surface water can be polluted. As a result, they are trying harder to avoid polluting it.

Groundwater Pollution

There is another kind of water pollution that is harder to control. Suppose you live in the country, near a big farm. The farmer sprays the fields with pesticides—chemicals that kill insects. When it rains, the pesticides seep into the soil.

If there is groundwater beneath the soil, it will be poisoned by the pesticides. Groundwater flows under the ground. The polluted groundwater may flow from the farm to your home's well, polluting your drinking water.

It is almost impossible to clean up polluted groundwater. Even if the farmer stopped using pesticides tomorrow, it might take about 6,000 years before the groundwater in your well would be pure again.

Other Forms of Pollution

Litter and other land pollution can be dangerous to health because of the bacteria and poisons that can come with it. Another form of pollution is noise pollution. Loud noise can damage hearing and cause stress. What are some things that might cause noise pollution where you live?

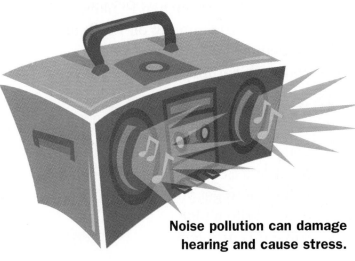

Noise pollution can damage hearing and cause stress.

Protecting Earth

Earth is made up of **natural resources**—natural substances or organisms that are useful or necessary for life. Soil, water, plants, and animals are all natural resources. People often overuse, destroy, and pollute natural resources. In time, some resources, such as coal and oil, may be all used up. The land might be destroyed.

A damaged Earth endangers all who depend on it. But people can take the following actions to help protect Earth's natural resources.

- Reduce, reuse, and recycle.

- Use renewable energy sources that do not run out or are easily replaced, such as the sun or the wind.

- Use energy sources that don't pollute.

Protecting natural resources will help save what is left of the natural world. Then you—and all living things—will enjoy a healthy environment.

HEALTH ACTIVITY
Digging for Coal

You will need: a chocolate chip cookie, a toothpick

1 Imagine that your cookie is Earth's surface. The chocolate chips are "coal" buried in it.

2 Pretend you are a coal miner. Use the toothpick to remove all the coal.

3 Write down what happened to your cookie as you dug for the chocolate chips. What does this tell you about how Earth could be changed by coal mining? How might people be affected? Discuss your findings with your class.

LESSON WRAP UP

Show What You Know

1. Choose one form of pollution. Make a list of possible health problems this form of pollution could cause.

2. Why is it important to protect Earth's natural resources? In what ways can these natural resources be protected?

3. **THINK CRITICALLY** How can using renewable energy sources help save Earth's natural resources?

Show What You Can Do

4. **PORTFOLIO** **APPLY HEALTH ACTIVITY**
   Science Connection Write a letter to your teacher. Explain the impact of coal mining on Earth and on people. Tell how people can conserve natural resources.

5. **LIFE SKILL** **PRACTICE LIFE SKILLS**
   Resolve Conflicts Suppose your brother is playing his drums for band practice. You're upset because you have to get your homework done. Write a plan or schedule to solve this problem.

CAREERS

Emergency Room Pediatrician

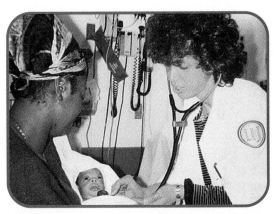

Dr. Nancy Rosenblum, Emergency Room Pediatrician

Q: Dr. Rosenblum, what are some of the most common problems that bring children to the emergency room?

DR. ROSENBLUM: The most common thing is asthma [breathing difficulty], which is on the increase. Then I'd have to say fevers caused by viruses.

Q: How do you treat a high fever?

DR. ROSENBLUM: Fever is a sign that something is wrong. We have to identify the source of the fever and treat it.

Q: What's the best way for kids to stay out of the emergency room?

DR. ROSENBLUM: They should see their own pediatricians regularly and get the screening and vaccinations they need. Injury prevention programs are also important—things like wearing helmets when biking or roller-skating, for example.

LIFE SKILL
SET GOALS
MAKE A PLAN FOR GOOD HEALTH

Dr. Rosenblum suggested a few ways that children can stay healthy and safe. What are some other ways to stay safe? On a piece of paper, set some goals for your good health. List five things you can start to do today that could keep you out of the emergency room in the future.

VOCABULARY

Write the word or words from the box that best completes each sentence.

emission

immunizations

natural resources

outbreaks

outpatient

ozone layer

pollution

recycle

1. Health departments watch for any unusual ___?___ of disease. (Lesson 1)

2. Putting harmful substances into the air and water causes ___?___. (Lesson 2)

3. You can reduce the amount of trash you produce if you ___?___. (Lesson 2)

4. What comes out of a factory smokestack is called a(n) ___?___. (Lesson 3)

5. The part of the atmosphere that blocks out harmful rays from the sun is the ___?___. (Lesson 3)

REVIEW HEALTH IDEAS

Use your knowledge of community and environmental health from Chapter 10 to answer these questions.

1. What does a medical specialist do? (Lesson 1)

2. When would you need emergency medical care? (Lesson 1)

3. How do health departments help prevent the spread of disease? (Lesson 1)

4. What are two laws that keep a community safe and clean? (Lesson 2)

5. What city facility treats polluted water to make it safe to drink? (Lesson 2)

6. Why are incinerators not the perfect solution to our solid waste problems? (Lesson 2)

7. How can breathing smog in affect your health? (Lesson 3)

8. Why are holes in the ozone layer damaging to people's health? (Lesson 3)

9. What are some effects of noise pollution? (Lesson 3)

10. What are some ways that Earth's natural resources can be protected? (Lesson 3)

APPLY HEALTH IDEAS

1. Why is it important that health departments find the sources of an outbreak of illness? (Lesson 1)

2. How might building a lot of new houses and apartments in your area affect your community's landfill? (Lesson 2)

3. Why might it be a good idea to use a carbon monoxide detector to tell you when there is carbon monoxide in your house? (Lesson 3)

4. **PORTFOLIO** **PRACTICE REFUSAL SKILLS** Some of your friends tease you because you refuse to litter. Write a paragraph explaining why you refuse to litter. Include at least three reasons. (Lessons 2 and 3)

5. **LIFE SKILLS** **OBTAIN HELP** You and your sister order the same meal at a restaurant. Later you both get ill and call a doctor. Who else should be notified? Why? (Lesson 1)

What did you learn in Chapter 10 that you can use at home every day?

Take a sheet of paper and label it with the headings shown.

Make a list of things your whole family can do to reduce, reuse, and recycle. Take time to talk to your family about what you have learned and why it is important. Post your list of ideas where the whole family can see it.

Things I Can Reduce (Use Less of)	Things I Can Reuse	Things I Can Recycle

Write True or False for each statement. If false, change the underlined word or phrase to make it true.

1. Educating the public about health is an important job for <u>water treatment plants</u>.

2. Picking up after your dog <u>is not</u> a way to protect the environment.

3. When released into the air, <u>CFCs</u> can destroy the ozone layer of the atmosphere.

4. The survival of fish and other animals living in rivers may depend a lot on <u>sewage treatment plants</u>.

5. Some companies make products out of used tires. This is an example of <u>solid waste</u>.

6. Coal and oil are examples of <u>natural resources</u>.

7. A health care worker who manages food preparation is a <u>pediatrician</u>.

8. There is a limited supply of oil in the world, which means this fuel is <u>renewable</u>.

9. The <u>ozone layer</u> protects us from harmful rays from the sun.

10. Burning coal causes <u>acid rain</u>.

Write a sentence to answer each question.

11–12. What are two things health departments do that improve public health?

13. How can lawn pesticides poison groundwater?

14. Describe the job of a counselor.

15. Why should everyone try to protect Earth's natural resources?

16. What are some results of using natural resources?

17. What are some things you can do to help reduce solid waste?

18. What are some ways to find emergency medical services in your community?

19–20. What are two sources of energy that are renewable?

/ **Performance Assessment**

 Suppose you belong to a group that wants to conserve natural resources. A paper company plans to cut down a huge forest. Write a letter explaining all of the effects of destroying the forest. Share your letter with the class.

![Life Skills logo] # HANDBOOK

Life Skill 1: Make Decisions

You make decisions every day. Some are pretty small, but even small decisions can affect your health. How much time will you spend brushing your teeth? Will you jog after school today or get home early to watch TV?

Other decisions may have a big impact on your health. When you have to make an important decision, you can follow the steps below to help you decide wisely.

Life Skill 1

MAKE DECISIONS

1. Name a decision you need to make.

2. List possible choices.

3. Think about the possible results of each choice. Which results are healthful? Are any results harmful to your health?

4. Think about your family's values. Which choices are in keeping with them?

5. Make a decision and take action.

6. Review your decision. Did your decision lead to the result you expected?

Practice Life Skills

Kerry has a few free hours every Saturday morning. He is trying to decide whether to join a local soccer team or take drum lessons. His decision will affect how he spends his weekends for months to come.

Kerry used the six decision making steps. He wrote down his ideas in the following way.

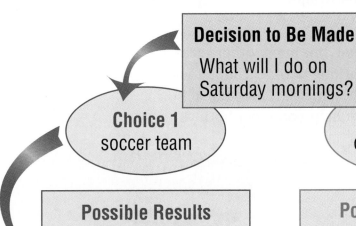

Decision to Be Made

What will I do on Saturday mornings?

Choice 1
soccer team

Choice 2
drum lessons

Possible Results

physical activity
meet new friends
improve my soccer skills
develop teamwork

Possible Results

learn a new instrument
play in a band when
    I'm ready
music helps me express
    myself

Consider Values

I'll keep fit.
I'll have fun.

Consider Values

I might annoy my new
    neighbors.
I'll have fun.

Decision

I'll join the soccer team because I really want to meet some new friends right away, plus the exercise is good for me.

MAKE DECISIONS

What Would You Do?

You've been working with a study group Mondays and Wednesdays to improve your grades. Now your club wants you to help out in a community center Mondays after school. Use the six steps to decide what you would do, and why.

Life Skill 2: Set Goals

A goal is something you wish to achieve. You might set a goal to be a great baseball pitcher or a terrific singer. Each of these goals takes more than just wishing. Achieving a goal takes work.

Many of your goals are personal, but many others are group goals. When you are working with a group, it is important to consider everyone's ideas. A six-step action plan—like the one below—can help you meet both your personal and your group goals.

Life Skill 2

SET GOALS

1. Choose one specific goal and write it down. It can be a small goal or a larger, long-term goal.

2. Decide what steps you will do to reach the goal.

3. List who can help and support you.

4. Set a time limit to reach your goal.

5. Check how you are doing several times before the time limit is up.

6. Reward yourself when you have reached your goal.

Practice Life Skills

During an afternoon break, Maria and two friends notice the snacks that many people in their class are eating. Chocolate bars and greasy chips are the clear favorites.

The three girls talk about the situation and decide they want to do something about it. They set a goal to hold a snack fair to help other students learn about healthful snacks. They use the six-step action plan to organize their thoughts.

1. Goal

Get people to eat healthful snacks.

2. Steps We Will Take

Plan to hold a snack fair.

3. Who Can Help

Students and parents can give ideas for healthful snacks. Teachers can arrange for school space.

4. Time Limit

We'll have a healthful snack fair in four weeks.

6. Rewards

We get to be the judges and taste all the snacks!

5. Checkpoints

Week 1: Talk to everyone about ideas and needs.
Week 2: Decide who'll do what.
Week 3: Review plans. Identify trouble spots.
Week 4: Prepare snacks and fair tables.

SET GOALS

What Would You Do?

You want to be a professional dancer. How can an action plan help you reach your goal? What are some short-term goals you can set to help you reach the long-term goal? Tell how you might reach any of these short-term goals.

Life Skill 3: Obtain Help

Obtaining help is another important skill for being healthy. What should you do if you are going to be in the sun all day? How can you get rid of that round rash on your arm?

The trusted adults you know are often your first resource when seeking help. A parent or guardian, a teacher, a coach, or a favorite relative may be able to offer you the help or facts you need. Other sources of information might be books, magazines, or videos.

Look at the five-step action plan for obtaining help. These steps can get you closer to the help you need.

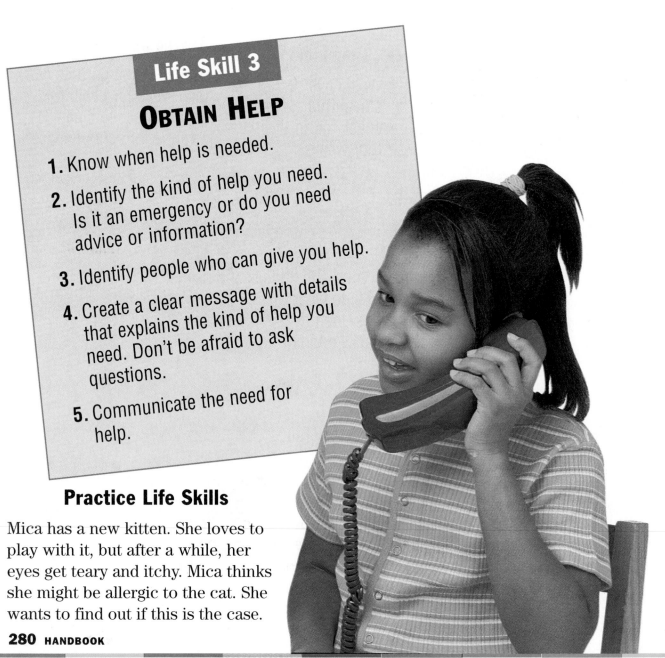

Life Skill 3

OBTAIN HELP

1. Know when help is needed.

2. Identify the kind of help you need. Is it an emergency or do you need advice or information?

3. Identify people who can give you help.

4. Create a clear message with details that explains the kind of help you need. Don't be afraid to ask questions.

5. Communicate the need for help.

Practice Life Skills

Mica has a new kitten. She loves to play with it, but after a while, her eyes get teary and itchy. Mica thinks she might be allergic to the cat. She wants to find out if this is the case.

Mica used the five-step plan to find out if she has an allergy. She created this flowchart as she thought about the kind of help she wanted.

1. Know when help is needed.

"Itchy, watery eyes may be the sign of an allergic reaction, so I should find out more about what's really happening."

2. Identify the kind of help you need.

"Some allergic reactions are emergencies, but I don't think watery eyes are. And they don't seem to be getting any worse."

3. Identify people who can give you help.

"I'll ask my parents about it. If they don't know, maybe I could talk to the school nurse or see Dr. Diaz."

4. Create a clear message about the help you need.

"My eyes begin to tear about 15 minutes after I start playing with my kitten. If it's really an allergy, what can I do and still keep him?"

5. Communicate the need for help.

"I'll talk to Mom and Dad about this problem at dinner tonight. I'm sure they'll be able to help or know whom to go to next."

OBTAIN HELP

What Would You Do?

When you visit your local playground in the afternoon, a tough gang of boys and girls is there. They tease you and push you and your friends around. You like the basketball court there, and it's the only one nearby. How can you get some help to solve this problem?

Life Skill 4: Manage Stress

Stress is the way your body and mind respond to unexpected changes. Unpleasant events—like being late for a doctor's appointment or getting caught in a storm—can create stress.

Learning how to manage stress is a key part of your health. Sometimes, you can avoid stressful situations. If you know that you get nervous when you're late, make sure you leave plenty of time. Other types of events—like the storm—are unavoidable, but you can still manage the stress they create.

Here's a four-step action plan for managing the stress in your daily life.

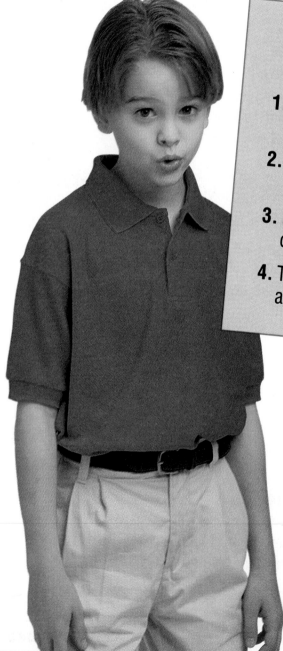

Life Skill 4

MANAGE STRESS

1. Be prepared. Plan your time. Don't leave important jobs for the last minute.
2. Get lots of rest, sleep, and physical activity.
3. In a stressful situation, try to relax. Take deep breaths.
4. Talk about the situation with a trusted adult or friend.

Practice Life Skills

One day, Ted and other classmates from the neighborhood were riding to school on the bus. Everyone felt relaxed and peaceful. Then, suddenly, KABOOM! A tire blows out, and the bus pulls over to the side of the road.

At first, everyone seems nervous. Then people begin to calm down. Ted decides to record what some of his classmates did to deal with the stress.

1. Be Prepared

"I didn't want to just waste time," said Aileen, "so I read a book. I always bring a book or magazine along, just in case I get stuck somewhere."

2. Get Sleep, Rest, and Physical Activity

Tai said, "I'm glad I got a good night's rest. I was wide awake when the school bag in the overhead rack began to fall."

Dealing with Stress the Day the Bus Got a FLAT

3. Relax and Take Deep Breaths

Jane said, "I helped some of the younger children stay calm. First, I showed them how to breathe deeply. Then I taught them a song."

4. Talk About It

Keith admitted to Jeff, "The sound of the tire popping scared me a little." Jeff said, "Well, I think everyone got a little scared when it happened."

MANAGE STRESS

What Would You Do?

Today is the day of your big speech. You've been practicing for weeks. But now you wake up so worried. Your stomach feels funny and your heart pounds a little faster when you think about the speech. What can you do throughout the day to prepare?

Life Skill 5: Practice Refusal Skills

Saying "no" is an important part of health. Refusal skills are the strategies you use to say "no." You might use them to turn something down because it isn't safe or doesn't fit in with your values and beliefs. For example, you might not want to go to the park with friends on Saturday or Sunday if that's a special day for your family.

Refusal skills will help you say "no" to people and show that you mean it. The five steps below can help you say "no" to an offer clearly and effectively.

Life Skill 5

PRACTICE REFUSAL SKILLS

1. Say "no" clearly to a dangerous situation or action or to a behavior you strongly believe is wrong.

2. Use a strong voice and a serious expression to show that you mean what you say.

3. Explain your reasons.

4. Suggest a possible alternative.

5. If necessary, walk away from the situation.

Practice Life Skills

Terry dares Stacey to stand on a swing and start swinging without holding on. Stacey knows that it would be too dangerous, and she might get hurt. Here are some things Stacey thought about to help her say "no."

1. Say No.
"*No* is the word I'm looking for, not *maybe* or *sort of* or *uh-uh*. I really want to be clear, so I really must say *no*."

2. Use a strong voice and a serious expression.
"If I mumble, it'll be hard for Terry to hear me. I've got to be firm and speak up, loud and clear. It's better not to grin or laugh it off."

3. Explain your reasons.
"Maybe the best thing to do is explain that it's just too dangerous to swing without holding on. I could fall and break something."

4. Suggest alternatives.
"I could challenge him to find out which of us can swing higher while sitting and holding on."

5. If necessary, walk away.
"If I get annoyed because Terry keeps asking me to do this, I can always tell him that I'm leaving and then really go."

 PRACTICE REFUSAL SKILLS

What Would You Do?

A woman asks you to walk her dog. You don't know her, but you've seen her around the neighborhood. You say "no," but she insists. What can you do?

Life Skill 6: Resolve Conflicts

A conflict is a strong disagreement between two people or two points of view. Some conflicts are avoidable. For example, cutting in line upsets people. You can avoid conflict by joining a line at the end.

However, you won't be able to avoid all conflicts. It's important to be able to resolve conflicts calmly and peacefully. Here are steps you can take to handle any conflict.

Life Skill 6

RESOLVE CONFLICTS

1. Be tolerant. Accept people as they are. Try to understand the other person's point of view.

2. Don't be prejudiced. It's never healthful to dislike people or ideas for their own sake. Avoid angry name calling and put-downs.

3. Communicate your thoughts and feelings clearly. Be respectful in what you say and how you listen to other people.

4. Try to reach a compromise without giving up safety, values, and basic rights.

5. If communication and compromise will not or cannot work, then try to delay the conflict or walk away.

Practice Life Skills

Jarod's team is creating a special presentation for the school assembly. All share ideas and chores—until they talk about the music to be used. Everyone's choice is different.

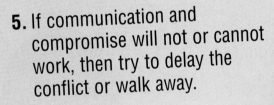

Jarod helped his group by suggesting ideas based on the five steps for resolving a conflict.

1. Be Tolerant
"Look, we all have the right to like whatever kind of music. We're not here to decide the best music ever, just what would be best for the presentation."

2. Avoid prejudices
"Let's not make fun of anyone's music. Just because you don't like it doesn't make it bad or the other person stupid."

3. Communicate
"Why don't we each think about our choice of music. Maybe we can bring in samples tomorrow and explain why we want certain music."

4. Compromise
"If we all are willing to listen and be honest, we should be able to figure out what's best for the presentation."

5. Delay or Walk Away
"Things may get heated in our discussion, so let's agree to disagree. If we can't reach a compromise today or tomorrow, then maybe we should try next week."

RESOLVE CONFLICTS

What Would You Do?

Kids in your neighborhood like to play softball at the local playground. However, picking teams almost always turns into a big fight. Everyone ends up angry and hurt before they even begin playing the game. How might you help your friends avoid these regular conflicts?

The Food Guide Pyramid

The Food Guide Pyramid can help you make healthful food choices. Use the following tips every day. Read the Food Guide Pyramid from the bottom up. Choose most of your foods from the bottom and second levels. Avoid choices from the top level of the pyramid.

MILK, YOGURT, AND CHEESE GROUP
2–3 Servings
These foods provide calcium and other minerals. Many are also high in protein.

VEGETABLE GROUP
3–5 Servings
Like fruits, vegetables are plant foods. They are naturally low in fat. Vegetables provide vitamins, minerals, and fiber.

FATS, OILS, AND SWEETS
Use sparingly.
You should eat few foods made mostly of fats, oils, or refined (processed) sugar. These are foods with many calories but few nutrients. This category is not considered one of the five food groups. You can find these ingredients in foods from other groups.

MEAT, POULTRY, FISH, DRY BEANS, EGGS, AND NUTS GROUP
2–3 Servings
These foods are high in protein. Most also have vitamins and minerals. These foods help your body grow and stay healthy.

FRUIT GROUP
2–4 Servings
Fruits provide vitamins and minerals. They have natural sugar for quick energy. Fruits also contain fiber and water, both important to your health.

BREAD, CEREAL, RICE, AND PASTA GROUP
6–11 Servings
Foods in this group are made from grains. Grains include wheat, corn, rice, and oats. Grains provide carbohydrates, protein, fiber, vitamins, and minerals.

KEY
- Fat (naturally occurring and added)
- Sugars (added)

These symbols show fats, oils, and added sugars in foods.

What Is a Serving?

The Food Guide Pyramid recommends a range of servings for each food group. For example, the Food Guide Pyramid shows that you should eat between 6–11 servings of food from the Bread, Cereal, Rice, and Pasta group. But how do you know whether to eat 6 servings or 11 servings or something in between? And how much food is one serving anyway?

- The number of servings depends largely on your age. The label "6–11 servings" includes all ages from age 5 to adults. Servings for young people ages 9 to 12 are from the lower number to a mid-range. See the chart below.

- Very active people may need more servings per day.

- Daily servings come from a combination of daily meals plus snacks.

- Remember that a single serving size is often smaller than what people may be served at a meal. Check food packages to find out how many servings are actually in the package. Study the chart below.

Food Group	One Serving Equals	Recommended Daily Servings for Ages 9–12
Bread, Cereal, Rice, and Pasta	1 slice bread; 1 ounce dry cereal; 1/2 cup cooked cereal, cooked rice, or pasta; 1/2 bagel	6 to 9 servings
Vegetables	1/2 cup chopped raw or cooked vegetables; 1 cup raw leafy vegetables; 1 medium potato; 3/4 cup vegetable juice	3 to 4 servings
Fruits	1 medium-sized apple, banana, or orange; 1/2 cup canned or cooked fruit; 1/2 grapefruit; 3/4 cup fruit juice	2 to 3 servings
Milk, Yogurt, and Cheese	1 cup milk or yogurt; 1 1/2 ounces natural cheese; 2 ounces processed cheese	2 to 3 servings
Meat, Poultry, Fish, Dry Beans, Eggs, and Nuts	2 1/2 to 3 ounces cooked lean meat, poultry, or fish; 2 tablespoons peanut butter; 1 egg or 1/2 cup cooked dry beans count as 1 ounce of meat	2 to 3 servings

Healthful Snacks

Everyone enjoys the right snack when hunger strikes. It's okay to snack. The goal is to choose foods that have a lot of nutrients and fiber but are low in calories and salt. Here are some suggestions for healthful snacking.

FRUITS

Apples, pears, nectarines, peaches
Fresh cherries, grapes, plums
Dried fruit, such as raisins or prunes
Baked apples and pears
Frozen bananas or grapes
Grapefruit or orange sections
Pineapple, apple, or melon spears
Chopped fruit mixed with nonfat yogurt

GRAINS, NUTS, AND BEANS

Shredded wheat, nuts, and raisins
Wheat germ and yogurt mixed with fruit
Whole wheat pretzels covered with sesame seeds
Unsalted, dry roasted peanuts
Unsalted almonds, pecans, or other nuts mixed with raisins
Air-popped popcorn (no salt, butter, or margarine)
Roasted pumpkin or sunflower seeds
Natural peanut butter or sesame butter (no salt or sugar) on crackers
Salt-free taco chips with chopped tomatoes, onions, and green pepper

UNCOOKED VEGETABLES

Carrot or celery sticks
Broccoli or cauliflower
Radishes
Zucchini strips or slices
Green or red pepper strips
Cherry tomatoes

THIRST QUENCHERS

Unsweetened fruit juices
Sparkling water or seltzer mixed with unsweetened grape juice
Vegetable juice (low salt)
Orange juice ice cubes
Lowfat or skim milk

PROTEIN POWER

Hummus (mashed chick peas mixed with lemon juice and chopped
   garlic) on pita bread
1/2 cup water-packed canned tuna mixed with
   2 tablespoons yogurt, dash of lemon juice, onion, celery, mustard
   and pepper on crackers or whole grain bread
Peanut butter and jelly on whole grain bread
Cottage cheese, seasoned cucumber slices, lettuce, and tomato in a
   pita pocket

Tips for a Healthy You

1. **Start each day with a healthful breakfast.**
   Try cold cereal with fruit and lowfat or skim milk.
   Breakfast gives you energy to start your day right.

2. **Balance your food choices.**
   Use the Food Pyramid on page 288 as your guide.
   You don't need to give up all your favorite foods as long as
   you have a balanced diet.

3. **Eat healthful snacks.**
   See the suggestions on page 290.

4. **Get physical!**
   Do 30 minutes of physical activity a day.
   Try brisk walks; climb stairs instead of using escalators;
   go for a jog or a bicycle ride. See page 292 for more ideas.

5. **Work up a sweat 3 to 5 times a week.**
   Try exercise routines that are about 20 minutes long.
   Include 5 minutes of warm-up and cool-down stretching
   and gentle movement.

6. **Get your family and friends to join in the fun.**
   Eat meals with your family when you're at home.
   Work out with friends.
   Join sports teams at school.
   Try new sports, games, and other activities—and sample
   new foods, too!

Daily Physical Activity

Getting 30 minutes of physical activity each day is important for your all-around health. If your activity is vigorous and uses a lot of energy, you can spend less time at it. If it is not vigorous, you may need to spend more time. Here are some examples of activities that require a lot of energy and others that take less energy and require more time.

less energy, more time

Playing baseball or softball for 45 minutes

Playing touch football for 30–45 minutes

Cleaning a room for 30–45 minutes

Wheeling self in wheelchair for 30–40 minutes

Walking 1 3/4 miles in 35 minutes (20 min/mile)

Shooting baskets for 30 minutes

Bicycling 5 miles in 30 minutes

Dancing fast for 30 minutes

Pushing a stroller 1 1/2 miles in 30 minutes

Raking leaves for 30 minutes

Walking 2 miles in 30 minutes (15 min/mile)

Swimming laps for 20 minutes

Playing wheelchair basketball for 20 minutes

Playing basketball for 15–20 minutes

Bicycling 4 miles in 15 minutes

Jumping rope for 15 minutes

Shoveling snow for 15 minutes

Stairwalking for 15 minutes

more energy, less time

The Activity Pyramid

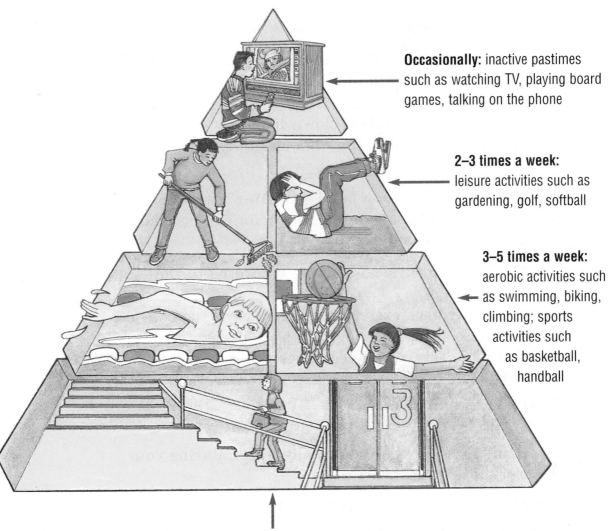

Occasionally: inactive pastimes such as watching TV, playing board games, talking on the phone

2–3 times a week: leisure activities such as gardening, golf, softball

3–5 times a week: aerobic activities such as swimming, biking, climbing; sports activities such as basketball, handball

Daily: substitute activity for inactivity—take the stairs, walk instead of riding, bike instead of taking the bus

Become an Active Person
- Turn off the TV and go outside.
- Walk every chance you get.
- Take the stairs when you can.

Be Active all the Time
- Play with your friends.
- Take an interest in sports and games.
- Look for activities that are fun for you.

Stay Active as You Grow Older
- Don't get stuck in a dull routine.
- Be open to new experiences.
- Ask friends and family to join you.

Guidelines for a Safe Workout

1. **Plan your activity.** Don't try to do more than you can do safely or are physically ready to do. (See physical activities on pages 292 and 298–299.)

2. **Do warm-up activities before beginning your workout, your main physical activity.** First, do muscle stretches. (See pages 295–297 of the Handbook.) Then begin your workout slowly to build your heart rate and avoid injury or strain. Work up slowly to the level you want for that day.

3. **Don't work out soon before or after a meal.** Stop physical activity at least one hour before a meal, and wait until two hours afterward.

4. **Modify your physical activity according to the weather.**
   - In hot weather, exercise less vigorously or do not exercise at all. The body loses a lot of water in hot weather. This condition is dangerous.
   - Outdoors in cold weather, be sure to wear layers of clothing and a hat. Up to fifty percent of your body heat can be lost through the top of the head.

5. **Drink lots of fluids, especially water, during your workout.**

6. **If you feel pain during physical activity, stop immediately.**

7. **Work out on surfaces that "give," such as grass or mats.** Don't work out on hard or bumpy surfaces. They can cause injury to joints and leg bones.

8. **Wear comfortable shoes that are right for the physical activity.** Walking shoes are different from running shoes or basketball shoes, for example.

9. **Don't jog or walk alone, especially at night.** If you are jogging near automobile traffic at night, wear reflective tape on your clothes.

10. **After your workout, do cool-down activities.** Slow down your workout and then do stretches again, as you did in your warm-ups.

Warm-Up and Cool-Down Stretches

A safe workout includes warm-up and cool-down activities. Always begin and end your workout with stretches; they keep you from having muscle and joint injuries. Choose stretches from these pages to warm up, cool down, and improve your flexibility.

Stretching Tips

- Spend about 5 minutes warming up and cooling down.

- Relax and breathe easily while stretching; don't bounce or jerk.

- Do each stretch until you feel a gradual pull in the muscles.

- Hold each stretch for 5–10 seconds. Work up to holding for 20 seconds.

- Do a stretch 3 to 5 times. Over time, increase to 10 times.

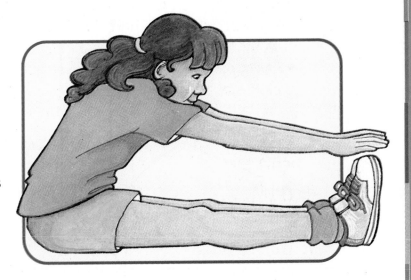

1. Reach for Your Toes
(Thigh–calf and lower-back stretch)
- Sit with legs straight out, heels about 5 inches apart.
- Slowly reach fingertips forward as far as you can.

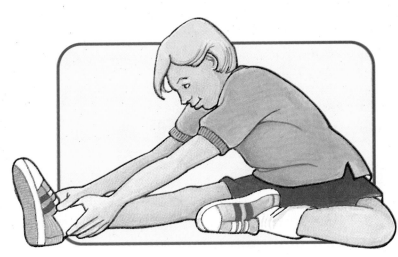

2. Ankle Grabber
(Thigh–calf stretch)
- Sit with legs straight out.
- Bend your left knee until that foot touches your right thigh.
- Reach forward to grasp your right ankle.
- Repeat with your right knee bent.

3. Wall Stretch

(Calf–heel stretch)

- Bend your left leg forward and lean against a wall.
- Stretch your right leg back.
- Keeping the right heel on the floor, bend the right knee slightly and lean forward.
- Repeat with your left leg back.

4. Ankle Pull

(Front-thigh stretch)

- Stand on your right leg.
- Bend your left leg up behind you.
- Grasp your left ankle with your left hand and pull gently.
- Repeat, bending your right leg.

5. Crouch and Stretch

(Back-thigh stretch)

- Crouch on the floor with your hands flat under your shoulders.
- Stretch your left leg straight back, leaning forward gently.
- Repeat with your right leg stretched back.

6. Wide Knee

(Inner-thigh stretch)

- Sit with the soles of your feet together.
- Grasp your ankles and press your elbows gently against your knees.

7. Elbows Over the Head

(Upper back–shoulder stretch)

- Put your arms over your head.
- Hold the elbow of one arm with the hand of the other.
- Stretch the other hand down your back.

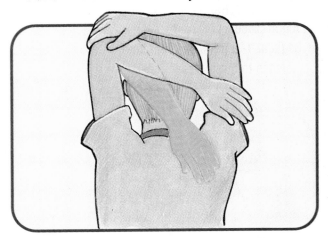

8. Shake Hands in Back

(Shoulder–chest stretch)

- Clasp your fingers together behind your back.
- Straighten your arms and stretch them downward.

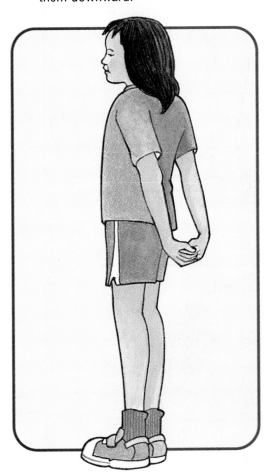

9. Toe Touch

(Lower back–leg stretch)

- Stand straight with slightly bent knees.
- Reach for your toes.

Exercises for Fitness

Here are some fun exercises to help strengthen your lungs, heart, and certain body muscles.

1. Standstill Jogging
- Jog in place.
- Begin at 1–2 minutes. Over time, increase to 5 minutes.

2. Cross-leg Hop
- Jump in place while moving your legs back and forth.
- Over time, work up to 1–2 minutes.

3. Push-ups
- Start on your hands and knees.
- Lower your chest to the floor, then push up.
- Be sure to keep your back straight.
- Start with 2 or 3 and increase over time.

4. Leg Raises

- Raise your top leg as high as you can.
- Start with 5 lifts and work up to 10 over time.
- Be sure to exercise both legs equally.

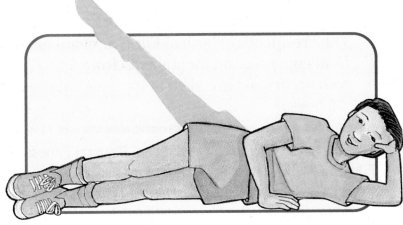

5. Jumping Jacks

- As you jump, spread your legs apart and swing your arms together.
- Jump again. This time bring your legs together and swing your arms apart.
- Start with 5 times and work up to 10.

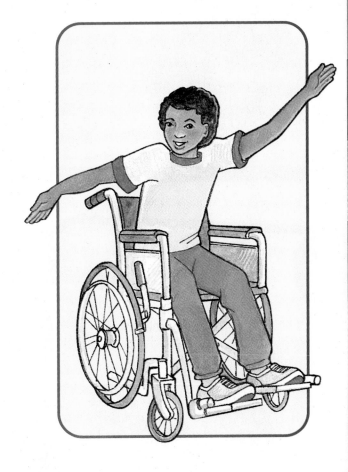

6. The Swim

- Reach forward and pull back with your left arm.
- Then reach and pull with your right arm.
- Make smooth movements as if you were swimming.
- Start with 10 strokes per side and work up to 20.

The President's Challenge

The Presidential Physical Fitness Award is a physical fitness challenge program for students from 6 to 17 years of age. Students who participate are eligible for one of these three awards:

Presidential Physical Fitness Award for students who score in the top 15 percent of their group.

National Physical Fitness Award for students who score in the top 50 percent of their group.

Participant Award for students who participate but do not score in the top 50 percent of their group.

1 Curl-ups or Sit-ups

This exercise measures your abdominal muscle strength.

Have a partner hold your feet down as you lift your upper body off the floor. Lower your upper body until it just touches the floor and start again.

2 Shuttle Run

This exercise measures leg strength and endurance.

Run to the blocks, pick up one block, and bring it to the starting line. Repeat with the second block.

3 One Mile Run/Walk

This exercise measures the strength of your leg muscles and your heart and lung endurance.

Complete the mile as fast as you can. You can walk if you get tired.

4 Pull-ups

This exercise measures the strength and endurance of your arm and shoulder muscles.

Hang by your hands from a bar. Pull your chin up until it is over the bar. Lower your body without touching the floor and start again.

5 V-sit Reach

This exercise measures the flexibility of your legs and back.

Sit on the floor with your feet behind the line. Reach forward as far as you can.

Indoor Safety

ELECTRICAL SAFETY

Do not overload outlets.

Do not use appliances with frayed cords.

Keep appliances away from water.

CHEMICAL SAFETY

Keep cleaners in a safe place.
Make sure cleaners have labels.

FIREARM SAFETY

Never touch or play with a weapon.
If you find one, tell an adult or call 911.

PREVENTING FALLS

Keep halls and stairways clear.

Turn lights on in dark rooms.

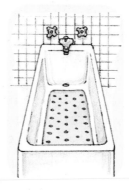

Use a nonslip mat in the tub.

Use a ladder to reach up high.

FIRE SAFETY

Turn off appliances.

Put fresh batteries in your smoke detector.

Keep a fire extinguisher handy.

Keep stoves and ovens clean.

Recycle old newspapers and rags.

Never play with matches.

Keep materials that burn away from electric heaters.

Obey all instructions during fire drills at school.

IN CASE OF FIRE

Get out fast if you can.

Stay low. Smoke rises.

Do not open a warm or hot door.

Line doors to keep smoke out.

Open a window and call for help.

Outdoor Safety

WATER SAFETY

DO:

- Learn to swim properly.
- Check water depth.
- Call for help if you need it.
- Wear a personal flotation device on a boat.

DON'T:

- Swim alone.
- Swim right after a meal.
- Swim in a storm.
- Try to carry a buddy.

WEATHER SAFETY

DO:

- In hot weather, wear loose-fitting clothes in light colors.
- In cold weather, wear layers of loose-fitting dark colors.
- Drink plenty of fluids when it's hot.

DON'T:

- Don't forget to use sunscreen when outside on sunny days.
- Forget your hat, gloves, and boots when it's cold.

PLAYGROUND SAFETY

DO:

- Always play with a buddy.
- Play inside the fenced area.
- Follow all playground rules.

DON'T:

- Play on broken equipment.
- Play near a construction site or in an abandoned building.

BICYCLE SAFETY

DO:

- Ride with a buddy single file whenever possible.
- Make sure your bike is safe to ride.
- Always wear a helmet.
- Obey traffic signs.
- Watch for cars pulling out.
- Use hand signals.

DON'T:

- Ride against traffic.
- Let a passenger share your bike.
- Ride barefoot.
- Ride at night without lights and reflectors.
- Try stunts like riding without holding on.
- Wear floppy clothes that can get caught in the chains.

HAND SIGNALS

LEFT   RIGHT   STOP

RURAL SAFETY

DO:

- Look for traffic at all crossroads.
- Keep chemicals locked up.
- Visit ponds and livestock with an adult.

DON'T:

- Operate farm machinery.
- Sit in the back of a moving pickup truck.
- Hitch rides on tractors or other vehicles.

CAR AND BUS SAFETY

- Always wear a safety belt.
- Don't distract the driver.
- Don't stick your head or hands out of the vehicle.
- Never ride or walk your bike behind any vehicle in operation.

STREET SAFETY

- Cross at crosswalks or intersections. Obey the crossing guard if one is present.
- Cross with the light.
- Look left, right, and left again before crossing.
- Pull away and run from a stranger who tries to touch or hold you.
- Don't walk alone, if possible.
- Avoid walking in deserted alleys or streets.
- Never touch animals (even pets) you do not know.
- Always walk away quickly if a stranger approaches you on the street.

HIKING AND CAMPING SAFETY

- Don't camp or hike alone.
- Let other people know where you will be camping or hiking.
- Dress appropriately for the weather.
- Bring a first-aid kit, a flashlight, a compass, and fresh water.
- Bring packaged food supplies when camping.
- Find out about possible poisonous snakes, insects, and plants at your campsite.
- Make sure your campfire is completely out. Cover with water or with dirt, if water is not available.

EARTHQUAKE SAFETY

- If you are inside during an earthquake, brace yourself in a hallway, door frame, or crawl under a piece of sturdy furniture.
- Be sure to keep away from windows, glass doors, tall shelves, chimneys, or anything that might collapse.
- If you are outdoors, move away from tall buildings, overhead electrical wires, and highway structures.

HURRICANE SAFETY

- Board up windows and doors.
- Have supplies of canned food and bottled water available.
- Have a battery-operated radio on hand. Listen for and obey instructions. You may have to leave your area.
- Have a battery-operated flashlight available.

TORNADO SAFETY

- Move to a storm cellar or basement, if possible. Otherwise, go to a hallway or other place with no windows.
- If you are outdoors, lie flat in a ditch.
- If the funnel of the tornado is approaching you, move away at right angles to its path. Run sideways from the funnel; do not run in front of it.

Safety When Babysitting

QUESTIONS TO ASK AHEAD OF TIME

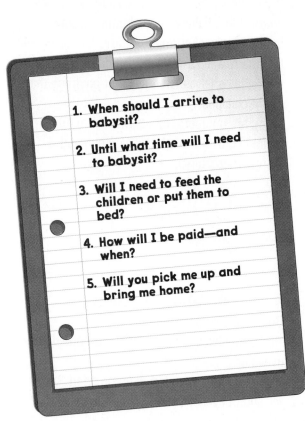

1. When should I arrive to babysit?

2. Until what time will I need to babysit?

3. Will I need to feed the children or put them to bed?

4. How will I be paid—and when?

5. Will you pick me up and bring me home?

QUESTIONS TO ASK WHEN YOU ARRIVE

1. When will you be back?

2. Where can you be reached?

3. What are some other emergency numbers I might need?

4. Would you like me to answer the phone if it rings?

5. Where can I find the children's toys, homework, pajamas, and/or dinners?

IMPORTANT RULES FOR BABYSITTERS

1. Never leave children alone.

2. Even if children are in bed, look in on them frequently.

3. Don't let children play with sharp objects, hot objects, or plastic bags.

4. Don't unlock the door unless the parents ask you to.

5. Don't tie up the phone or eat things you weren't invited to eat.

6. Don't invite friends over; they can distract you from your job.

7. Never take your eyes off children in the bathtub or swimming pool.

8. Keep children away from strangers at parks and playgrounds.

First Aid

HOW TO TREAT INSECT STINGS

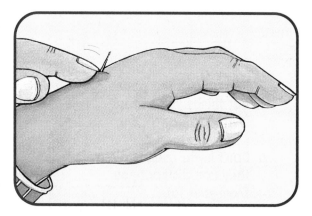

Remove the stinger with a fingernail.
Wash the injury with soap and water.

Apply a cold cloth and some first aid cream.
In case of serious swelling or trouble breathing,
get emergency help.

HOW TO TREAT POISONOUS PLANT RASHES

Wash your skin with soap and water.
This will remove the sap.

Do not scratch bumps or break blisters.

HOW TO TREAT A NOSEBLEED

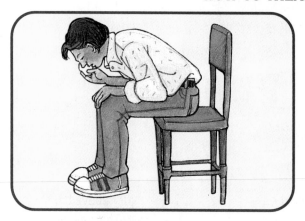

Sit and lean forward in a chair.

Pinch both nostrils shut with your thumb
and index finger.

HOW TO TREAT BURNS AND BLISTERS

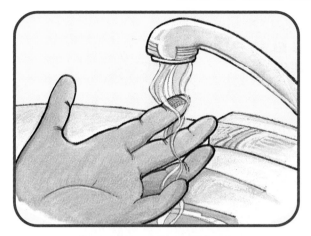

Run cold water over a burn.

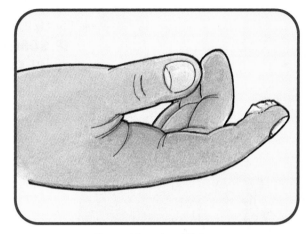

Do not break a blister.

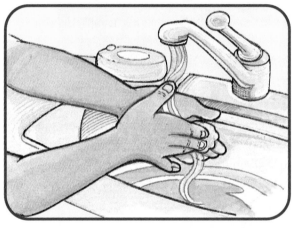

If a blister breaks on its own, wash it with soap and water. Pat it dry with a clean cloth.

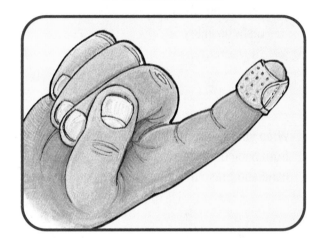

Put on a bandage.

HOW TO TREAT A SPRAIN

Don't move the injured area. You might have a break instead of a sprain. Get help from an adult.

Put something cold on the sprain. Ask someone to get you an ice pack.

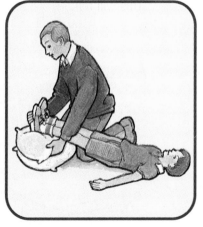

Raise the injury above the level of your heart. This will help the swelling go down.

First Aid for Choking

IF SOMEONE ELSE IS CHOKING

Wrap your arms around the person from behind. Make a fist with one hand and grasp it with the other.

Pull the thumb side of your fist into the person's stomach. Use quick, hard, upward pulls to press your fist into the person's stomach.

IF YOU ARE ALONE AND CHOKING

Lean with your stomach against the back of a chair.

Press against the chair with a quick, hard push. Be sure not to press so hard that you break or injure a rib.

In Case of Emergency

Call 911 or your local emergency number. Tell the operator what happened, who is injured, and where you are. Stay on the line until the operator tells you to hang up.

Do not move an injured person.

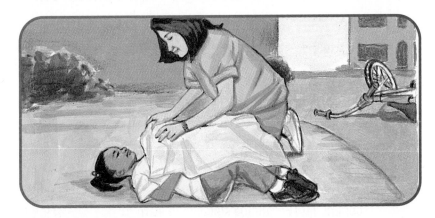

Cover the person with a blanket.

Stay with the person and keep him or her calm.

Field Trips and Class Visitors

These places can be field trips or a visitor from any of them may be invited to your school to speak to the students.

A DENTAL CLINIC

Dentists need to know the most up-to-date techniques for cleaning and repairing teeth and gums. Encourage students to learn about new advances in taking care of teeth.

QUESTIONS TO ASK

- How often should I brush and floss?
- Are some toothpastes better than others?
- How do you keep people from fearing dental checkups?

Bring two or three questions of your own, too.

LIFE SKILL

SET GOALS

Follow-Up Activity

NO FEAR Now that you've learned about a modern dental office, you should feel more comfortable at your next dental checkup. Finish this sentence to set your own goals for dental checkups without fear.

I'm not afraid of the dentist, because I know _____ .

THE RED CROSS

Your local chapter of the Red Cross provides a number of services to the community. Encourage students to learn how The Red Cross helps others.

QUESTIONS TO ASK

- What would you do if there were an earthquake or flood?
- Why is it important for people to donate blood?

Bring two or three questions of your own, too.

LIFE SKILL

MAKE DECISIONS

Follow-Up Activity

HELPING OUT Now that you know what your local Red Cross does, think about ways you might help. What do they do that interests you most? Write a paragraph telling how you might donate your own services to help the Red Cross.

A RECYCLING PLANT

Encourage students to learn about a recycling center and how it helps keep the community clean.

QUESTIONS TO ASK
- What are we allowed to recycle? What can't be recycled?
- Where do these recycled items end up?

Bring two or three questions of your own, too.

PRACTICE REFUSAL SKILLS

Follow-Up Activity

GIVE THE EARTH A BREAK You now know what can and can't be recycled in your community. Suppose some people you know keep throwing out things that can be recycled. What could you say to change their minds? Write a dialogue between a non-recycler and yourself.

A HOSPITAL

Encourage students to learn about the services and support provided at a local hospital.

QUESTIONS TO ASK
- What skills do nurses need to have?
- When should people go to their doctor instead of to the hospital?
- Do most people go to the hospital because of emergencies?

Bring two or three questions of your own, too.

MANAGE STRESS

Follow-Up Activity

FINDING YOUR WAY The stress of an emergency can be greatly relieved if you know your way around your hospital. If your tour guide gave you a map, circle the main check-in, the emergency entrance, and other important areas. If not, work with a partner to draw a map from your notes and memory.

Books About Health Topics

PHYSICAL, EMOTIONAL AND INTELLECTUAL, AND SOCIAL HEALTH

Colt
by Nancy Springer
Dial Books, 1991

Colt's health is not good; he spends his time moping in his wheelchair. When he participates in a special horseback riding program, the progress he makes affects his physical, emotional and intellectual, and social health.

Follow-Up Activity

Think about how physical activity improved the three parts of Colt's health. Write a short story in which someone improves the three parts of health by taking part in a special activity.

FAMILY LIFE

Superfudge
by Judy Blume
Yearling Books (Reprint Edition), 1991

Peter Hatcher has his hands full with his younger brother, Fudge. Matters get more complicated when the family has to move, too.

Follow-Up Activity

Write another scene for the book. Show how Peter handles a stressful situation with a family member in a healthy way.

NUTRITION

Travel-the-World Cookbook
by Pamela Marx
GoodYear Books, 1996

Are you interested in discovering new flavors, tastes, cultures, and customs? Here are 60 easy-to-make dishes from around the world to enjoy.

Follow-Up Activity

Try one of the recipes and share the results with some classmates. Compare and discuss your responses to the food you prepared.

CANCER

Understanding Cancer
by Susan N. Terkel and Marlene Lupiloff-Brazz
Franklin Watts, 1993

Just what is cancer? Knowing about cancer is important for friends and relatives of people who have cancer, this book gives recent information on the disease and its treatments.

Follow-Up Activity
This book probably told you many things you never knew before. Think of three new facts you learned about cancer. Share them with a group.

ALCOHOL, TOBACCO, AND DRUGS

Poison! Beware! Be an Expert Poison Spotter
by Steve Skidmore
Millbrook, 1991

You may not think of tobacco, alcohol, and drugs as poisons, but the author of this book does. He shows you how poisons that enter the body change the way the body works and cause harm.

Follow-Up Activity
What does the author want you to learn? Write a paragraph that summarizes the main point of this book.

FIRST AID

Kids to the Rescue! First-Aid Techniques for Kids
by Maribeth and Darwin Boelts
Parenting Press, 1992

What would you do in an emergency? Here are step-by-step proper actions to follow in 14 different emergency situations.

Follow-Up Activity
Pick an emergency situation from the book, and pretend that you are there. Write a short story telling how you saved the day by following proper first-aid procedures.

COMMUNITY AND ENVIRONMENTAL HEALTH

50 Simple Things Kids Can Do to Save the Earth
by The EarthWorks Group
Andrews and McMeel, 1990

How can you help to save the environment? This classic book offers 50 easy ways any kid can help protect Earth.

Follow-Up Activity
Pick one activity from the book and do it. Write a letter to a friend describing what you did, the results, and how you felt about them.

Media

VIDEOTAPES

I'm Joe's Stomach (VHS)
Pyramid Film and Video
P.O. Box 1048
Santa Monica, CA 90406
1-310-828-7577

Three-dimensional animation illustrates how the digestive system works as well as the effects of overeating, stress, and medication.

My Self Esteem (VHS)
Pyramid Film and Video
P.O. Box 1048
Santa Monica, CA 90406
1-310-828-7577

Follow Molly as she improves her self-concept and learns to make changes in her life by communicating effectively, setting goals, and accepting differences in other people.

My Friends and Me (VHS)
Quest International
537 Jones Road
Granville, OH 43023
1-800-446-2700

Having problems making or keeping friends? This video helps young people develop skills needed for building and maintaining friendships.

Kid Safe (VHS)
American Academy of Pediatrics
141 Northwest Point Blvd.
Elk Grove Village, IL 60009-0927
1-847-228-5005

This video is designed to help kids deal with first aid, fire safety, and the 911 emergency system.

COMPUTER SOFTWARE

How Your Body Works
(CD-ROM for Mac and Windows)
Mindscape
60 Leveroni Court
Novato, CA 94947
1-415-883-3000

This software allows you to tour various body systems. It includes videos of professionals discussing health issues and a file cabinet of research.

Dole's 5 A-day Adventures
(CD-ROM for Mac and Windows)
Dole, Inc.
155 Bovet Road
San Mateo, CA 94402
1-415-570-4378

Travel to the land of 5 A-Day where you'll learn about the Food Guide Pyramid and how to make healthful food choices.

Substance Abuse: Decisions, Decisions
(CD-ROM for Mac and Windows)
Tom Snyder Productions
80 Coolidge Hill Road
Watertown, MA 02172
1-617-926-6000

Students must make decisions as they face unexpected drug-related predicaments.

Smart Team
(CD-ROM for Mac and Windows)
Glencoe Publishing
P. O. Box 508
Columbus, OH 43216
1-800-334-7344

Learn what makes you angry and strategies to avoid violence and stay safe.

Web Sites

Web sites change frequently. Some of those listed below may have changed or been eliminated by the time of publication. For updated information on health organizations, check the McGraw-Hill School Division Web site at: http://mhschool.com.

http://www.kidshealth.org/kid

This award-winning Web site is designed by the staff of the duPont Hospital for Children. It features health games, cartoons, a "Health Tip of the Day," and a "KidsVote" health poll.

http://sln2.fi.edu/biosci/heart.html

Believe it or not, a sixth-grader designed this site, which describes the circulatory system and suggests ways to keep your heart healthy.

http://ificinfo.health.org

This home page for the International Food and Information Council contains information on nutrition and food safety.

http://www.cycling.org

If you love riding bikes, this site will connect you to hundreds of organizations, clubs, and other bicycle buffs.

http://www.autonomy.com/smoke.html

This is a great resource for learning about tobacco and its effects on the body. You can connect from here to many home pages that tell about the effects of tobacco.

http://www.envirolink.org

If you're interested in keeping up on environmental news and views, this Web site is for you. You can shop for "green" products, talk to environmentalists, and learn the latest about what's happening to the environment around the world.

http://www.drugfreeamerica.org/drug—info.html

This Web site offers a large menu of information about illegal and abused drugs and their effects on the body.

http://www.uoknor.edu/oupd/kidsafe/start.htm

This award-winning Web site focuses on Kids Safety on the Internet. It answers frequently asked questions about how kids can stay safe in the real world and in cyberspace.

Health Organizations

For updated information on health organizations, check the McGraw-Hill School Division Web site at: http://mhschool.com.

ALCOHOL, TOBACCO, AND DRUGS

Parents' Resource Institute for Drug Education
100 Edgewood Avenue, #1210
Altanta, GA 30303
1-404-761-6700
http://www.prideusa.org

COMMUNITY AND ENVIRONMENTAL HEALTH

Environmental Protection Agency
Public Information Center
PM 211-B
401 M Street, NW
Washington, DC 20460
1-202-260-2080
http://www.epa.gov

CONSUMER HEALTH

Food and Drug Administration
Office of Consumer Affairs, Public Inquiries
5600 Fishers Lane
Rockville, MD 20857
1-301-443-3170
http://www.fda.gov.fdahomepage.html

Consumer Information Center
P.O. Box 100
Pueblo, CO 81009
1-719-948-3334
http://www.pueblo.gsa.gov.

Consumer Product Safety Commission
Office of Information and Public Affairs
5401 Westbard Avenue
Washington, D.C. 20207
1-800-638-2772
gopher://cpsc.gov/

DISEASE PREVENTION AND CONTROL

American Cancer Society
1599 Clifton Road, NE
Atlanta, GA 30329
1-404-320-3333
http://www.cancer.org

American Heart Association
7272 Greenville Avenue
Dallas, TX 75231
1-214-373-6300
http://www.amhrt.org

Centers for Disease Control and Prevention
1600 Clifton Road, NE
Atlanta, GA 30333
1-404-639-3534
http://www.cdc.gov

Juvenile Diabetes Foundation
International Hotline
1-800-223-1138
http://www.jdfcure.com

EMOTIONAL AND INTELLECTUAL HEALTH

National Institute of Mental Health
Science Communication Branch
Public Inquiries Section
5600 Fishers Lane
Room 15C-17
Rockville, MD 20857
1-301-443-4513
http://gopher.nimh.nih.gov

National Mental Health Association
1021 Prince Street
Alexandria, VA 22314
1-703-684-7722
http://www/worldcorp.com/dc-online/nmha

NUTRITION

National Dairy Council
O'Hare International Building
10255 West Higgins, Suite 900
Rosemont, IL 60019
1-847-803-2000
http://www.dairyinfo.com

Food and Nutrition Information Education Resouces Center
National Agriculture Library
10301 Baltimore Blvd
Beltsville, Maryland 20705
http:/www.nalusda.gov/fnic/

PERSONAL HEALTH AND PHYSICAL ACTIVITY

American Dental Association
211 East Chicago Avenue
Chicago, IL 60611
1-312-440-2500
http://www.ada.org

President's Council on Physical Fitness and Sports
Suite 250
701 Pennsylvania Avenue, NW
Washington, DC 20004
1-202-272-3421

SAFETY AND INJURY PREVENTION

National Safety Council
444 N. Michigan Avenue
Chicago, IL 60611
1-312-527-4800
http://www.nsc.org

TOLL-FREE NUMBERS FOR INFORMATION ON VARIOUS HEALTH TOPICS

Automobile Safety 1-800-424-9393
Cancer 1-800-4-CANCER
Consumer Product Safety 1-800-636-CPSC
Diabetes 1-800-ADA-DISC
Eating Disorders 1-800-334-8415
Hazardous Waste 1-800-424-9346
Headaches 1-800-843-2256
Physical Fitness 1-800-227-3988
Vision Problems 1-800-232-5463

GLOSSARY

This Glossary gives the pronunciation and meanings of the vocabulary and other important terms in this book. It also tells where these items can be found.

A

abuse (ə būz′) to use an illegal drug; to use a legal drug in an unsafe way on purpose (p. 190)

acid rain (as′id rān) rain that contains high levels of dangerous chemicals that can harm the environment (p. 266)

acquired (ə kwīrd′) gotten from (as in a disease that is caught from other people) (p. 169)

addictive (ə dik′tiv) causing dependence, or a strong need to have a substance (p. 198)

additive (ad′i tiv) a substance put in a food to make it more healthful, last longer, look better, or taste better (p. 114)

aerobic exercise (â rō′bik ek′sər sīz) physical activity that uses oxygen over a long time to provide energy for working muscles (p. 142)

agility (ə jil′i tē) the ability to move easily (p. 136)

AIDS (Acquired Immune Deficiency Syndrome) (ādz) a very serious disease in which the immune system is extremely weak; caused by infection with HIV (p. 168)

alcohol (al′kə hôl′) a drug found in beer, wine, liquor, and some medicines (p. 204)

allergic (ə lûr′jik) having a sensitivity to a certain substance (p. 175)

allergy (al′ər jē) an unpleasant reaction by the body to a substance; a sensitivity to certain substances that can cause people to have rashes, run fevers, or have trouble breathing (pp. 174, 191)

alveoli (al vē′ə lī) small air sacs in the lungs (p. 44)

anemia (ə nē′mē ə) a condition in which the blood has too few red blood cells (p. 118)

antibody (an′ti bod′ē) chemical made by the body that helps destroy or weaken bacteria, viruses, and other microbes (p. 162)

anus (ā′nəs) the opening through which solid waste left over from digestion leaves the body (p. 52)

appreciate (ə prē′shē āt′) to understand the value of someone or something (p. 68)

artery (är′tə rē) a blood vessel that carries blood away from the heart (p. 44)

attitude (at′i tüd′) thoughts and feelings about something (p. 6)

B

bacteria (sing. bacterium) (bak tîr′ē ə) a type of one-celled organism, or living thing (pp. 124, 156)

balance (bal′əns) the ability to keep your body in a steady position (p. 136)

balanced diet (bal′ənsd dī′it) eating the right variety and amounts of healthful foods every day (p. 110)

ball-and-socket joint (bôl ənd sok′it joint) a joint that allows movement in several directions—circular, back and forth, and side to side, such as in the hips and shoulders (p. 40)

behavior (bi hāv′yər) the way a person acts; something that a person does (p. 6)

biceps (bī′seps) a muscle in the upper arm that bends the arm by contracting (p. 43)

bicuspids (bī kus′pidz) teeth that crush food (p. 11)

blister (blis′tər) a swelling of the skin filled with a watery fluid (p. 244)

blood vessel (blud ves′əl) long, thin tube through which blood moves around the body (pp. 37, 46)

body system (bod′ē sis′təm) a group of organs that work together to perform a particular job for the body (p. 34)

brain (brān) organ that controls your body's systems and coordinates your actions, emotions, and thoughts (p. 54)

bronchi (brong′kē) the two tubes into which the trachea divides; they carry air into the lungs (p. 47)

C

calorie (kal′ə rē) a unit for measuring the amount of energy contained in food (pp. 116, 118)

cancer (kan′sər) a group of diseases caused when cells multiply in ways that are not normal (p. 176)

capillary (kap′ə ler′ē) a narrow blood vessel that connects an artery and a vein (p. 44)

carbohydrates (kär′bo hī′drāts) nutrients used by the body as its main source of daily energy (p. 104)

carbon monoxide (kär′bən mon ok′sīd) a poisonous gas produced when tobacco burns as well as when a motor vehicle gives off exhaust (p. 194)

cartilage (kär′tə lij) flexible tissue that covers and protects the ends of some bones (p. 38)

cavity (kav′i tē) a place that has worn away in a tooth; a hole in a tooth (p. 10)

cell (sel) the basic structural unit of life (p. 34)

chronic (kron′ik) lasting for a long time (p. 174)

circulatory system (sûr′kyə lə tôr′ē sis′təm) a body system that transports blood throughout the body, delivering oxygen and food to the cells and taking away wastes. (pp. 37, 45)

classroom rules (klas′rüm rülz) guidelines that keep a classroom safe, fair, and quiet (p. 92)

cocaine (kō kān′) a stimulant made from the coca plant (p. 210)

communicable disease (kə mū′ni kə bəl di zēz′) a disease that can be spread to a person from another person, an animal, or an object (p. 162)

communicate (kə mū′ni kāt′) to talk with and listen to others (p. 88)

communication (kə mū′ni kā′shən) exchanging or sharing feelings, thoughts, or information (p. 90)

competition (kom′pi tish′ən) a contest between people or teams (p. 146)

compromise (kom′prə mīz′) to settle an argument or reach an agreement by give and take (p. 74)

conflict (kon′flikt) a struggle or disagreement between two or more people or points of view (p. 74)

consideration (kən sid′ə rā′shən) thoughtfulness toward other people and their feelings (p. 68)

contract (kən trakt′) to get shorter, as the action of a muscle (p. 43)

cool-down (kül′doun) gentle movement that relaxes the body after exercise (p. 142)

cooperation (kō op′ə rā′shən) working together for the same purpose or goal (p. 68)

pronunciation key

a at; ā ape; ä far; âr care; e end; ē me; i it; ī ice; îr pierce; o hot; ō old; ô fork; oi oil; ou out; u up; ū use; ü rule; ù pull; ûr turn; hw white; ng song; th thin; th this; zh measure; ə about, taken, pencil, lemon, circus

coordination (kō ôr'də nā'shən) the ability to use more than one body part at a time to perform a task (p. 136)

crack (krak) an especially harmful form of cocaine (p. 212)

crown (kroun) the part of a tooth that you can see (p. 11)

cuspids (kus'pidz) teeth that tear food apart (p. 11)

D

dandruff (dan'drəf) pieces of dead scalp seen in the hair and on the clothes (p. 20)

deficiency (di fish'ən sē) a lack of something important (p. 122)

deficiency disease (di fish'ən sē di zēz') a disease caused by the lack of a nutrient (p. 118)

deficient (di fish'ənt) lacking something important (p. 169)

dentin (den'tin) the material comprising much of the inside of a tooth, which covers the pulp (p. 11)

dependence (di pen'dəns) a strong need or desire for a medicine or drug (p. 190)

depressant (di pres'ənt) a drug that slows down the activity of the body (p. 210)

dermis (dûr'mis) the layer of skin just beneath the epidermis (p. 18)

digestion (di jes'chən) a process that turns food into a form body cells can use (p. 50)

digestive system (di jes'tiv sis'təm) a body system that breaks down food for your cells to use (pp. 37, 51)

disease (di zēz') a condition that keeps the body from feeling or working well; an illness (p. 156)

disrespectful touch (dis'ri spekt'fəl tuch) a touch that shows a lack of caring for another person, such as hitting or kicking (p. 228)

dosage (dō'sij) how much of a medicine to take (p. 187)

drug (drug) a substance, other than food, that causes changes in the body (p. 186)

E

eardrum (îr'drum') a thin membrane inside the ear that makes hearing possible by vibrating when sound waves hit it (p. 14)

emergency (i mûr'jən sē) a situation that requires immediate help, usually from the police, the fire department, or medical personnel (pp. 220, 244)

emission (i mish'ən) a substance that is released into the air, such as smoke from a factory smokestack or exhaust from a bus or car (p. 266)

emotion (i mō'shən) a strong feeling, such as love, sadness, or anger (p. 74)

emotional health (i mō'shə nəl helth) health of the mind; health having to do with feelings (p. 2)

emotional skills (i mō'shə nəl skilz) the ability to deal with your emotions (p. 30)

emotional violence (i mō'shə nəl vī'ə ləns) acts such as using mean words and making fun of people (p. 225)

enamel (i nam'əl) the hard, white, protective outer layer of teeth (p. 10)

endocrine system (en'də krin sis'təm) a body system that is made up of glands and hormones (p. 33)

endurance (en dûr'əns) the ability to be active for a while without getting too tired to continue (p. 132)

environment (en vī'rən mənt) everything in your surroundings that influences you (p. 28)

epidermis (ep'i dûr'mis) the outer layer of the skin (p. 18)

esophagus (i sof'ə gəs) a tube that connects the mouth and stomach (p. 51)

expiration date (ek′spə rā′shən dāt) date on a medicine label after which medicine should not be used (p. 188)

F

fallacy (fal′ə sē) a false or mistaken belief; misconception

family (fam′ə lē) a group of people usually made of parents, children, and relatives (p. 86)

farsighted (fär′sī′tid) being able to see objects that are far away better than objects that are near (p. 14)

fats (fats) nutrients that provide large amounts of long-lasting energy (p. 104)

fever (fē′vər) a body temperature higher than normal (pp. 157, 165)

fiber (fī′bər) the part of a plant that is eaten but cannot be digested (p. 108)

fire extinguisher (fīr ek sting′gwi shər) a machine that sprays chemicals onto a fire to put it out (p. 232)

first aid (fûrst ād) immediate treatment for minor injury or illness; in an emergency, treatment given until medical help arrives (p. 220)

flexibility (flek sə bi′lə tē) the ability to bend and move your body easily (p. 132)

fluoride (flùr′īd) a substance that strengthens tooth enamel and helps prevent cavities (p. 10)

food group (füd grüp) various foods that are grouped together because they contain the same nutrients (p. 110)

Food Guide Pyramid (füd gīd pir′ə mid′) a chart of the different food groups that helps you understand how to maintain a healthful diet (p. 110)

food label (füd lā′bəl) information about the product, including the name and address of the manufacturer, printed on the packaging (p. 114)

fungus (fung′gəs) an organism that feeds off other living or dead organisms (p. 156)

G

gender (jen′dər) the sex of a person, male or female (p. 29)

germ (jûrm) a microbe that can make you ill (p. 158)

gland (gland) a part of the body that produces substances needed by the body, including liquid such as sweat or oil (p. 18)

H

hazard (haz′ərd) a thing or an action that creates a dangerous situation or risk of harm (p. 220)

head lice (hed līs) tiny flat insects without wings that can live on a person's scalp (p. 20)

health department (helth di pärt′mənt) a local or state government agency that promotes community health (p. 254)

heart (härt) a hollow, muscular organ that pumps blood throughout the body (p. 35)

heart attack (härt ə tak′) a serious condition caused when blood vessels to the walls of the heart are blocked (p. 176)

heart disease (härt di zēz′) any of many serious illnesses caused by the heart not working properly (p. 176)

heredity (hə red′i tē) passing of traits from parents to children (p. 28)

hinge joint (hinj joint) a joint that allows back-and-forth movements, such as in knees and elbows (p. 40)

pronunciation key

a at; ā ape; ä far; âr care; e end; ē me; i it; ī ice; îr pierce; o hot; ō old; ô fork; oi oil; ou out; u up; ū use; ü rule; ù pull; ûr turn; hw white; ng song; th thin; th this; zh measure; ə about, taken, pencil, lemon, circus

HIV (Human Immunodeficiency Virus) (āch ī vē) a virus that attacks the body's immune system and leads to AIDS (p. 168)

home remedy (hōm rem′i dē) treatment for illness using natural substances (p. 191)

hormones (hôr′mōnz) chemicals made by your body that control growth and some body processes (p. 28)

hunger center (hung′gər sen′tər) the part of the brain that receives the message that a person is hungry (p. 105)

I

immovable joint (i mü′və bəl joint) a place where bones fit together too tightly to move, such as in the skull (p. 40)

immune system (i mūn′ sis′təm) all of the parts and functions of your body that fight germs (p. 162)

immunity (i mū′ni tē) protection against or ability to fight a disease (p. 162)

immunizations (im′yə ni zā′shənz) vaccines to prevent certain diseases (p. 254)

incinerator (in sin′ə rā′tər) a community facility that burns trash (p. 263)

incisors (in sī′zərz) teeth that bite into food (p. 11)

incurable (in kyūr′ə bəl) not capable of being cured or healed (p. 172)

influence (in′flü ənts) to have either a positive or negative effect on people (p. 68)

ingredient (in grē′dē ənt) a substance mixed together with others to make food (p. 114)

inhalant (in hā′lənt) a legal substance that gives off gas at room temperature; may be abused by inhaling (p. 210)

inherited trait (in her′it əd′ trāt) a trait that is passed from parent to child (p. 31)

injury (in′jə rē) any kind of physical damage or harm to a person (p. 220)

intellectual health (in′tə lek′chü əl helth) health of the mind, health having to do with thoughts (p. 2)

intellectual skills (in′tə lek′chü əl skilz) talking, solving problems, reading, and writing (p. 30)

intentional injury (in ten′shə nəl in′jə rē) an injury in which someone harms another person on purpose (p. 220)

interact (in′tə rakt′) to deal with others (p. 90)

interpret (in tûr′prit) to make sense of (p. 15)

involuntary muscle (in vol′ən ter′ē mus′əl) a muscle you cannot control by thinking about it (p. 38)

J

joint (joint) where two bones meet (p. 38)

K

keratin (ker′ə tin) the substance from which fingernails and toenails are made (p. 21)

L

landfill (land′fil) land where garbage is dumped (p. 263)

large intestine (lärj in tes′tin) an organ that absorbs water from undigested food and stores the wastes (p. 50)

life cycle (līf sī′kəl) the stages, or steps, of growth and development throughout a person's life (p. 29)

life preserver (līf pri zûr′vər) a belt, vest, or ring made from a material that keeps a person afloat in water (p. 238)

lifestyle (līf′stīl) a person's pattern of behaviors (p. 175)

ligament (lig′ə mənt) a tough band of tissue that holds two bones together at a joint (p. 38)

liver (liv′ər) an organ that produces bile, which helps break down fats (p. 52)

lungs (lungz) two large organs inside the chest where blood picks up oxygen and gets rid of carbon dioxide (p. 44)

M

marijuana (mar′ə wä′nə) a drug made from the crushed leaves, flowers, and seeds of the cannabis plant (p. 210)

marrow (mar′ō) a tissue found in the center of long bones in which most blood cells form (p. 39)

medicine (med′ə sin) a drug used to prevent, treat, or cure disease or injury (p. 186)

melanin (mel′ə nin) a chemical made by the skin cells that gives skin its color (p. 19)

membrane (mem′brān) a lining that surrounds the outside of a cell (p. 35)

microbe (mī′krōb) a tiny organism or particle, visible only with a microscope (p. 156)

minerals (min′ər əlz) nutrients found in the soil that are needed by plants and animals (p. 107)

misuse (mis ūz′) to use a legal drug improperly or in an unsafe way (p. 190)

molars (mō′lərz) teeth that grind up food (p. 11)

mold (mōld) an organism that can spoil food; can appear as a fuzzy growth (p. 124)

motor nerve cell (mō′tər nûrv sel) a nerve cell that carries messages from your brain or spinal cord to other parts of your body (p. 54)

mucus (mū′kəs) a slippery substance in the mouth (part of saliva); a thick fluid that protects the insides of your nose, mouth, throat, and other parts of your body (pp. 51, 164)

muscles (mus′əlz) the tissues that make your body move (pp. 42, 142)

muscular system (mus′kyə lər sis′təm) a body system made up of muscles that helps your body move (pp. 37, 42)

N

nail bed (nāl bed) the soft skin under the nail (p. 21)

natural resource (nach′ər əl rē′sôrs) a substance or organism found in nature that is useful or necessary for life, such as water (p. 266)

nearsighted (nîr′sī′tid) being able to see objects that are near better than objects that are far away (p. 14)

need (nēd) something that you must have to stay alive or be healthy (p. 64)

nerve cell (nûrv sel) a cell that consists of a cell body with nerve fibers extending out from it (p. 55)

nerve tissue (nûrv tish′ü) tissue made up of nerve cells (p. 35)

nervous system (nûr′vəs sis′təm) a body organ system made up of the brain, the spinal cord, and the nerves that control most body functions and movement (pp. 37, 54)

nicotine (nik′ə tēn′) a drug; a poisonous, oily substance found in tobacco (p. 194)

noncommunicable disease (non′kə mū′ni kə bəl di zēz′) a disease that cannot be spread to a person from another living being (p. 174)

pronunciation key

a at; ā ape; ä far; âr care; e end; ē me; i it; ī ice; îr pierce; o hot; ō old; ô fork; oi oil; ou out; u up; ū use; ü rule; ù pull; ûr turn; hw white; ng song; th thin; th this; zh measure; ə about, taken, pencil, lemon, circus

nonsmoking section (non smōk′ing sek′shən) a part of a public place set aside for people who do not smoke (p. 200)

nucleus (nü′klē əs) the control center of a cell (p. 35)

nutrient (nü′trē ənt) a substance in food that the body needs to stay healthy (pp. 51, 104)

O

oral health (ôr′əl helth) the health of the teeth and gums (p. 10)

organ (ôr′gən) a structure, made of two or more tissues, that has a job (p. 34)

organism (ôr′gə niz′əm) a living thing (p. 158)

outbreak (out′brāk) a sudden increase in the number of people with a disease or illness (p. 254)

outpatient (out′pā′shənt) a patient admitted to a hospital or other health care facility for treatment and released the same day (p. 254)

over-the-counter medicines (ō′vər thə koun′tər med′ə sinz) medicines that can be bought off the shelf for which a doctor's order is not needed (p. 188)

overweight (ō′vər wāt′) weighing more than is normal for a given height and build (p. 120)

ozone layer (o′zōn lā′ər) a naturally occurring layer of a special kind of oxygen in the atmosphere; keeps some of the sun's harmful rays from reaching Earth (p. 266)

P

pancreas (pan′krē əs) an organ that adds juices to help break down proteins, fats, and starches in the small intestine (p. 52)

passive smoke (pas′iv smōk) tobacco smoke that is inhaled by someone other than the smoker (p. 200)

permanent teeth (pûr′mə nənt tēth) the 32 adult teeth (p. 11)

personality (pûr′sə nal′i tē) all of the ways you feel, think, and act (p. 64)

pharmacist (fär′mə sist) a person trained and licensed to prepare medicines and give them out to doctors' patients (p. 186)

physical activity (fiz′i kəl ak tiv′i tē) a game, sport, exercise or other action that involves moving your body (p. 132)

physical fitness (fiz′i kəl fit′nəs) the condition in which your body works at its best (p. 132)

physical health (fiz′i kəl helth) health of the body (p. 2)

pituitary gland (pi tū′i ter′ē gland) a gland found at the base of the brain; makes the hormone that controls growth (p. 33)

pivot joint (piv′ət joint) a joint that allows bones to move in a ring, such as in the neck (p. 40)

plaque (plak) a sticky film left on teeth by food and germs; if not removed, it can harm tooth enamel (p. 10)

pollution (pə lü′shən) unhealthful substances that make the air, water, or soil dirty or impure (p. 260)

pore (pôr) a tiny opening in the skin through which liquids such as oil or sweat move (p. 18)

posture (pos′chər) the way a person "carries" his or her body when sitting, standing, and walking (p. 6)

power (pou′ər) the combination of strength and speed (p. 136)

prescription (pri skrip′shən) a written order from a doctor, usually for medicine (p. 186)

preventable injury (pri vent′ə bəl in′jə rē) a potential injury that you can keep from happening (p. 221)

primary teeth (prī′mer ē tēth) the 20 baby teeth (p. 11)

privilege (priv′ə lij) a special favor granted to a person or group (p. 86)

proteins (prō′tēnz) nutrients needed for growth and to build and repair body cells (p. 104)

puberty (pū′bər tē) time during which a person first becomes able to reproduce (p. 28)

pulp (pulp) the soft inner part of a tooth, made up of blood vessels and nerves (p. 11)

pulse (puls) the rhythmic beating of the arteries caused by the heart as it pumps blood (p. 45)

R

reaction time (rē ak′shən tīm) the time it takes to notice and respond to something (p. 136)

recycle (rē sī′kəl) to set certain types of trash aside to be made into other products (p. 260)

reduce (ri düs′) to decrease the number of things you throw out (p. 260)

reflex (rē′fleks′) a quick, automatic action (p. 57)

relax (ri laks′) to lengthen, as in the action of a muscle (p. 43)

reproduce (rē′prə düs′) to have a baby (p. 29)

resolve (ri zolv′) to settle a problem (p. 74)

respect (ri spekt′) consideration or esteem (p. 90)

respectful touch (ri spekt′fəl tuch) a touch that shows caring for another person, such as a handshake or pat on the back (p. 228)

respiratory system (res′pər ə tôr′ē sis′təm) a body system that takes in oxygen from the air and gets rid of waste gases (pp. 37, 47)

responsibility (ri spon′sə bil′i tē) a job or duty (p. 86)

responsible (ri spon′sə bəl) being in charge, especially in taking care of your own health (p. 6)

reuse (rē ūz′) to find a new use for something that might otherwise be thrown out (p. 260)

right (rīt) something a person needs and deserves because it is fair, moral, or lawful (p. 86)

risk (risk) the chance of injury, damage, or loss (p. 2)

risk factor (risk fak′tər) something that increases the possibility that a person will get a certain disease (p. 174)

root (rüt) the part of a tooth that attaches the tooth to the jawbone (p. 11)

S

safety equipment (sāf′tē i kwip′mənt) materials designed to reduce the risk of injury (p. 146)

saliva (sə lī′və) a mixture of water, mucus, and chemicals in your mouth (p. 51)

salivary glands (sal′ə ver′ē glandz) three pairs of glands in your mouth that make saliva (p. 51)

self-concept (self′kon′sept) the thoughts you have about yourself (p. 64)

self-esteem (self′e stēm′) the level of respect you have for yourself (p. 64)

self-medication (self′med′i kā′shən) treating oneself when ill such as by taking over-the-counter medications (p. 191)

sense organs (sens ôr′gənz) the eyes, ears, nose, tongue, and skin, which receive messages from the outside world and send the messages to the brain (p. 55)

pronunciation key

a at; ā ape; ä far; âr care; e end; ē me; i it; ī ice; îr pierce; o hot; ō old; ô fork; oi oil; ou out; u up; ū use; ü rule; ù pull; ûr turn; hw white; ng song; th thin; th this; zh measure; ə about, taken, pencil, lemon, circus

sensory nerve cell (sen′sə rē nûrv sel) a nerve cell that carries messages from your sense organs to your spinal cord or brain (p. 54)

serving (sûr′ving) a certain amount of food (p. 110)

sewage (sü′ij) liquid waste from household or public facilities (p. 262)

share (shâr) to use together in common (p. 92)

side effect (sīd′ i fekt′) an unwanted result of using a medicine (p. 190)

skeletal system (skel′i təl sis′təm) a body system that gives your body shape, protects many of your organs, and helps you walk, sit, and stand (pp. 37, 39)

small intestine (smôl in tes′tin) an organ that finishes breaking down food after it leaves the stomach (p. 50)

smog (smog) a combination of smoke and fog (p. 267)

smoke detector (smōk di tek′tər) a machine that sounds an alarm when it senses smoke (p. 232)

smokeless tobacco (smōk′lis tə bak′ō) chewing tobacco or snuff that is held between the cheek and the gums (p. 197)

social group (sō′shəl grüp) two or more people who interact (p. 90)

social health (sō′shəl helth) health having to do with relationships with other people (p. 2)

social skills (sō′shəl skilz) trusting, sharing with, talking to, and making friends with others (p. 30)

solid waste (sol′id wāst) any solid material that is thrown out; trash; garbage (p. 263)

specialist (spesh′ə list) a doctor who has a lot of training with certain illnesses or health problems (p. 255)

speed (spēd) how quickly you move (p. 136)

spinal cord (spī′nəl kôrd) the long bundle of nerves that extends down the back from the brain (pp. 39, 54)

spine (spīn) the backbone that protects the spinal cord (p. 55)

spoil (spoil) to become rotten and unhealthy (p. 124)

sprain (sprān) an injury caused by twisting muscles around a joint such as the ankle or wrist (p. 244)

stamina (stam′ə nə) another word for endurance; see *endurance* (p. 133)

stimulant (stim′yə lənt) a drug that speeds up the activity of the body (p. 210)

stomach (stum′ək) muscular organ where food is broken down and mixed with digestive juices (p. 50)

strength (strengkth) the ability to lift, push, and pull (p. 132); also something a person does well (p. 66)

stress (stres) emotional or intellectual pressure or strain (p. 78)

stressor (stre′sər) something that causes stress (p. 78)

sunscreen (sun′skrēn) a cream or lotion that blocks the sun's dangerous rays and prevents or minimizes sunburn (pp. 20, 238)

symptom (simp′təm) a sign of a disease (p. 156)

T

tar (tär) a sticky, brown substance found in tobacco (p. 194)

tartar (tär′tər) yellowish substance that forms on the teeth when plaque hardens (p. 10)

tendon (ten′dən) tough cord of tissue that attaches muscles to bones (p. 42)

tissue (tish′ü) a group of cells, usually of the same type, that work together to do a certain job (p. 34)

tobacco (tə bak′ō) a plant whose leaves are dried and made into cigarettes, cigars, or smokeless tobacco (p. 194)

trachea (trā′kē ə) windpipe, or hollow tube through which air travels when you breathe (p. 47)

trait (trāt) characteristic, such as a person's hair color or eye color (p. 31)

triceps (trī′seps) a muscle on the outside of the upper arm; causes arm to straighten when it contracts (p. 43)

trustworthy (trust′wûr′the̅) honest and truthful; able to be trusted (p. 94)

tumor (tü′mər) a growth made of cancer cells (p. 176)

U

underweight (un′dər wāt′) weighing less than is normal for a given height and build (p. 120)

unintentional injury (un′in ten′shə nəl in′jə rē) an injury that is the result of an unexpected event (p. 220)

V

vaccine (vak sēn′) a substance that protects the body against a certain disease by causing the body to produce antibodies (p. 178)

vein (vān) a blood vessel that carries blood back to the heart (p. 44)

villi (vil′ī) tiny, fingerlike projections that line the small intestine (p. 52)

violence (vī′ə ləns) physical force intended to cause bodily injury or harm; behavior intended to cause emotional harm (p. 224)

virus (vī′rəs) a tiny particle that can only reproduce inside living cells (p. 156)

vision (vizh′ən) the ability to see; eyesight (p. 14)

vitamins (vī′tə minz) nutrients, found in small amounts in food, needed by the body to grow and function (p. 104)

voluntary muscle (vol′ən ter′ē mus′əl) a muscle you can control by thinking about it (p. 38)

W

want (wont) something a person would like to have, but not a need (p. 67)

warm-up (wôrm′up) gentle movement that prepares the body for exercise (p. 142)

water (wô′tər) an essential nutrient that helps the body dissolve some vitamins and helps bring other nutrients to the cells of the body (p. 107)

weakness (wēk′nis) something a person does not do well (p. 66)

weapon (wep′ən) a knife, gun, or other object used in an attack (p. 224)

pronunciation key

a **at**; ā **ape**; ä **far**; âr **care**; e **end**; ē **me**; i **it**; ī **ice**; îr **pierce**; o **hot**; ō **old**; ô **fork**; oi **oil**; ou **out**; u **up**; ū **use**; ü **rule**; u̇ **pull**; ûr **turn**; hw **white**; ng **song**; th **thin**; <u>th</u> **this**; zh **measure**; ə **about, taken, pencil, lemon, circus**

INDEX

This Index lists many topics that appear in the book,
along with the pages on which they are found.

CREDITS